TEA PLANTATIONS
VIEW IN THE GREEN TEA DISTRICT

A JOURNEY

TO THE

TEA COUNTRIES OF CHINA;

INCLUDING

SUNG-LO AND THE BOHEA HILLS;

WITH

A SHORT NOTICE OF THE EAST INDIA COMPANY'S TEA PLANTATIONS
IN THE HIMALAYA MOUNTAINS.

BY

ROBERT FORTUNE,

AUTHOR OF THREE YEARS' WANDERINGS IN CHINA.

WITH MAP AND ILLUSTRATIONS.

MILDMAY BOOKS
LONDON

Mildmay Books Limited
Venture House
29 Glasshouse Street
London W1R 5AP

First published by John Murray,
London, 1852
This edition 1987

Printed in Great Britain by
Redwood Burn Limited, Trowbridge,
Wiltshire and bound by Pegasus
Bookbinding, Melksham, Wiltshire

British Library Cataloguing in Publication Data

Fortune, Robert
    A Journey to the tea countries of China and
    India.
    1. China——Description and travel——To
    1900
    I. Title
    915.1'043   DS709

    ISBN 1–869945–07–7
    ISBN 1–869945–10–7 Pbk

PREFACE.

IT is now about five years since I submitted to
the public my 'Three Years' Wanderings in the
Northern Provinces of China.' Shortly after the
publication of that volume I was deputed by the
Honourable the Court of Directors of the East India
Company to proceed to China for the purpose of
obtaining the finest varieties of the Tea-plant, as well
as native manufacturers and implements, for the
Government Tea plantations in the Himalayas. On
the 20th of June, 1848, I left Southampton, with
many other passengers, in the Peninsular and Oriental
Company's steam-ship 'Ripon,' Captain Moresby,
I.N., and landed in Hong-kong on the 14th of
August.

As I went far inland, and visited many districts
almost unknown to Europeans, I now venture to lay
an account of my travels and their results before the
public. Blessed with a sound constitution and good
health, I cared little for luxuries, and made light of

the hardships of a traveller's life. New scenes, new
countries, and new plants were day by day spread out
before me and afforded gratification of the highest and
purest kind. And even now, when on a different side
of the globe and far removed from such scenes and
such adventures, I often look back upon them with
feelings of unalloyed pleasure.

The important objects of my mission have been
brought to a successful termination. Upwards of
twenty thousand tea-plants, eight first-rate manufacturers, and a large supply of implements were
procured from the finest tea-districts of China, and
conveyed in safety to the Himalayas. In the course
of my travels I discovered many useful and ornamental trees and shrubs, some of which, such as the
Funereal Cypress, will one day produce a striking
and beautiful effect in our English landscape and
in our cemeteries.

In publishing this account of my journey I may
repeat what I said in the introduction to my former
' Wanderings :'—" I have no intention of writing or
making a book upon China." My object is to give
a peep into the Celestial Empire, to show its strange
hills and romantic valleys, its rivers and canals, its
natural productions, whether in the field, on the hill-
side, or in the garden, and its strange and interesting
people, as they were seen by me in their every-day

life. As I hope my readers will accompany me through the whole of my journey, I shall have the pleasure of taking them to India and the Himalayas, and showing them the Government Tea plantations, from which much is expected, and which are likely to prove of great advantage, not only to India but also to England and her wide-spreading colonies.

Having thus given an idea of what may be expected in the following pages, I have only to express a hope that the work may be received by the public in the same kind spirit, and with the same indulgence and favour, that were shown to my former 'Wanderings.'

Brompton, April, 1852.

CONTENTS.

CHAPTER I.

Arrive at Hong-kong — Excitement on the arrival of the mail — Centipede boats — Bay of Hong-kong by moonlight — Town of Victoria — Its trees and gardens — Mortality amongst the troops — Its cause — A remedy suggested — Sail for Shanghae — Its importance as a place of trade — New English town and shipping — The gardens of the foreign residents . . . . . Page 1

CHAPTER II.

My object in coming north — Difficulty in procuring tea-plants — No dependence can be placed upon the Chinese — Adopt the dress of the country — Start for the interior — Mode of getting my head shaved — City of Kea-hing-foo and its old cemetery — Lakes and " ling "— Mode of gathering the ling — Great silk country — Increase in exports — City of Seh-mun-yuen — Fear of thieves — Hang-chow-foo — The " Garden of China "— Description of the city and its suburbs — Gaiety of the people — Adventure in the city — Kan-du — A " chop "— A Chinese inn — I get no breakfast and lose my dinner — Boat engaged for Hwuy-chow — Importance of Hang-chow both for trading and *"squeezing"* . . . 19

CHAPTER III.

Leave Hang-chow-foo — A China passage-boat — Scenery and natural productions — Remarkable hills — Our fellow-passengers — A smoker of opium — I am discovered to be a foreigner — City of Yen-chow-foo — A Chinaman cheats a Chinaman !—The river and

water-mills — Botany of the country — A valuable palm-tree —
Birds — Lime-kilns and green granite — Tea-plant met with —
The new FUNEREAL CYPRESS discovered — Its beauty — How its
seeds were procured — Dr. Lindley's opinion of its merits — Strange
echo — River and land beggars — Charity .   .   .   Page 45

CHAPTER IV.

City of Wae-ping — Threatened attack from boatmen — A false alarm
— A border country and a border guard — Enter the district of
Hwuy-chow — The tea-plant and other crops — A Chinese play —
Ferry-boat and ladies — Cargo transshipped — Two coffins below
my bed — A mandarin's garden — Botany of the hills — A new
plant (*Berberis japonica*) — My servant's advice — Leave the boat —
The opium-smoker outwitted — Town of Tun-che — Its importance
in connection with the tea-trade — Features of country, soil, and
productions — First view of Sung-lo-shan   67

CHAPTER V.

Sung-lo-shan — Its priests and tea — Its height above the sea — Rock
formation — Flora of the hills — Temperature and climate —
Cultivation of the tea-shrub — Mode of preserving its seeds — The
young plants — Method of dyeing green teas — Ingredients employed
— Chinese reason for the practice — Quantity of Prussian blue and
gypsum taken by a green-tea drinker — Such teas not used by
the Chinese — Mr. Warrington's observations .   .   .   86

CHAPTER VI.

My reception in the house of Wang's father — A smoky Chinese
cottage — My coolie and the dwarf — The dangers to which they
had been exposed — Chinese mode of warming themselves on a
cold day — Tea-seeds, &c., obtained — Anecdote of the new
Berberis — Obtain some young plants of it — Deceitful character
of the Chinese — Leave the far-famed Sung-lo-shan — Wang tries
to cheat the chairmen — Invents a story of a "great general" —
Leave Tun-che — Mountain scenery — Pleasure of going down the
river — Gale of wind amongst the mountains — Arrive at Nechow —
Shaou-hing-foo — Tsaou-o — Pak-wan — Arrive at Ning-po .   96

CHAPTER VII.

Kintang or Silver Island — Its inhabitants and productions — Bay of Chapoo — Advantages of an inland route — New year at Shanghae — Flower-shops and flowers — Sacred bamboo — The Chrysanthemum — Mode of cultivating it — Weather-prophets — Sail for Hong-kong — A game-ship — The Enkianthus — Canton seeds, and mode of packing them — False notion regarding their being poisoned
Page 115

CHAPTER VIII.

Foo-chow-foo — Jealousy of the mandarins — A polite way of getting rid of a spy — Scenery amongst the mountains — Temple of Koo-shan — Its priests and idols — Buddha's tooth and other relics — Trees and shrubs — City of Foo-chow-foo — Chinese mode of getting out when the gates are shut — Journey up the Min — Chinese sportsmen and their dogs — A deer-hunt — Scenery about Tein-tung — Wild flowers — Roadside temples — The bamboo — A priest and siphon — Lakes of Tung-hoo 133

CHAPTER IX.

Leave Ning-po for the Bohea mountains — My guides — A flag and its history — The Green River again — Spring scenery on its banks — Yen-chow and Tā-yang — A storm in a creek — Boatwomen — A Chinese Mrs. Caudle and a curtain lecture — Natural productions — Funereal cypress and other trees — Our boat seized for debt and the sail taken away — A Chinèse creditor — Town of Nan-che — Its houses, gardens, and trade — Vale of Nan-che — Productions and fertility — City of Chu-chu-foo — Moschetoes and Moscheto " tobacco " — Arrive at Chang-shan 159

CHAPTER X.

City of Chang-shan and its trade — Land journey — My chair and chair-bearers — Description of the road — Trains of tea coolies — Roadside inns — Boundary of two provinces — Dinner at a Chinese inn — Value of the chopsticks — Adventure with two Canton men — City of Yuk-shan — Its trade and importance — Quan-sin-foo — My servant speculates in grass-cloth — A Chinese test of respecta-bility — Description of the country and its productions — Arrive at the town of Hokow 182

CHAPTER XI.

Town of Hokow — Its situation, trade, and great importance — Bohea
mountain chair — Mountain road — Beggars by the wayside —
Beautiful scenery — the priest and his bell — Town of Yuen-shan
— Appearance of the road — Tea coolies — Different modes of
carrying the tea-chests — Large tea-growing country — Soil and
plantations — My first night in a Chinese inn — Reception — Dirty
bed-rooms — I console myself, and go to dinner   .   . Page 197

CHAPTER XII.

First view of the Bohea mountains — Mountain pass — A noble fir-
tree — Its name and history — Flora of the mountains — New plants
— Source of the river Min — Entertainment for man and beast —
A rugged road and another pass — A gale amongst the mountains —
An amusing old China-woman — Sugar and tea-spoons — A kind
landlord — The Tein-sin — Arrive at the city of Tsong-gan-hien —
Its situation, size, and trade — Tea-farms   208

CHAPTER XIII.

Woo-e-shan — Ascent of the hill — Arrive at a Buddhist temple —
Description of the temple and the scenery — Strange rocks — My
reception — Our dinner and its ceremonies — An interesting conversation — An evening stroll — Formation of the rocks — Soil —
View from the top of Woo-e-shan — A priests' grave — A view by
moonlight — Chinese wine — Cultivation of the tea-shrub — Chains
and monkeys used in gathering it — Tea-merchants — Happiness
and contentment of the peasantry   223

CHAPTER XIV.

Stream of "nine windings" — A Taouist priest — His house and temple
— Du Halde's description of these hills — Strange impressions of
gigantic hands on the rocks — Tea-plants purchased — Adventure
during the night — My visitors — Plants packed for a journey —
Town of Tsin-tsun and its trade — Leave the Woo-e hills — Mountain scenery — The lance-leaved pine — Rocks, ravines, and waterfalls — A lonely road — Trees — Birds and other animals — Town of
She-pa-ky — Productions of the country — Uses of the Nelumbium
— Pouching teas — City of Pouching-hien   240

CHAPTER XV.

Some advice to the reader — Botany of the black-tea country — Geological features — Soil — Sites of tea-farms — Temperature — Rainy season — Cultivation and management of tea-plantations — Size of farms — Mode of packing — Chop names — Route from the tea-country to the coast — Method of transport — Distances — Time occupied — Original cost of tea in the tea-country — Expenses of carriage to the coast — Sums paid by the foreign merchant — Profits of the Chinese — Prospect of *good* tea becoming cheaper — Tüng-po's directions for making tea — His opinion on its properties and uses .   .   .   . Page 253

CHAPTER XVI.

Geography of the tea-shrub — Best tea districts of China — Names of tea-plants — Black and green tea made from the same variety — My Chinamen asked to make tea from *Pongamia glabra* — They succeed ! —Difference between black and green tea depends upon manipulation — Method of making green tea — Of making black — Difference in the manipulation of the two kinds — Mr. Warrington's remarks on this subject—A familiar illustration—The tea-plant—Inferior teas made from *Thea bohea* — Best teas made from *Thea viridis* — The Woo-e-shan variety — The tea-plant affected by climate and reproduction — Tea cultivation in America and Australia — In English gardens   272

CHAPTER XVII.

Inn at Pouching-hien — Opium-smokers and gamblers — Value of life in China — A midnight disturbance — Sing-Hoo fights with a joss-stick — Difficulty of procuring men next day — Sing-Hoo carries the luggage, and we march — His bamboo breaks — Scene amongst beggars — Description of beggars in China — A " king of the beggars " — Charity always given — I continue my journey — Mountain passes and Buddhist temples — A border town and Tartar guard — We are inspected and allowed to pass on .   .   . 288

CHAPTER XVIII.

A celebrated Buddhist temple — Scenery around it — Its trees and shrubs — Buddhist worship — Leave the temple — Reflections on Buddhism — Important station for Christian missionaries — Privations they would have to endure — Roman Catholics and their labours — Christian charity — Protestant missionaries — Their views as to the interior of China — A day-dream of China opened — Bamboo paper — A mandarin on a journey — Town of Ching-hoo — Engage a boat for Nechow — Return to Shanghae . Page 302

CHAPTER XIX.

Tea-plants, &c., taken to Hong-kong — Shipped for India — I sail again for the north — Shanghae gardens in spring — " South Garden " — Double-striped peach and other plants — Moutan gardens — Fine new varieties of the tree-pæony — Chinese method of propagating them — Mode of sending them to Canton — Value there — Introduction to Europe — Size in England — Azalea gardens — Skimmia Reevesiana — New Azaleas — The " Kwei-wha " — The Glycine — Its native hills — Chinese mode of training it — The yellow Camellia   315

CHAPTER XX.

Safe arrival of tea-plants in India — Means taken in China to engage tea-manufacturers — I visit Chusan — My lodgings — A mandarin who smoked opium — His appearance at daylight — A summer morning in Chusan — An emperor's edict — The Yang-mae — Beauty of its fruit — City of Ting-hae — Poo-too, or Worshipping Island — Ancient inscriptions in an unknown language — A Chinese caught fishing in the sacred lake — He is chased by the priests — The bamboo again — The sacred Nelumbium — My holidays expire — Collections of tea-seeds and plants made — Return to Shanghae — Tea-manufacturers engaged — We bid adieu to the north of China   340

CHAPTER XXI.

Experiments with tea-seeds — Best method of sending them to distant countries — How oaks and chestnuts might be transported — Arrive at Calcutta — Condition of the collections — East India Company's botanic garden — Amherstia and other plants in bloom — Proceed onwards — The Sunderbunds — Arrive at Allahabad — Land journey — Reach Saharunpore — State of the tea-plants — Saharunpore garden — Mussooree garden — Its trees and other productions — Its value to the country and to Europe . Page 355

CHAPTER XXII.

Ordered to inspect the tea-plantations in India — Deyra Doon plantation — Mussooree and Landour — Flora of the mountains — Height and general character — Our mode of travelling — Hill-plants resemble those of China — Guddowli plantation — Chinese manufacturers located there — I bid them farewell — The country improves in fertility — Tea-plantations near Almorah — Zemindaree plantations — Leave Almorah for Bheem Tal — View of the Snowy range — Bheem Tal tea-plantations — General observations on tea culture in India — Suggestions for its improvement — Other plants which ought to be introduced — Nainee Tal — Arrive at Calcutta — The Victoria regia 368

LIST OF ILLUSTRATIONS.

1. View in the Green Tea Country   –   –   *Frontispiece*

2. Engraved Title-page.

3. Map   –   –   –   –   –   –   *to face page*   1

4. Curious mode of gathering the Ling near Kea-hing-foo   ,,   27

5. Palm-tree (*Chamærops excelsa ?*)   –   –   –   –   59

6. Funereal Cypress   –   –   –   –   –   –   63

7. Relic-Cage   –   –   –   –   –   –   –   138

8. Buddha's Tooth   –   –   –   –   –   –   139

9. Crystal Vase   –   –   –   –   –   –   –   140

10. Mo-ze, the Chinese Sportsman   –   –   –   –   151

11. Roadside Altar –   –   –   –   –   –   –   154

12. Mode of carrying the finest Tea across the Bohea mountains –   –   –   –   –   –   –   202

13. Mode of carrying common Tea   –   –   –   –   203

14. Chinese Tomb –   –   –   –   –   –   –   239

15. Chinese Bird's-eye View of the "Stream of Nine Windings" and strange Rocks   –   –   –   –   –   –   241

16. Ancient Inscription   –   –   –   –   –   –   347

17. Old Stone at Poo-too   –   –   –   –   –   –   348

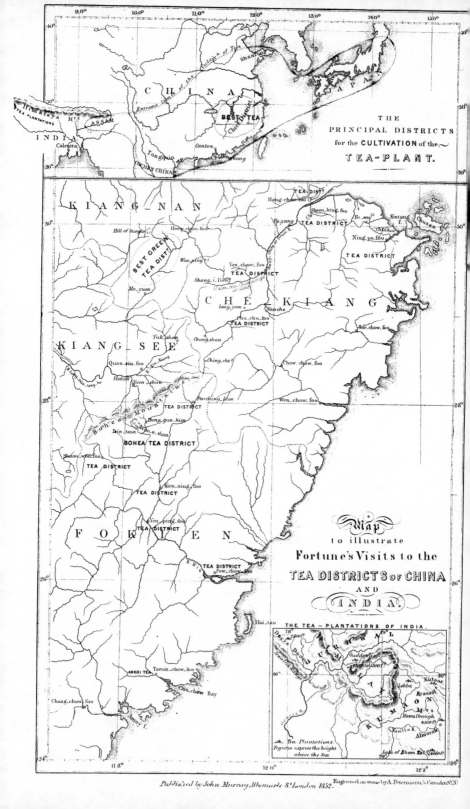

THE
PRINCIPAL DISTRICTS
for the CULTIVATION of the
TEA-PLANT.

Map
to illustrate
Fortune's Visits to the
TEA DISTRICTS OF CHINA
AND
INDIA

THE TEA-PLANTATIONS OF INDIA.

Tea Plantations.
Figures express the height
above the sea

Published by John Murray, Albemarle St London 1852.

Engraved on stone by A. Petermann, Camden St N

JOURNEY

TEA DISTRICTS OF CHINA.

CHAPTER I.

Arrive at Hong-kong — Excitement on the arrival of the mail —
Centipede boats — Bay of Hong-kong by moonlight — Town of
Victoria — Its trees and gardens — Mortality amongst the troops
— Its cause — A remedy suggested — Sail for Shanghae — Its
importance as a place of trade — New English town and shipping
— The gardens of the foreign residents.

On the 14th of August, 1848, the Peninsular and
Oriental Company's steam-ship "Braganza," in which
I was a passenger, dropped her anchor in the Bay of
Hong-kong, at nine o'clock in the evening. In a few
seconds our decks were crowded with the inhabitants of
the place, all anxious to meet their friends, or to hear
the news from home. As I did not intend to go on
shore until the following morning, I had sufficient leisure to survey the busy and exciting scene around me.

Amongst the numerous boats which came off to us
there were two which presented a most striking appearance. They were very long and narrow, and
were each propelled by about fifty oars. They had
been built by the English and American merchants

B

to convey the news to Canton on the arrival of the
mail. The moment these boats received their de-
spatches they started on their journey, and, as they
belonged to opposition parties, each did its best to
outstrip the other; and, as it was often a matter of
considerable importance to get the earliest news, a
large sum of money was distributed amongst the crew
of the winning boat.

The boatmen made a great noise ; Chinamen like,
all were talking, all were giving orders, for each had
a stake in the winning of the race. At last the
papers, letters, or whatever they had to take, were
put on board, and off they started across the bay for
the mouth of the Canton or "Pearl" river. They
ploughed the water like two enormous centipedes,
and, although they were going very fast, they were
visible for some time in the clear moonlight. I
watched them from the deck of the steamer until
they were lost in the distance, but even then and for
some time afterwards I could hear distinctly the
quick splash of the oars and the noise of the boisterous
crews. Steam has now invaded the quiet waters of
the Pearl river, and these boats are numbered amongst
the things that were.

The noise and excitement connected with the
arrival of the mail gradually subsided ; those of our
visitors who had been lucky enough to get hold of a
' Straits Times,' ' Home News,' or ' Times,' returned on shore to peruse it, while others hastened
home to communicate to their friends the news they
had been able to pick up from the officers or passen-

gers of the ship. By eleven o'clock at night all was
perfectly quiet. Captain Potts and myself had our
chairs taken up on deck, and we sat down to breathe
the cool air and enjoy the scene by which we were
surrounded.

It was a clear moonlight night; such a night as
one sees only in the sunny lands of the East. Those
who have anchored in the Bay of Hong-kong by
moonlight will agree with me that the scene at such
a time is one of the grandest and most beautiful
which can be imagined. On this evening the land-
locked bay was smooth as glass, scarcely a breath of
air fanned the water, and as the clear moonbeams
played upon its surface it seemed covered with glit-
tering gems. Numerous vessels, from all parts of
the world, lay dotted around us, their dark hulls and
tall masts looming large in the distance. The view
was bounded on all sides by rugged and barren hills,
and it required no great stretch of fancy to imagine
oneself on a highland lake.

The white town of Victoria was distinctly visible
from where we lay, and very pretty it appeared in
the moonlight. It is built along the southern shores
of the bay, and in some places extends a considerable
way up the side of the hill. The background of the
picture consisted of a chain of rugged mountains,
which are nearly two thousand feet above the level of
the sea. Altogether the view was a charming one.

When I went on shore the following morning I
found a great change had taken place since 1845;
many parts of the town, then bare, were now densely

covered with houses. Our merchant-princes had
built themselves houses not inferior to those in the
far-famed "City of Palaces;" and the barracks for
the troops were equally handsome and expensive,
although unfortunately not equally healthy. And,
last of all, a pretty English church was rising slowly
on the hill side.

An interest in gardening and planting had sprung
up which promises to lead to most satisfactory results.
When I was formerly in Hong-kong every one complained of the barren appearance of the island, and of
the intense heat and glare of the sun. Officers in
the army, and others who had been many years in
the hotter parts of India, all agreed that there was a
fierceness and oppressiveness in the sun's rays here
which they had never experienced in any other part
of the world. From 1843 to 1845 the mortality was
very great; whole regiments were nearly swept away,
and many of the Government officers and merchants
shared the same fate. Various opinions were expressed regarding the cause which produced these
great disasters; some said one thing and some another; almost all seemed to think that imperfect
drainage had something to do with it, and a hue and
cry was set up to have the island properly drained.
But the island is a chain of mountains; there is very
little flat ground anywhere upon it, and hence the
water which flows from the sides of the hills gushes
rapidly down towards the sea. Imperfect drainage,
therefore, could have very little to do with its un-
healthiness.

I have always thought that, although various causes may operate to render Hong-kong unhealthy, yet one of the principal reasons is the absence of trees and of the shade which they afford. In a communication which I had the honour to make to the Government here in 1844 I pointed out this circumstance, and strongly recommended them to preserve the wood then growing upon the island from the Chinese, who were in the habit of cutting it down annually, and at the same time to plant extensively, particularly on the sides of the roads and on the lower hills. I am happy to say that these recommendations have been carried out to a certain extent, although not so fully as I had wished. It is well known that a healthy vegetation, such as shrubs and trees, decomposes the carbonic acid of the atmosphere, and renders it fit for respiration; besides which there is a softness and coolness about trees, particularly in a hot climate, that is always agreeable.

Many of the inhabitants have taken up the matter with great spirit, and have planted all the ground near their houses. Some of them have really beautiful gardens. I may instance those of His Excellency the Governor at "Spring Gardens," of Messrs. Dent and Co. at "Green Bank," and of Messrs. Jardine and Matheson at "East Point." In order to give some idea of a Hong-kong garden I shall attempt to describe Messrs. Dent's, which was then in the possession and under the fostering care of Mr. Braine :—

This garden is situated on the sloping sides of a valley near the bottom of one of the numerous ravines

which are seen on the sides of the Hong-kong hills.
It is near the centre of the new town of Victoria, and
is one of its greatest ornaments. On one side nothing
is seen but rugged mountains and barren hills, but
here the eye rests upon a rich and luxuriant vegetation, the beauty of which is greatly enhanced by the
contrast.

Every one interested in Chinese plants has heard
of the garden of the late Mr. Beale at Macao, a friend
of Mr. Reeves, and like him an ardent botanical
collector. Nearly the whole of the English residents
left Macao and went to Hong-kong when that island
was ceded to England, and all the plants in Mr.
Beale's garden which could be moved with safety
were brought over in 1845 and planted in the garden
at " Green Bank."

On entering the garden at its lower side there is a
wide chunamed walk leading in a winding manner up
the side of the hill, in the direction of the house.
On each side of this walk are arranged the trees and
shrubs indigenous to the country, as well as many of
the fruits, all of which grow most luxuriantly. *Ficus
nitida,* the Chinese banyan, grows on the right-hand
side, and promises soon to form a beautiful tree.
This is one of the most valuable trees for ornamental
purposes met with in the south of China. It grows
rapidly with but little care, its foliage is of a glossy
green colour, and it soon affords an agreeable shade
from the fierce rays of the sun, which renders it peculiarly valuable in a place like Hong-kong. The
India-rubber tree (*Ficus elastica*) also succeeds well

in the same part of the garden, but it grows much slower than the species just noticed. On the other side of the main walk I observed several specimens of the Indian "neem" tree (Melia Azedarach), which grows with great vigour, but is rather liable to have its branches broken by high winds, owing to the brittle nature of the wood. This defect renders it of less value than it otherwise would be, particularly in a place so liable to high winds and typhoons. This same Melia seems to be found all round the world in tropical and temperate latitudes; I believe it exists in South America, and I have seen it in Gibraltar, Malta, Egypt, Aden, Ceylon, the Straits, and in the south and north of China, at least as far north as the 31st degree of north latitude. Amongst other plants worthy of notice in this part of the garden are the Chinese cinnamon, the pretty *Aglaia odorata*, and *Murraya exotica*, both of which are very sweet scented and much cultivated by the Chinese. Two specimens of the cocoa-nut palm imported from the Straits are promising well. Other fruits—such as the loquat (*Eriobotrya japonica*), the Chinese gooseberry (*Averrhoa Carambola*), the wangpee (*Cookia punctata*), and the longan and leechee—are all succeeding as well as could be expected, considering the short time they have been planted. The *Pinus sinensis*, which is met with on the sides of every barren hill, both in the south and north of China, and which is generally badly used by the natives, who lop off its under branches for fuel, is here growing as it ought to do. The Chinese have been prevented, not without some

difficulty, from cutting off the under branches, and
the tree now shows itself in its natural beauty. It
does not seem to grow large, but in a young state,
with its fine green foliage reaching to the ground, it is
not unhandsome.

As the main walk approaches the terrace on which
the house stands it turns to the right, between two
rows of beautiful yellow bamboos. This species of
bamboo is a very striking one, and well worthy of
some attention in England ; the stems are straight, of
a fine yellow colour, and beautifully striped with
green, as if done by the hand of a first-rate artist. I
sent a plant of it to the Horticultural Society in 1844.

At the bottom of the terrace on which the house
stands there is a long narrow bamboo avenue, which
is called the " Orchid Walk." This always affords a
cool retreat, even at mid-day, as the rays of the sun
can only partially reach it, and then they are cooled
by the dense foliage. Here are cultivated many of
the Chinese orchids and other plants which require
shade. Amongst them I observed *Phaius grandifo-
lius, Cymbidium sinense* and *aloifolium, Aerides odo-
ratum, Vanda multiflora* and *teretifolia, Renanthera
coccinea, Fernandezia ensifolia, Arundina sinensis,
Habenaria Susannæ,* a species of *Cypripedium,* and
Spathoglottis Fortuni. There are also some other
plants, such as *Chirita sinensis,* the " man-neen-
chung " (a dwarf species of *Lycopodium,* highly
prized by the Chinese), and various other things
which, taken all together, render this shaded " Orchid
Walk " a spot of much interest.

Above the "Orchid Walk" is a green sloping bank, on which are growing some fine specimens of bamboos, *Poinciana pulcherrima*, myrtles, *Gardenias*, oleanders (which thrive admirably in China), *Croton variegatum* and *pictum*, *Magnolia fuscata*, *Olea fragrans*, *Dracœna ferrea*, and *Buddlea Lindleyana*. The latter was brought down from Chusan by me in 1844, and is now common in several gardens on the island, where it thrives well, and is almost always in bloom, although the flower-spikes are not so fine as they are in a colder climate. A large collection of plants in pots are arranged on each side of the broad terrace in front of the mansion. These consist of camellias, azaleas, roses, and such plants as are seen in the Fa-tee gardens at Canton; many of the pots are prettily painted in the Chinese style, and placed upon porcelain stands.

When it is remembered that six years before Hong-kong was but a barren island, with only a few huts upon it, inhabited by pirates or poor fishermen, it is surprising that in so short a time a large town should have risen upon the shores of the bay, containing many houses like palaces, and gardens, too, such as this, which enliven and beautify the whole, and add greatly to the recreation, comfort, and health of the inhabitants.

If we except the troops in the new barracks, the inhabitants generally—at least those who use common precaution—are now enjoying as good health as falls to the lot of our countrymen elsewhere in Eastern countries; but the state of the troops has been, until

very lately, most melancholy and alarming. General
D'Aguilar, when commander-in-chief in the colony,
predicted the loss, in three years, of a number equal
to the strength of one regiment, and his prediction
has been almost verified. This sacrifice of human
life is fearful to contemplate. The merchant may
complain of the dulness of trade in the colony, the
political economist may cry out about its expensive-
ness, but these matters sink into insignificance when
compared with such loss of human life.

' The question " Why do soldiers suffer more than
other men?" naturally presents itself, and I humbly
think it is not difficult to answer. They have not
the same occupation for the mind as tradesmen, merchants, and others; of excitement they have little or
none; day after day the same dull routine of duty
has to be got through, and, in addition to this, they
are often exposed to the night air. When some of
them get an attack of fever, others who look on
become nervous and predisposed to disease, and are
soon laid up in hospital with their comrades. And
add to all these things the effects of the Chinese
spirit called "Samshoo," which drives men mad,
and, as Captain Massie, of the "Cleopatra," so justly
observed in the Supreme Court, "makes bad men of
the best in the ship."

If these are the main causes of fever and death
amongst the troops, it surely is not difficult to point
out a remedy. The editor of the 'China Mail'
justly remarks that "the climate was blamed for
much that arose from a blind adherence to regulations

as to diet, drill, discipline, and quarters, which, if
tried on the civil community, would, in all probability, have produced similar disastrous effects." It
is satisfactory to observe that now the system of
treatment has been completely changed, and apparently with the most satisfactory results. The editor
of the paper already quoted observes that General
Jervois "has done much to improve the condition of
the soldiers, *by considering them as men, and not mere
machines.* They have more freedom, and, it is said,
better food and more airy quarters. Something has
been done also to relieve the ennui of idleness, by the
introduction and encouragement of amusements."*
It is to be hoped that these measures will be crowned
with entire success, and that the soldiers will soon be
as healthy as the rest of the community.

Having nothing to detain me in Hong-kong, I
took the earliest opportunity of going northwards to
Shanghae. This town is the most northerly of the
five ports at which foreigners are permitted to trade,
and is situated nearly one thousand miles north-east
from Hong-kong. In 1844 I published an account
of it in the 'Athenæum,' and in 1846 I described it
more fully in my 'Wanderings.' In both these
works I ventured to point it out as a place likely to
become of great importance both to England and
America as a port of trade easy of access from the sea.
"Taking into consideration its proximity to the large
towns of Hangchow, Souchow, and the ancient capital
of Nanking; the large native trade; the convenience

* Overland China Mail, June, 1851.

of inland transit by means of rivers and canals; the fact that teas can be brought here more readily than to Canton; and, lastly, viewing this place as an immense mart for our cotton manufactures,—there can be no doubt that in a few years it will not only rival Canton, but become a place of far greater importance."*

When these remarks were written the war had just been brought to a satisfactory termination, and the treaty of Nanking had been wrung from the Chinese. The first merchant-ship had entered the river, one or two English merchants had arrived, and we were living in wretched Chinese houses, eating with chop-sticks, half starved with cold, and sometimes drenched in bed with rain. When the weather happened to be frosty we not unfrequently found the floors of our rooms in the morning covered with snow. A great change has taken place since those days. I now found myself (September, 1848), after having been in England for nearly three years, once more in a China boat sailing up the Shanghae river towards the city. The first object which met my view as I approached the town was a forest of masts, not of junks only, which had been so striking on former occasions, but of goodly foreign ships, chiefly from England and the United States of America. There were now twenty-six large vessels at anchor here, many of which had come loaded with the produce of our manufacturing districts, and were returning filled with silks and teas. But I was much more surprised with the appearance which the shore presented than

* Three Years' Wanderings in China.

with the shipping. I had heard that many English and American houses had been built, indeed one or two were being built before I left China; but a new town, of very considerable size, now occupied the place of wretched Chinese hovels, cotton-fields, and tombs. The Chinese were moving gradually backwards into the country, with their families, effects, and all that appertained unto them, reminding one of the aborigines of the West, with this important difference, that the Chinese generally left of their free will and were liberally remunerated for their property by the foreigners. Their chief care was to remove, with their other effects, the bodies of their deceased friends, which are commonly interred on private property near their houses. Hence it was no uncommon thing to meet several coffins being borne by coolies or friends to the westward. In many instances when the coffins were uncovered they were found totally decayed, and it was impossible to remove them. When this was the case, a Chinese might be seen holding a book in his hand, which contained a list of the bones, and directing others in their search after these the last remnants of mortality.

It is most amusing to see the groups of Chinese merchants who come from some distance inland on a visit to Shanghae. They wander about along the river side with wonder depicted in their countenances. The square-rigged vessels which crowd the river, the houses of the foreigners, their horses and their dogs, are all objects of wonder, even more so than the foreigners themselves. Mr. Beale, who has one of the finest houses here, has frequent applications from respectable Chinese who are anxious to see the inside of an English dwelling. These applications are always complied with in the kindest manner, and the visitors depart highly delighted with the view. It is to be hoped that these peeps at our comforts and refinements may have a tendency to raise the "barbarian race" a step or two higher in the eyes of the "enlightened" Chinese.

A pretty English church forms one of the ornaments of the new town, and a small cemetery has been purchased from the Chinese; it is walled round, and has a little chapel in the centre. In the course of time we may perhaps take a lesson from the Chinese, and render this place a more pleasing object than it is at present. Were it properly laid out with good walks, and planted with weeping willows, cypresses, pines, and other trees of an ornamental and appropriate kind, it would tend to raise us in the eyes of a people who of all nations are most particular in their attention to the graves of the dead.

The gardens of the foreign residents in Shanghae are not unworthy of notice; they far excel those of the Chinese, both in the number of trees and shrubs which they contain, and also in the neat and tasteful manner in which they are laid out and arranged. The late Mr. Hetherington* was the first to

---

* Mr. Hetherington fell a victim to a fever of a very fatal kind which prevailed in the autumn of 1848. He was a true specimen of the old English gentleman, and was deeply regretted by all who had the pleasure of knowing him.

attempt rearing vegetables on a large scale.   He introduced asparagus, which now succeeds admirably at Shanghae, rhubarb, seakale, and all the vegetables common in English gardens.   He also raised the strawberry from some seeds I sent him in 1846, and large quantities of this fine fruit were seen for the first time in Shanghae in the summer of 1850.   The ground about the town is too low and wet for the growth of the potato, and hence no one has succeeded in rearing what would be called a good crop of this desirable vegetable.   In the course of time, however, when the cultivation is attempted in the higher parts of the country, we may expect to get better potatoes here than at Macao, although the latter are usually most excellent.

The English consul, Mr. Alcock, has also a good vegetable garden on the grounds attached to the consulate.   There is a noble plant of the *Glycine sinensis* in this garden, which flowers most profusely, and becomes covered with its long legumes, or pea-like fruit, which ripen to perfection.

The two most beautiful ornamental gardens are those of Mr. Beale and the Messrs. Mackenzie.   Mr. Beale's house, a fine square building of two stories, is placed in the centre of the garden.   In front is a fine grass lawn, which extends from the house to the boundary-wall near the river.   Behind the house there is another lawn surrounded with a dwarf ornamental wall.   A wide gravel walk, leading from the entrance to the back part of the garden, divides the house from the business part of the premises.   This garden is rich in plants indigenous to China, and also contains many which have been introduced from other parts of the world. On entering the gate the first thing which strikes a botanist is a fine specimen of the new funereal cypress, nearly six feet high, and just beginning to show its beautiful weeping habit. This has been obtained from the interior, as it is not found in the neighbourhood of Shanghae. Mr. Beale intends to plant another on the opposite side of the gate, and, when the two grow up, a very striking and pretty effect will be produced. In the same border there are fine specimens of *Weigela rosea*, *Forsythia viridissima*, *Chimonanthus*, *Moutans*, *Lagerstrœmias*, roses, &c., and of nearly all the new plants sent home to the Horticultural Society from 1843 to 1846. In this part of the garden there is also a fine plant of the new *Berberis japonica*, lately obtained from the interior.

The American *Magnolia grandiflora* has been introduced here, and promises to be a very ornamental tree; its fine green leaves and noble flowers are much admired by the northern Chinese. Several plants of *Cryptomeria japonica* are succeeding admirably, and will soon be much more beautiful than any in this part of the country. The garden has been raised with a large quantity of fresh soil considerably above the level of the surrounding ground, so that all the family of the pines succeed much better than in those places where they are usually planted by the Chinese; besides, the latter generally spoil all the trees belonging to this family by lopping off the lower branches for firewood.

Large quantities of the *Olea fragrans*, the Qui Wha, are planted in different parts of the garden. These succeed much better here than in the south of China. In the autumn, when they are in bloom, the air is perfumed with the most delicious fragrance. Another most fragrant plant is the new *Gardenia* (*G. Fortuniana*), now common in English gardens, to which it was introduced by the Horticultural Society in 1845. In Mr. Beale's garden many of the bushes of this charming species are ten or twelve feet in circumference, and in the season are covered with fine double white flowers, as large as a camellia, and highly fragrant. Altogether this is a most interesting garden, and promises to be to Shanghae what the well-known garden of Mr. Beale's father was to Macao.

The Messrs. Mackenzie's garden here is also well worthy of notice. It resembles some of those attached to the neat suburban residences near London. The shrubs are arranged with great taste in groups and single specimens on the lawn, and consist of all the species and varieties common in this part of China. The collection of Azaleas is particularly fine. During the summer time, when these plants are in bloom, they are placed on a stage, and protected from the sun and rain. They flower in great profusion; the individual flowers are larger, and the colours are more brilliant, than they are in England. Here, too, are gorgeous specimens of the new Viburnums (*V. plicatum* and *V. macrocephalum*) sent to Chiswick in 1845. The first English apple-tree fruited in this garden about a year ago.

c

The gentlemen connected with the London Missionary Society have a village of their own about a quarter of a mile back from the English town. Each house has a good garden in front of it, full of interesting Chinese shrubs and trees. Dr. Lockhart has the finest collection.

These short statements are sufficient to show what has been done since the last war. Chinese plants have not only been introduced to Europe and America, to enliven and beautify our parks and gardens, but we have also enriched those of the Celestial Empire with the productions of the West. Nothing, I believe, can give the Chinese a higher idea of our civilisation and attainments than our love for flowers, or tend more to create a kindly feeling between us and them.

Before all these gardens could be stocked the demand for shrubs and trees was necessarily great, and varieties which in former days were comparatively rare about Shanghae have been brought down in boat-loads and sold at very low prices. Good young plants of *Cryptomeria*, three to four feet in height, are now sold for thirty cash each, about a penny of our money; a hundred fine bushy plants of the new *Gardenia* just noticed have frequently been bought for a dollar. It is amusing to see the boat-loads of plants ranged along the river banks to tempt the eye of the English planter. They are chiefly brought from the large towns of Soo-chow and Hang-chow, the former fifty miles distant, and the latter about a hundred.

CHAPTER II.

My object in coming north — Difficulty in procuring tea-plants — No
dependence can be placed upon the Chinese — Adopt the dress of
the country — Start for the interior — Mode of getting my head
shaved — City of Kea-hing-foo and its old cemetery — Lakes and
" ling " — Mode of gathering the " ling " — Great silk country —
Increase in exports — City of Seh-mun-yuen — Fear of thieves —
Hang-chow-foo — The " Garden of China" — Description of the city
and its suburbs — Gaiety of the people — Adventure in the city
— Kan-du — A " chop " — A Chinese inn — I get no breakfast
and lose my dinner — Boat engaged for Hwuy-chow — Importance
of Hang-chow both for trading and " *squeezing*."

My object in coming thus far north was to obtain
seeds and plants of the tea shrub for the Hon. East
India Company's plantations in the north-west provinces
of India.   It was a matter of great importance to procure them from those districts in China where the
best teas were produced, and I now set about accom-
plishing this object.   There were various tea districts
near Ning-po where very fair green teas were prepared
for Chinese use ; but these teas were not very well
suited to the foreign market.   It might be that the
plant was precisely the same variety from which the
finer sorts were made, and that the difference consisted
only in climate, in soil, or, more likely still, in a
different mode of manipulation.   This might or might
not be the case ; no one, so far as I knew, had ever
visited the Hwuy-chow district and brought away
plants from the tea hills there.   In these circum-

stances I considered that it would be a most unsatisfactory proceeding to procure plants and seeds from the Ning-po district only, or to take it for granted that they were the same as those in the great green-tea country of Hwuy-chow.

It was a very easy matter to get plants and seeds from the tea countries near Ning-po. Foreigners are allowed to visit the islands in the Chusan archipelago, such as Chusan and Kin-tang, in both of which the tea shrub is most abundant. They can also go to the celebrated temple of Tein-tung, about twenty miles inland, in the neighbourhood of which tea is cultivated upon an extensive scale.

But the Hwuy-chow district is upwards of 200 miles inland from either of the northern ports of Shanghae or Ning-po. It is a sealed country to Europeans. If we except the Jesuit missionaries, no one has ever entered within the sacred precincts of Hwuy-chow.*

Having determined, if possible, to procure plants and seeds from this celebrated country, there were but two ways of proceeding in the business. Either Chinese agents must be employed to go into the country to procure them and bring them down, or I must go there myself. At first sight the former way seemed the only one possible—certainly it was the easiest. But there were some very formidable objections to this course. Suppose I had engaged Chinese agents for this purpose—and plenty would have

---

* Since this was written I have been informed that the Rev. Mr. Medhurst passed through some part of this district.

undertaken the mission—how could I be at all certain that the plants or seeds which they would have
brought me had been obtained in the districts in
question?   No dependence can be placed upon the
veracity of the Chinese.   I may seem uncharitable,
but such is really the case; and if it suited the purpose of the agents employed in this matter they
would have gone a few miles inland to the nearest
tea district—one which I could have visited myself
with ease and safety—and have made up their collection there.   After staying away for a month or
two they would have returned to me with the collection, and, if requisite, have sworn that they had
obtained it in the country to which I had desired
them to proceed.   It is just possible that they might
have done otherwise; but even if they had I could
not have been certain that such was the case, and I
therefore abandoned all idea of managing the business
in that way, and determined to make an effort to
penetrate into the Hwuy-chow country myself, where
I could not only procure the true plants which produce the finest green teas of commerce, but also gain
some information with regard to the nature of the
soil of the district and the best modes of cultivation.

I had two Hwuy-chow men in my service at this
time.   I sent for them, and inquired whether it was
possible to penetrate so far into the country.   They
replied that we could easily do so, and that they were
quite willing to accompany me, only stipulating that
I should discard my English costume and adopt the

dress of the country. I knew that this was indispensable if I wished to accomplish the object in view,
and readily acceded to the terms.

My servants now procured me a Chinese dress,
and had the tail which I had worn in former years
nicely dressed by the barber. Everything was soon
in readiness except the boat which had to be engaged
for the first stage of our journey. This was, just
then, a difficult matter, owing to some boatmen having been severely punished by the Chinese authorities for taking three or four foreigners some distance
inland to see the silk districts. These gentlemen
went in the English dress, and complaints were consequently made by the officers in the districts through
which they passed to the mandarins in Shanghae.
On this account it was impossible to engage a boat as
a foreigner, and I desired my servant to hire it in
his own name, and merely state that two other persons were to accompany him. He agreed to this
plan, and soon returned with a "chop," or agreement, which he had entered into with a man who
engaged to take us as far as the city of Hang-
chow-foo.

Thus far all was right; but now my two men
began to be jealous of each other, each wanting to
manage the concern, with the view, as it proved
ultimately, of getting as many dollars out of me
as possible. One of them had been engaged as a
servant and linguist, and the other was little better
than a common coolie. I therefore intrusted the
management of our affairs to the former, much to

the disgust of the other, who was an older man.   In
an ordinary case I would have sent one of them
away, but, as I had but little confidence in either, I
thought that in their present jealous state the one
would prove a check upon the other.   The projected
journey was a long one, the way was unknown to me,
and I should have been placed in an awkward position had they agreed to rob me, and then run off and
leave me when far inland.   The jealous feeling that
existed between them was therefore, I considered,
rather a safeguard than otherwise.

As I was anxious to keep the matter as secret as
possible, I intended to have left the English part of
the town at night in a chair, and gone on board the
boat near to the east gate of the city, where she lay
moored in the river.   Greatly to my surprise, however, I observed a boat, such as I knew mine to be,
alongside of one of the English jetties, and apparently
ready for my reception.   " Is that the boat that you
have engaged ?" said I to my servant Wang.   " Yes,"
said he, " that coolie has gone and told the boatman
all about the matter, and that an Englishman is
going in his boat."   " But will the boatman consent
to go now ?"   " Oh ! yes," he replied, " if you will
only add a trifle more to the fare."   To this I consented, and, after a great many delays, everything
was at last pronounced to be ready for our starting.
As the boatman knew who I was, I went on board
in my English dress, and kept it on during the first
day.

When I rose on the morning of the second day,

we were some distance from Shanghae, and the boatman suggested that it was now time to discard the
English dress, and adopt that of the country, according to our agreement. To put on the dress was an
easy matter, but I had also to get my head shaved—
an operation which required a barber. Wang, who
was the most active of my two men, was laid up that
morning with fever and ague, so that the duty de-
volved upon the coolie. The latter was a large-
boned, clumsy fellow, whose only recommendation to
me was his being a native of that part of the country
to which I was bound. Having procured a pair of
scissors, he clipped the hair from the front, back, and
sides of my head, leaving only a patch upon the
crown. He then washed those parts with hot water,
after the manner of the Chinese, and, having done so,
he took up a small razor and began to shave my
head. I suppose I must have been the first person
upon whom he had ever operated, and I am charitable enough to wish most sincerely that I may be
the last. He did not shave, he actually scraped my
poor head until the tears came running down my
cheeks, and I cried out with pain. All he said was,
" Hai-yah—very bad, very bad," and continued the
operation. To make matters worse, and to try my
temper more, the boatmen were peeping into the
cabin and evidently enjoying the whole affair, and
thinking it capital sport. I really believe I should
have made a scene of a less amusing kind had I not
been restrained by prudential motives, and by the
consideration that the poor coolie was really doing

the best he could.   The shaving was finished at last;
I then dressed myself in the costume of the country,
and the result was pronounced by my servants and
boatmen to be very satisfactory.

The whole country to the westward of Shanghae
is intersected with rivers and canals, so that the traveller can visit by boat almost all the towns and
cities in this part of the province.   Some of the
canals lead to the large cities of Sung-kiang-foo, Soo-
chow-foo, Nanking, and onward by the Grand Canal
to the capital itself.   Others, again, running to the
west and south-west, form the highways to the Tartar
city of Chapoo, Hang-chow-foo, and to numerous other
cities and towns, which are studded over this large
and important plain.

We proceeded in a south-westerly direction—my
destination being the city of Hang-chow-foo.   Having
a fair wind during the first day, we got as far as the
Maou lake, a distance of 120 or 130 le * from
Shanghae.   Here we stopped for the night, making
our boat fast to a post driven into the grassy banks
of the lake.   Starting early next morning, we reached
in the forenoon a town of considerable size, named
Kea-hing-yuen, and a little farther on we came to the
city of Kea-hing-foo, a large place walled and fortified.

This city seems nearly as large as Shanghae, and
probably contains about the same number of inha-

* A *le* has generally been set down as the third part of an English
mile, but if we suppose a fourth, or even a fifth, we shall be nearer the
truth.

bitants—270,000. Its walls and ramparts had been
in a most dilapidated and ruinous condition, but the
people got such a fright when the English took
Chapoo—which is not a very great distance off—
that they came forward with funds, and had the de-
fences of their city substantially repaired. Such was
the boatmen's story when accounting for the excellent order in which the fortifications were. A number of old grain junks, of great size considering the
depth of water, are moored in the canal abreast of
the city, and are apparently used as dwelling-houses
by the natives; some, however, are half sunk in the
water, and appear entirely abandoned. Junks of the
same description as these are seen abreast of all the
large towns on the grand canal. When too old for
the Government service they seem to be drawn up to
the nearest city, and either used by Government
officers as dwelling-houses, or sold to the highest
bidder.

We had now entered the great Hang-chow silk
district, and the mulberry was observed in great
abundance on the banks of the canal, and in patches
over all the country.

I was greatly struck with the appearance of a
cemetery on the western side of the city of Kea-
hing-foo, not very far from the city walls. Its large
extent gave a good idea of the numerous and dense
population of the town. It had evidently existed for
many ages, for a great number of the tombstones
were crumbling to pieces, and mingling with the
ashes of the dead. But this "place of skulls" was

no barren waste, like those churchyards which we see
in large towns at home. Here the dead were interred
amidst groves of the weeping willow, mulberry-trees,
and several species of juniper and pine. Wild roses
and creepers of various kinds were scrambling over
the tombs, and the whole place presented a hallowed
and pleasing aspect.

Leaving the old town behind us, and sailing westward, we entered a broad sheet of water of considerable size, which is probably part of, or at least joins,
the celebrated Tai-ho lake. The water is very shallow, and a great part of it is covered with the *Trapa
bicornis*—a plant called *ling* by the Chinese. It
produces a fruit of a very peculiar shape, resembling
the head and horns of a bullock, and is highly
esteemed in all parts of the empire. I have seen
three distinct species or varieties, one of which has
fruit of a beautiful red colour.

Women and boys were sailing about on all parts of
the lake, in tubs of the same size and form as our
common washing-tubs, gathering the fruit of the *ling*.
I don't know of any contrivance which would have
answered their purpose better than these rude tubs,
for they held the fruit as it was gathered as well as
the gatherer, and at the same time were easily propelled through the masses of *ling* without doing the
plants any injury. The sight of a number of people
swimming about on the lake, each in his tub, had
something very ludicrous about it.

After we had passed the lake, the banks of the
canal, and indeed the greater part of the country,

were covered with mulberry trees.   Silk is evidently
the staple production in this part of China.   During
the space of two days—and in that time I must have
travelled upwards of a hundred miles—I saw little
else than mulberry trees.   They were evidently carefully cultivated, and in the highest state of health,
producing fine, large, and glossy leaves.   When it is
remembered that I was going in a straight direction
through the country, some idea may be formed of the
extent of this enormous silk district, which probably
occupies a circle of at least a hundred miles in
diameter.   And this, it must be remembered, is only
one of the silk districts in China, but it is the principal and the best one.   The merchant and silk-
manufacturer will form a good idea of the quantity
of silk consumed in China, when told that, after the
war, on the port of Shanghae being opened, the
exports of raw silk increased in two or three years
from 3000 to 20,000 bales.   This fact shows, I
think, the enormous quantity which must have been
in the Chinese market before the extra demand
could have been so easily supplied.   But as it is
with tea, so it is with silk,—the quantity exported
bears but a small proportion to that consumed by the
Chinese themselves.   The 17,000 extra bales sent
yearly out of the country have not in the least degree
affected the price of raw silk or of silk manufactures.
This fact speaks for itself.

Seh-mun-yuen, a town about 140 le north-east
from Hang-chow-foo, was the next place of any note
which I passed.   It is apparently a very ancient

city, but has no trade, and is altogether in a most dilapidated condition. The walls were completely overrun with wild shrubs, and in many places were crumbling into ruins. It had evidently seen better and more prosperous days, which had long ago passed by. The boatmen informed me that this part of the country abounded in thieves and robbers, and that they must not all go to bed at night, otherwise something would be stolen from the boat before morning.

We reached the city about three o'clock in the afternoon. The morning had been cold and rainy, and the boatmen, who were all wet to the skin, refused to proceed further that day. I was therefore obliged to make up my mind to stay there all that night, and a more disagreeable one I never spent. After dark my servants and the boatmen told stories of celebrated pirates and robbers, until they frightened themselves, and almost made me believe myself to be in dangerous company. The wind was very high, and, as it whistled amongst the ruinous ramparts, the sound was dismal enough; and what added still more to our discomfort, the rain beat through the roof of our boat, and kept dripping upon our beds.

Before retiring to sleep it had been arranged that my coolie and one of the boatmen were to sit and keep watch during the night for our protection from thieves. The coolie's station was inside the boat, where I was, and the other man was to keep watch in the after-part of the boat, where the cooking department was carried on. How long these sentries

kept watch I cannot tell, but when I awoke, some
time before the morning dawned, the dangers of the
place seemed to be completely forgotten, except perhaps in their dreams, for I found them sound asleep.
The other men were also sleeping heavily, and no
one seemed to have harmed us during our slumbers.
I now roused the whole of them, and, the morning
being fine, we proceeded on our journey towards the
city of Hang-chow-foo.

During this three days' journey we had been
passing through a perfectly level country, having
seen only three or four small hills near the city of
Sung-kiang-foo. Now, however, the scene began to
change, and the hills which gird this extensive plain
on the west and south-west sides came into view.
We passed a town named Tan-see, which is on the
side of the grand canal on which we were now sailing.
Tan-see is a bustling town of considerable size, a few
miles to the north-east of Hang-chow-foo. The appearance of the flat country here was rich and beautiful. Still the mulberry was seen extensively cultivated on all the higher patches of ground, and rice
occupied the low wet land.

As we approached Hang-chow the vegetation of
the country was richer and under a higher state of
cultivation than any which had come under my
notice in other parts of China. It reminded me of
the appearance which those highly cultivated spots
present near our large market towns in England.
Here were beautiful groves of the loquat (*Eriobotrya
japonica*), yang-mai (*Myrica sp.*), peaches, plums,

oranges, and all the fruits of Central China, in a high state of cultivation.

The country around Hang-chow-foo may well be called "the garden of China." The grand canal, with its numerous branches, not only waters it, but also affords the means of travelling through it, and of conveying the productions for which it is famous to other districts. The hills in the background, the beautiful bay which comes up to the town and stretches far away towards the ocean, and the noble river which here falls into the bay, all contribute to render the scenery strikingly beautiful.

On the evening of the 22nd of October I approached the suburbs of Hang-chow-foo—one of the largest and most flourishing cities in the richest district of the Chinese empire. The Chinese authorities have always been most jealous of foreigners approaching or entering this town. It is generally supposed that, in addition to the natural antipathy which they manifest to the "outside barbarians," they have a custom-house here in which they levy duties on merchandise imported or exported by foreigners, which duties are opposed to the terms of the treaty of Nanking. They know well enough that, if foreigners were allowed to come here, this system of extortion would soon be exposed and broken up.

As I drew nearer the city, everything which came under my observation marked it as a place of great importance. The grand canal was deep and wide, and bore on its waters many hundreds of boats of

different sizes, all engaged in an active bustling trade.
Many of these were sailing in the same direction as
ourselves, whilst others were leaving the city and
hurrying onwards in the direction of Soo-chow, Hoo-
chow, Kea-hing, and other towns. Canals were seen
branching off from the grand canal in all directions,
and forming the high roads of the country.

When I reached the end of this part of my
journey my boatmen drew up and moored the boat
amongst thousands of the same class, and, it being
now nearly dark, I determined to rest there for the
night. When the next morning dawned, and I had
time to take a survey of our position, I found that
we had been moored on the edge of a large broad
basin of water which terminates the grand canal.
As I had nothing to do in the city, and merely
wanted to pass onwards on my journey to the green-
tea country, I did not wish to run the risk of passing
through it. Before leaving Shanghae, when consulting the map and fixing my route, I asked if it were
possible to get to the mouth of the Hang-chow river
without actually passing through the city itself. Both
my men informed me that this was quite easy, and
even protested strongly against my entering the town.
They said we could go by the See-hoo lake, at which
place we could leave the Shanghae boat, and then
proceed on foot or in chairs a distance of 30 le. By
this means we should merely skirt the town, and
attain the object we had in view. This plan seemed
feasible enough. When we reached the suburbs of
Hang-chow, therefore, not knowing the locality, I

naturally supposed that we were at See-hoo, which is only a part of the suburbs. This, however, was not the case.

Wang, who had been sent on shore at daybreak to procure a chair, and coolies for our luggage, now came back and informed me that he had succeeded in arranging all this at an inn hard by, to which we must now go. Leaving the boat, we walked up a crowded street for nearly a quarter of a mile, and then entered the inn in question. No one took the slightest notice of me, a circumstance which gave me a good deal of confidence, and led me to conclude that I was dressed in a proper manner, and that I made a pretty good Chinaman.

Our Shanghae boatmen accompanied us, carrying our luggage; indeed I believe they had recommended us to the inn at which we had now arrived. To my astonishment they at once informed their friend the innkeeper that I was a foreigner. Having been paid their fare, they had nothing more to expect, and I suppose could not contain the secret any longer. I now expected that some difficulties would be experienced in procuring a chair, either through fear of the mandarins, or with the view of extorting money. The old man, who made his living by letting chairs and selling tea, took everything very quietly, and did not seem to despise a good customer, even if he was a foreigner. A chair was soon ready for me to proceed on my journey. The bearers were paid by the master of the house to take me one stage—about half way—and a sum of money was

given them to engage another chair for the remainder
of the journey, to a place called Kan-du, which is
situated on the banks of the large river which here
falls into the bay of Hang-chow.

Everything being satisfactorily arranged, I stepped
into the chair, and, desiring my two servants to follow
me, proceeded along the narrow streets at a rapid
pace. After travelling in this way for about a mile,
and expecting every moment to get out into the open
country, I was greatly surprised by finding that I was
getting more and more into a dense town. For the
first time I began to suspect that my servants were
deceiving me, and that I was to pass through the city
of Hang-chow after all. These suspicions were soon
confirmed by the appearance of the walls and ramparts of the city. It was now too late to object to
this procedure, and I thought the best way to act
was to let matters take their course and remain
passive in the business.

We passed through the gates into the city. It
seemed an ancient place : the walls and ramparts were
high and in excellent repair, and the gates were
guarded as usual by a number of soldiers. Its main
street, through which I passed, is narrow when compared with streets in European towns; but it is well
paved, and reminded me of the main street of Ning-
po. Hang-chow, however, is a place of much greater
importance than Ning-po, both in a political and
mercantile point of view. It is the chief town of
the Chekiang province, and is the residence of many
of the principal mandarins and officers of govern-

ment, as well as of many of the great merchants.   It
has been remarked not unfrequently, when comparing the towns of Shanghae and Ning-po, that the
former is a trading place, and the latter a place of
great wealth.   Hang-chow-foo has both these advantages combined.   Besides, it is a fashionable place,
and is to the province of Chekiang what Soo-chow-foo
is to Kiang-nan.   Du Halde quotes an old proverb
which significantly says that "Paradise is *above*, but
below are Soo-chow and Hang-chow."

The walls of this terrestrial paradise are said to
be forty le in circumference, that is, about eight
English miles.   Although there are a great many
gardens and open spaces inside, yet the extent of the
city is very great, and in many parts the population
is most dense.   The suburbs also are very extensive,
and must contain a very large population.   Sir
George Staunton supposed that the population of the
city and suburbs was equal to that of Peking, and
Du Halde estimates it at a million of souls.

The houses bear a striking resemblance to those
of Ning-po, Soo-chow, and other northern towns.
Were I set down blindfolded in the main street of
one of these Chinese towns, even in one which I
knew well, and the bandage removed from my eyes,
I should have great difficulty in saying where I was.
There are doubtless distinctions with which the
" barbarian" eye is unacquainted, but which would
be plain enough to a Chinese.

I observed in many parts of the city triumphal
arches, monuments to great men, and gorgeous-look-

ing Buddhist temples; but although these buildings
have a certain degree of interest about them, and
many of them are certainly curious, yet as works of
art they are not to be compared with the buildings of
the same class which one meets with at home.

The shops in the main streets have their fronts
entirely removed by day, so that the passenger may
have an opportunity of seeing and of forming a good
idea of the wares which are for sale. I observed
many shops where gold and silver ornaments and
valuable Jade stone were exposed for sale. Old
curiosity shops were numerous, and contained articles
of great value amongst the Chinese, such as ancient
porcelain jars, bronzes, carved bamboo, jars cut out
of the beautiful Jade stone, and a variety of other
things of like description. I observed some large
silk-shops as I passed along, and, judging from the
number of people in the town who wear silk dresses,
they must have a thriving trade. Everything, indeed,
which met the eye, stamped Hang-chow-foo as a place
of wealth and luxury. As usual in all the Chinese
towns which I have visited, there were a vast number
of tea and eating houses for the middle classes and
the poor. They did not seem to lack customers, for
they were all crowded with hundreds of natives, who,
for a few cash or "tseen," can obtain a healthy and
substantial meal.

Besides the officers of Government, merchants,
shopkeepers, and common labourers connected with
any of these professions, the city contains a large
manufacturing population. Silk is the staple article

of manufacture. Du Halde estimates the numbers engaged in this operation at sixty thousand. I observed a great number employed in the reeling process, and others were busily engaged with the beautiful embroidery for which this part of China is so famous.

The people of Hang-chow dress gaily, and are remarkable amongst the Chinese for their dandyism. All except the lowest labourers and coolies strutted about in dresses composed of silk, satin, and crape. My Chinese servants were one day contrasting the natives of Hang-chow in this respect with those of the more inland parts from which they came. They said there were many rich men in their country, but they all dressed plainly and modestly, while the natives of Hang-chow, both rich and poor, were never contented unless gaily dressed in silks and satins. "Indeed," said they, "one can never tell a rich man in Hang-chow, for it is just possible that all he possesses in the world is on his back."

When we were about half way through the city the chairmen set me down, and informed me that they went no farther. I got out and looked round for my servants, from whom I expected an explanation, for I had understood that the chairmen had been paid to take me the whole way through. My servants, however, were nowhere to be seen—they had either gone some other road, or, what was more probable, had intentionally kept out of the way in case of any disturbance. I was now in a dilemma, and did not clearly see my way out of it. Much to

my surprise and pleasure, however, another chair
was brought me, and I was informed that I was to
proceed in it.   I now understood how the business
had been managed.   The innkeeper had intrusted
the first bearers with a sum of money sufficient to
hire another chair for the second stage of the journey.
Part of this sum, however, had been spent by them
in tea and tobacco as we came along, and the second
bearers could not be induced to take me on for the
sum which was left.   A brawl now ensued between
the two sets of chairmen, which was noisy enough;
but as such things are quite common in China, it
seemed, fortunately for me, to attract but little notice.
The situation in which I was now placed was rather
critical, and far from an enviable one.   Had it been
known that a foreigner was in the very heart of the
city of Hang-chow-foo, a mob would have soon collected, and the consequences might have been
serious.

" Take things coolly and never lose your temper"
should be the motto of every one who attempts to
travel in China.   This is always the best plan, for, if
you allow things to take their course, ten to one you
will get out of a dilemma like that in which I was now
placed; but if you attempt to interfere, you will probably make matters worse.   These were the principles on which I generally acted; but in the present
instance I was not allowed to carry them out to their
fullest extent.

I had taken my seat in the second chair, and was
patiently waiting until such time as the first men

could give the second satisfactory reasons for spending part of their cash in tea and tobacco. The first notice, however, which I received of the unsuccessful result of this attempt, was an intimation that I was to be ejected from the chair. I knew this would not do, as from my imperfect knowledge of the language I might have some difficulty in finding another conveyance, and I did not know one foot of the way which I was going. I was therefore obliged to inquire into the dispute, and put an end to it by promising to pay the difference when we arrived at the end of our stage. This was evidently what the first rascals had been calculating upon; but it had the effect of stopping all further disputes, and my bearers shouldered their burthen and jogged onwards.

The distance from the basin of the Grand Canal to the river on the opposite side is 28 or 30 le, between five and six miles. After leaving the city behind us, we passed through a pretty undulating country for about two miles, and then entered the town of Kan-du, which is built along the banks of the river Tcien-tang-kiang, sometimes called the Green River, which here falls into the Bay of Hang-chow. Kan-du is the seaport of Hang-chow.

I had seen nothing of my servants during the whole way, and was beginning to expect a scene or adventure at the end of this part of the journey. The chair-bearers spoke a peculiar dialect, which I could scarcely make out, and I kept wondering as we went along what would happen next. The only thing I could make out was, that they were taking me to a

Hong-le, but what a Hong-le was, was beyond my comprehension.

To carry out my own principles and trust to circumstances seemed to be the only way of proceeding, and I gave myself very little uneasiness about the result. At length I heard the men say that here was the Hong-le, and, as I was about to look and see what this might be, the chair was set down, and it was intimated to me that we had reached the end of the journey. Greatly to my surprise and pleasure I now found that this Hong-le was a quiet and comfortable Chinese inn, which was frequented by passengers from all parts of the country. Getting out of my chair, I walked quietly up to the farther end of the large hall, and began to look amongst a number of packages which were heaped up there for my own luggage. I had seen nothing of either that or my servants since I left the former inn. It had arrived, however, quite safely, having been sent on by a coolie before me, and in a few minutes my two men also made their appearance.

We now informed the innkeeper that we wanted to go up the river to Hwuy-chow, and made inquiries regarding a boat. We soon found that it was part of his trade to give " chops," or to " secure" boatmen. Everything is done upon this plan in China. When a servant is engaged, or a boat hired, it is always necessary for the said servant or boatman to produce some respectable householder, who for a certain sum becomes bound for him in a written " chop" or agreement. This " chop" is handed over

to the master of the servant, or to the hirer of the
boat, who retains it until his contract is satisfactorily
fulfilled. This system is practised universally amongst
the Chinese, who seem to have no faith in the lower
orders of the people.

I quickly despatched Wang to look after a boat,
and desired him to bring the boatman with him to
the inn, to have his agreement drawn up and signed.
The other man ran out along with him, and I was
again left in a strange place amongst strangers.

The inn in which I was located was a large old
building, pleasantly situated on the banks of the
Green River. All the lower part formed a sort of
shed or warehouse, which was filled with goods of
various kinds and the luggage of passengers. At
the upper end of this apartment a table was placed
in the middle of the floor, and served for the host and
his guests to dine upon. Around this table were
sitting five or six respectable-looking Chinese merchants smoking from long bamboo pipes, and discuss-
ing the news of the day and the state of trade.
These men politely made way for me at the table.
I took the seat offered, and to be neighbour-like
commenced smoking as fast as any of them. In
other parts of the warehouse the servants of these
men, and other travelling servants, were lolling about,
or sound asleep upon the chairs or goods. No one
seemed to take any particular notice of me, and I
soon sat perfectly at my ease.

A little incident happened which gave me some
uneasiness at the time, but at which I have often had

a good laugh since. Preparations began to be made
for dinner, and the travellers who were seated around
the table arose and wandered about the other parts of
the house. It was mid-day, and, as I had eaten no
breakfast, I felt rather hungry. In these circumstances it may be thought that the appearance of
dinner would have afforded me some pleasure. This,
however, was not the case, and for the following
reason: I had not eaten with chop-sticks for three
years, and I had no confidence in my talents in the
use of them. This important circumstance had not
struck me before, otherwise I would have practised
all the way from Shanghae to Hang-chow, and might
have been proficient by this time. As it was I was
quite certain that I should draw the eyes of the Chinamen upon me, for nothing would astonish them so
much as a person using the chop-sticks in an awkward manner. I was therefore obliged, reluctantly I
confess, to abandon all ideas of a dinner on that day.

Meanwhile the dishes were placed upon the table,
and the guests were called by their names and requested to sit down. " Sing Wa, Sing Wa " (the
name I bore amongst the Chinese), " come and sit
down to dinner." I felt much inclined to break my
resolution and sit down, but prudence came to my
aid, and I replied, " No, I thank you, I shall dine by
and by, when my servants come back." I believe it
is common enough for travellers to dine at different
hours and in different ways, according to circumstances, so that my refusal did not seem to attract
much notice.

A short time afterwards my servants returned, bringing a boatman with them to have a chop made out, and to have him "secured" by the innkeeper. As soon as this was done to our satisfaction we left the inn and walked down to the boat, which lay alongside of one of the wharfs at the river side. Several other passengers had also arrived, and we were all to sleep on board, as the boat was to start at daybreak on the following morning. To me this had been an exciting and adventurous day, and I was not sorry when the darkness closed around us and we all retired to rest.

The river Tcien-tang-kiang, on which I was now, has its sources far away amongst the mountains to the westward. One of its branches rises amongst the green-tea hills of Hwuy-chow, another near to the town of Changshan, on the borders of Kiang-see, and a third on the northern side of the Bohea mountains. These streams unite in their course to the eastward, and, passing Hang-chow, fall into the bay which bears the same name. All the green and black tea comes down this river on its way to Shanghae, and at Hang-chow is transhipped from the river-boats into those which ply upon the Grand Canal. The importance of Hang-chow-foo, in a mercantile point of view, is therefore very great. All goods from the south and westward must of necessity pass through this town on their way to the large and populous districts about Soo-chow, Sung-kiang, and Shanghae. In the same manner all foreign imports, and the products of the low countries, such as silk and cotton, in going to the southward and westward, must also pass through Hang-chow. It therefore appears to be like a great gate on a public highway, through which nothing can pass or repass without the consent and cognizance of the authorities.

The power which this place gives the Chinese authorities over our imports and exports through Shanghae is very great, and hence complaints of stoppages and illegal charges, or " *squeezes,*" have been not unfrequent. The day cannot be very far distant when we shall be allowed to trade and travel in China as in other countries—when all those foolish regulations regarding boundary-lines will be swept away; but, in the event of these changes being gradual, it may be a question whether our Government should not endeavour to open the town of Hang-chow-foo, or at all events have a consular agent there for the encouragement and protection of our trade.

CHAPTER III.

Leave Hang-chow-foo — A China passage-boat — Scenery and natural productions — Remarkable hills — Our fellow-passengers — A smoker of opium — I am discovered to be a foreigner — City of Yen-chow-foo — A Chinaman cheats a Chinaman ! — The river and water-mills — Botany of the country — A valuable palm-tree — Birds — Lime-kilns and green granite — Tea-plant met with — The new FUNEREAL CYPRESS discovered — Its beauty — How its seeds were procured — Dr. Lindley's opinion of its merits — Strange echo — River and land beggars — Charity.

WHEN the next morning dawned we got under way and steered out into the river, which is here three or four miles in width. The boat was strongly built, flat-bottomed, and very sharp both fore and aft. Ordinary boats, such as those seen at Shanghae, would be perfectly useless here, for they would soon be broken to pieces on the rocks and stones which abound in this shallow but rapid river.

We were deeply laden with cargo, and carried about twenty passengers. The cargo was packed in the bottom of the boat, and the passengers above it. Two rows of sleeping-berths were constructed along each side of the boat, and a passage between them, so that both passengers and boatmen could walk from stem to stern without any inconvenience. The first-class passengers occupied the side-berths, and their servants and coolies slept in the passage.

A Chinese bed is not a very luxurious one. It

consists simply of a mat to lie upon, a hard square
pillow for the head, and a coverlet stuffed with cotton
to draw over the body as a protection from the
cold.

I had the berth nearest the stern of the boat, a
dwarf occupied the one opposite, and my two servants
slept in the passage between us. The galley, or, I
should rather say, cooking apparatus, was placed outside in the stern, near to the steersman.

Each passenger, when he takes his passage in these
boats, agrees for three meals a-day at a certain fixed
rate. We were to have congé in the morning, rice
at mid-day, and rice-congé again in the evening.
Anything else the passengers wanted, such as tea,
fish, meat, or vegetables, they had to provide and
cook for themselves. The arrangement seems a good
one, and it enables those who are so inclined to travel
at a very small cost. Many of the passengers had
nothing else than what was provided by the boatmen,
excepting perhaps a little tea, which they all carried
with them, and which in this country is cheap
enough.

In the morning a basin of hot water, with a cloth
in it, was brought to me to perform my ablutions.
The following is the Chinese way of using this: the
cloth is dipped in the hot water and then wrung until
the greater part of the water is pressed out. In this
hot and damp state it is spread out on both hands,
and the face, neck, and head rubbed over with it.
This mode of washing is not the most effectual, but
there is nothing more refreshing on a warm day, if

one comes in from a walk hot and weary; it is far more refreshing than bathing in cold water, and perhaps more conducive to health.

After I was dressed I received a cup of tea—tea in the strict sense of the word—without sugar or milk, these additions never being used in this part of China. About eight o'clock the cook had six large earthenware basins placed at the side of the rice-pot; each of these he filled brim full of congé, and set them in the open air to cool. When it was cool enough to be eaten, the basins were placed in a row in the passage between our berths; the passengers then arranged themselves into messes, four in each, and breakfast began. By this arrangement the dwarf, who occupied the berth opposite to mine, my two Chinese servants, and myself formed the mess nearest to the stern of the boat. Each man was furnished with a small basin and a pair of chop-sticks; a wooden ladle was placed in the earthen pan, with which each filled his basin.

Having had little to eat the day before, except some sweet potatoes which one of my men brought me, I was hungry enough not only to eat the congé, uninviting as it certainly was, but also to disregard the presence of the Chinese, or what they might think of the awkward way in which I used the chopsticks. I got on very well, however, and found that I had not quite forgotten the art of eating with these highly-civilized instruments. It is, however, easier to eat rice and congé with them than other kinds of food, for the basin is generally brought quite close up to the mouth, and its contents partly sucked and partly shovelled in.

The tide and wind were both fair, so that we glided up the river with great rapidity; it was a beautiful autumnal day, and the scene altogether was a most charming one. We had left behind us the great plain of the Yang-tse-kiang, and the country was now hilly and most romantic. The hills were richly wooded; pines, cypresses, and junipers clothed their sides from the base nearly to the top, and their foliage of a sombre green contrasted strongly with the deep-red, ripened leaves of the tallow-tree, which grows in great abundance on the plains. A few mulberry-trees were seen in the neighbourhood of Hang-chow, but, as we got higher up the river, their cultivation appeared to cease. Tobacco, Indian corn, millet, and a small portion of rice seemed to be the staple productions of the plains; millet and Indian corn were also observed on the lower sides of the hills.

Buddhist temples and pagodas were observed, here and there, rising high above the trees; one of the latter is called Lui-foong-ta, or the "temple of the thundering winds." It stands on the borders of the Se-hoo lake, and appeared to be a very ancient edifice. Wild briers and other weeds were growing out of its walls, even up to its very summit, and it was evidently fast going to decay. It formed a striking feature in the landscape, and reminded me of those ancient castle ruins which are so common on the borders of England and Scotland.

At night, when it became too dark to see our course, the boat was anchored abreast of a small village until the following morning, when we again got under way. We were now forty or fifty miles to the south-west of Hang-chow-foo.

The hills here had not that rich appearance which those nearer the sea had presented, but they were far more striking in their formation. Their sides were ridged and furrowed in a most remarkable manner, and their summits broken up into many curious peaks and cones. Some were low, others were three or four thousand feet in height, and all were rugged, barren, and wild.

The river now became narrow, shallow, and in many parts very rapid. Near Hang-chow-foo the country seemed densely populated, but up here there is so little ground capable of cultivation that a numerous population could not find subsistence. We only passed two towns of any note, named Fu-yang and Tung-yu, all the way from Hang-chow to Yen-chow-foo, a distance of 380 le. The people in the villages amongst these hills seemed to earn a scanty subsistence by cutting firewood and sending it down to the lowland towns for sale.

My fellow-passengers, who were chiefly merchants and servants, were quiet and inoffensive, indeed they did little else but loll in bed and sleep, except when they were eating or smoking. One of them was a confirmed opium-smoker, and the intoxicating drug had made him a perfect slave. I have seen many opium-smokers in my travels, but this one was the

E

most pitiable of them all; he was evidently a man of some standing in society, and had plenty of money. His bed was surrounded with silk curtains, his pillows were beautifully embroidered, and his coverlet was of the richest and softest satin. Everything about him told of luxury and sensual pleasures.

But let me take a peep inside his bed-curtains and describe what I saw on the first day of our acquaintance. The curtains were down and drawn close round, particularly on that side from which the wind came. He was clothed in the finest silks, and had lain down on his side upon a mat; his head was resting on one of the embroidered pillows. A small lamp was burning by his side, an opium-pipe was in his mouth, and he was inhaling the intoxicating fumes. After smoking for a few minutes he began to have the appearance which a drunken man presents in the first stage of intoxication; the fumes had done their work, and he was now in his "third heaven of bliss."

In a minute or two he jumped up and called for his teapot, from which he took a good draught of tea; he then walked about the boat evidently a good deal excited, and talked and joked with every one he met. After spending some time in this manner he began to smoke tobacco; he then took another draught out of his teapot and lay down to sleep; but his slumbers were not of long duration, and were evidently disturbed by strange and frightful dreams. He awoke at last, but it was only to renew the dose as before; and so on from day to day. Even in the silent night, when all around was sunk in repose, his craving for the stimulant was beyond his feeble powers of resistance. Often and often during this passage, when I happened to awake during the night, I could see his little lamp burning, and could smell the sickening fumes as they curled about the roof of the boat.

The effects which the immoderate use of opium had produced upon this man were of the most melancholy kind. His figure was thin and emaciated, his cheeks had a pale and haggard hue, and his skin had that peculiar glassy polish by which an opium-smoker is invariably known. His days were evidently numbered, and yet, strange to tell, this man tried to convince others and himself also that he was smoking medicinally, and that the use of opium was indispensable to his health. As I looked upon him in these moments of excitement I could not help feeling what a piteous object is man, the lord of Creation, and noblest work of God, when sensual pleasures and enjoyments take such a hold upon him as they had upon this poor opium-smoker.

During the first day all the passengers looked upon me as one of themselves, and I fancied I had become a very fair Chinaman; but my coolie, who was a silly, talkative fellow, imagined he was in possession of a secret, and doubtless felt the weight of it rather uncomfortable. I observed him once or twice in close conversation with one of the boatmen, and it turned out afterwards that he told this man, as a great secret of course, that I was a foreigner,—one

of those *Hong-mous* who were so numerous in Shanghae.   By-and-by the *secret* began to ooze out, and
both boatmen and passengers were taking sly peeps at
me when they thought I did not see them.   Suspecting that all was not right, I called Wang aside, and
asked him how it was that I had become all at once
such an object of interest.   "Oh," he said, "that
coolie he too much a fool-o; he have talkie all that
men you no belong this country; you more better
sendie he go away, suppose you no wantye too much
bobly."   In plain English, he informed me that the
coolie was a fool, that he had told all the people that
I was a foreigner, and that I had better send him
away if I did not wish to have a disturbance.

It was too true, my secret was such no longer.   I
felt much inclined to punish the coolie for his conduct, and he had to thank the peculiar circumstances
in which I was placed for getting off "scot free."   I
believe the poor fellow was sufficiently punished
afterwards by his own countrymen, who thought they
had him, to a certain extent, in their power.   Nothing
more occurred worthy of notice until we arrived at
the city of Yen-chow-foo, a large town about 380 le
from Hang-chow, in latitude 29° 37′ 12″ north, and
in longitude 119° 32′ 47″ east.   It is walled and
fortified in the same manner as all Chinese towns;
the walls are fully four miles in circumference.   It
seems an ancient place, but, judging from the small
number of boats moored in the river opposite, I
should not imagine it of much importance as a place
of trade.   A considerable quantity of rough lacquered

ware is manufactured here, and sold much cheaper than in the towns nearer to the sea. It is a place of call for all the Hwuy-chow boats, and a considerable trade is carried on in all the common necessaries of life. Judging from its size, it may contain about 200,000 inhabitants. They do not seem so rich, or at all events they are not so gaily dressed, as their neighbours in Hang-chow.

A little below the town there are two very pretty pagodas; one of these is built on a curious conical hill, and is named the Hoo-lung-tâ. Here the river divides, or, I should rather say, two streams unite, one of which comes down from the southward, taking its rise partly on the borders of Kiang-see and Kiang-nan, and partly on the northern sides of the Great Bohea mountains. To this I may return afterwards. In the mean time I went up the northern branch, which comes down from the green-tea country of Hwuy-chow.

The hills about Yen-chow-foo are barren, but the valleys and low lands are rich and fertile. This city is considered half-way between Hang-chow and Hwuy-chow, and our boatmen seemed to think themselves entitled to make it serve the purpose of a half-way house, at which they could remain some time. Moreover the river had increased much in rapidity, and it was necessary to add considerably to the number of our crew. Two days were spent here in making these arrangements, and in making various purchases, such as straw shoes for the men, rice to serve us during the remainder of the journey, and also articles which would sell at a profit further up the country. I did not regret this delay, as it gave me an opportunity of seeing the old town, as well as a portion of the country which was entirely new to me.

During our stay here, my servant Wang, who was a foolish, obstinate man, nearly got us all into a very serious scrape. It seemed he had given one of our boatmen a bad dollar in payment of a debt, which the latter brought back, not being able to pass it in the town. In the mean time Wang had been indulging in a little sam-shoo (a Chinese spirit), and was in a very excited state when the dollar was brought back. He affirmed that it was not the same one he had given the boatman, and that he would have nothing to do with it. After some altercation, however, he took it back, and set off into the city, as he said, to change it himself. In a few minutes he returned with a dollar's worth of copper cash strung over his shoulders, exclaiming, in triumph, that "the dollar was good enough, and that he had found no difficulty in passing it, although the fool of a boatman had." He now threw down the dollar's worth of cash to the other, and asked him, in an enraged and excited manner, if he was satisfied now. The latter took up the strings of cash very quietly, and began counting and examining them. In a second or two he returned them, saying that they were so mixed and inferior that it would be impossible to pay them away, except at a considerable loss, and that he would not receive them. He again demanded to be paid in good and perfect coin. Wang now pretended to be very indignant. "I gave you a dollar," said he, "and you said that was bad; I changed it, and gave you copper cash, and you return them; pray what do you want?" The passengers now gathered round them, and there was every prospect of a serious riot. After a great deal of noise, however, the poor fellow pocketed his cash, protesting, at the same time, that he had been badly used, and threatening to have his revenge on Wang at some future time.

At the end of two days, the additional men having been engaged, and all the purchases completed, we passed up the river, and left the town of Yen-chow behind us. Our course was now in a north-westerly direction. The stream was very rapid in many parts, so much so that it is used for turning the water-wheels which grind and husk rice and other kinds of grain. The first of these machines which I observed was a few miles above Yen-chow-foo. At the first glance I thought it was a steamboat, and was greatly surprised. I really thought the Chinese had been telling the truth when they used to inform our countrymen in the south that steamboats were common in the interior. As I got nearer I found that the "steamboat" was a machine of the following description. A large barge or boat was firmly moored by stem and stern near the side of the river, in a part where the stream ran most rapidly. Two wheels, not unlike the paddles of a steamer, were placed at the sides of the boat, and connected with an axle which passed through it. On this axle were fixed a number of short cogs, each of which, as it came round, pressed up a heavy mallet to a certain height, and then allowed it to fall down upon the grain placed in a basin below. These mallets were continually rising and falling, as the axle was driven rapidly round by the outside wheels, which were turned by the stream. The boat was thatched over to afford protection from the rain. As we got farther up the river we found that machines of this description were very common.

About ten or twelve miles above Yen-chow the country appears more fertile; the hills are covered again with low pines, and the lowlands abound in tallow-trees, camphor-trees, and bamboos. Large quantities of Indian corn and millet are grown in this part of the country, which is, for the most part, too hilly for rice crops.

Our progress upwards was now very slow, owing to the great rapidity of the river. Every now and then we came to rapids, which it took us hours to get over, notwithstanding that fifteen men, with long ropes fastened to the mast of our boat, were tracking along the shore, and five or six more were poling with long bamboos. Nothing shows so much as this the indefatigable perseverance of the Chinese. When looking upon a river such as this is, one would think it quite impossible to navigate it, yet even this diffi-culty is overcome by hard labour and perseverance.

The slow progress which we necessarily made suited my purposes exactly, and enabled me to ex-plore the botanical riches of the country with conve-nience and ease. I used to rise at break of day, and spend the morning inspecting the hills and valleys near the sides of the river, and then return to the boat in time for breakfast. Breakfast over, I generally went on shore again, accompanied by my men, who carried the seeds, plants or flowers we might discover during our rambles. The first thing we did on these occasions was to ascend the nearest hill and take a survey of the windings of the river, with the number of rapids, in order that we might form some idea of the progress our boat would make during our absence. If the rapids were numerous we knew that she would progress slowly, and that we might wander to a considerable distance with perfect safety; if, on the other hand, the river seemed smooth, and its bed comparatively level, we were obliged to keep within a short distance of the banks.

During these rambles I met with many plants growing wild on the hills, which I had never seen before, except in gardens. Here the curious and much-prized *Edgworthia chrysantha* was growing in great abundance. Reeves's Spiræa and *Spiræa prunifolia* were found in great profusion. Several species of the *Chimonanthus* or Japan allspice, *Forsythia viridissima*, *Buddlea Lindleyana*, and numerous Daphnes, Gardenias, and Azaleas, were also met with. Many kinds of mosses and Lycopods were growing out of the crevices of the moist rock; amongst the latter, and very abundant, was a fine species named *Lycopodium Willdenovii*.

Amongst the trees the most common were the *Dryandra cordata* of Thunberg, the tung-eu of the

Chinese, which is valuable on account of the quantity of oil found its seeds, and the tallow-tree, which furnishes both tallow and oil. Here and there were plantations of the common Chinese pine, and the lance-leaved one known to botanists as *Cunninghamia lanceolata*. A palm-tree, and the only species of the genus indigenous to, or cultivated in, the northern or central provinces of the empire, was seen on the hill-side here in a high state of perfection. It seems a species of *Chamærops*. It is particularly valuable to the northern Chinese, who use its large, brown, hair-like bracts for many purposes. Ropes and cables for their junks are made out of this substance, and seem to last, even under water, for a very long time. It is probably better and stronger for those purposes than the fibre of the cocoa-nut, which it resembles to a certain extent. Bed-bottoms are wrought out of this, and are largely used in the country by all classes of the natives. Agricultural labourers and coolies are fond of wearing hats and cloaks made out of the same substance, which in wet weather keeps out a great deal of rain ; and there are many other purposes to which this useful tree is applied. Besides all this, it is most ornamental in the country where it grows.

I am in hopes that one day we shall see this beautiful palm-tree ornamenting the hill-sides in the south of England, and in other mild European countries. With this view I sent a few plants home to Sir William Hooker, of the Royal Gardens at Kew, with a request that he would forward one of them to the garden of His Royal Highness Prince Albert, at Osborne House, Isle of Wight.*

For the accompanying sketch of this interesting palm, and for several others in this work, I am indebted to the kindness of Captain Cracroft, R.N., a gentleman whose services in China, when in command of the "Reynard," were highly and justly appreciated by the foreign community.

[The Hemp Palm.]

* In the 'Botanical Magazine' for March, 1850, Sir Wm. Hooker thus writes of it :—"A palm, *Chamærops excelsa*, (?) sent to the Royal gardens by Mr. Fortune, has braved, unharmed, and unprotected by any sort of covering, the severe winter now passed" (1849-50).

Limestone rock is very plentiful in this district, and there are a great number of kilns for burning it, constructed exactly like those we see at home. Large quantities of water-fowl, such as geese, ducks, teal, and several fine varieties of the kingfisher, were common about the river. Inland, on the hill-sides, pheasants, woodcocks, and partridges were most abundant. I believe deer are also plentiful, but I did not see any.

Thus day after day passed pleasantly by ; the weather was delightful, the natives quiet and inoffensive, and the scenery picturesque in the highest degree. My Chinamen and myself, often footsore and weary, used to sit down on the hill-top and survey and enjoy the beautiful scenery around us. The noble river, clear and shining, was seen winding amongst the hills ; here it was smooth as glass, deep and still, and there shallow, and running rapidly over its rocky bed. At some places trees and bushes hung over its sides, and dipped their branches into the water, while at others rocks reared their heads high above the stream, and bade defiance to its rapid current.

The whole country was hilly, and the distant mountains, varying in height from three hundred to three thousand feet, were peaked, ridged, and furrowed in a most remarkable manner. Altogether the views were most charming, and will long remain vividly impressed upon my memory.

On the 29th and 30th of October we passed the towns of Tsa-yuen, Tsasa-poo, Kang-koo, and Shang-i-yuen, all places of considerable note, particularly the last, which must contain at least 100,000 inhabitants.

Opposite to the town of Tsa-yuen there is a curious shaped hill, which is composed chiefly of granite of a beautiful greenish colour, much prized by the Chinese. The slabs which are quarried out of the hill are used for various ornamental purposes, but they are more particularly in demand for the building of tombs. Large quantities are taken down the river to Yen-chow and Hang-chow for this purpose.

The tea-plant was now frequently seen in cultivation on the hill sides, this being the outskirt of the great green-tree country to which I was bound. Large camphor-trees were frequently seen in the valleys, particularly near the villages. Tallow-trees were still in extensive cultivation, and at this season of the year, being clothed in their autumnal hues, they produced a striking effect upon the varied landscape. The leaves had changed from a light-green to a dark blood-red colour. Another tree, a species of maple, called by the Chinese the fung-gze, was also most picturesque from the same cause. These two trees formed a striking contrast with the dark-green foliage of the pine tribe.

But the most beautiful tree found in this district is a species of weeping cypress, which I had never met with in any other part of China, and which was quite new to me. It was during one of my daily rambles that I saw the first specimen. About half a mile distant from where I was I observed a noble-looking fir-tree, about sixty feet in height, having a stem as straight as the Norfolk Island pine, and weeping branches like the willow of St. Helena. Its branches grew at first at right angles to the main stem, then described a graceful curve upwards, and bent again at their points. From these main branches others long and slender hung down perpendicularly, and gave the whole tree a weeping and graceful form. It reminded me of some of those large and gorgeous chandeliers, sometimes seen in theatres and public halls in Europe.

What could it be? It evidently belonged to the pine tribe, and was more handsome and ornamental than them all. I walked, no,—to tell the plain truth, I ran up to the place where it grew, much to the surprise of my attendants, who evidently thought I had gone crazy. When I reached the spot where it grew it appeared more beautiful even than it had done in the distance. Its stem was perfectly straight, like *Cryptomeria*, and its leaves were formed like those of the well-known arbor-vitæ, only much more slender and graceful.

This specimen was fortunately covered with a quantity of ripe fruit, a portion of which I was most anxious to secure. The tree was growing in some grounds belonging to a country inn, and was the property of the innkeeper. A wall intervened between us and it, which I confess I felt very much inclined to get over; but remembering that I was acting Chinaman, and that such a proceeding would have been very indecorous, to say the least of it, I immediately gave up the idea. We now walked into the inn, and, seating ourselves quietly down at one of the tables, ordered some dinner to be brought to us. When we had taken our meal we lighted our

[Cupressus funebris]

Chinese pipes, and sauntered out, accompanied by our polite host, into the garden where the real attraction lay. "What a fine tree this of yours is! we have never seen it in the countries near the sea where we come from; pray give us some of its seeds." "It is a fine tree," said the man, who was evidently much pleased with our admiration of it, and readily complied with our request. These seeds were carefully treasured; and as they got home safely, and are now growing in England, we may expect in a few years to see a new and striking feature produced upon our landscape by this lovely tree. Afterwards, as we journeyed westward, it became more common, and was frequently to be seen in clumps on the sides of the hills.

This tree has been named the Funereal Cypress. Professor Lindley—to whom I sent one of the dried specimens procured during this journey—pronounces it "an acquisition of the highest interest;" and adds, "We have received a specimen of it, which enables us to say that it must be a plant of the greatest beauty. It may be best described as a tree like the weeping willow in growth, with the foliage of the savin, but of a brighter green; it is, however, not a juniper, as the savin is, but a genuine cypress. It has long been a subject of regret that the Italian cypress cannot be made to endure our climate, and to decorate our burial-places; but we have now a finer tree, still better adapted for the purpose."*

Leaving the town of Shang-i-yuen, abreast of which

* Gardener's Chronicle, 1849, p. 243.

we had anchored during the night, we proceeded on
our journey on the morning of the 31st of October.
After going a short distance we came to a wild-look-
ing part of the hills where there was a most curious
and distinct echo, called by the Chinese *Fung-shu*.
The boatmen and passengers amused themselves by
yelling and uttering strange sounds at the highest
pitch of their voices; these were taken up and distinctly repeated again and again, first by the nearest
hills, and then by others more distant, until they
gradually died away. The Chinese have strange
prejudices and opinions about this place. They told
me that the spirits of men after death often chose to
dwell amidst this wild and beautiful scenery; and
they said it was they that now repeated these sounds,
and echoed them from hill to hill.

As the day wore on we came to one of those rapids
which were so difficult to pass, and observed a great
number of small boats waiting for and visiting all
the larger ones as they came up. These were river
beggars. Each of them had a very old man or
woman on board, whose hair in most instances was
whitened with age, and who was evidently in a state
of imbecility and second childhood. They all expected alms from the boatmen who arrived from the
rich towns of the east near the sea. The Chinese,
to their honour, revere and love old age. It was
said that a celebrated English admiral was once in
danger of an attack from the Canton mob, but the
moment he lifted his hat and showed his gray hairs
they drew back and allowed him to pass on unmo-

F

lested. Be this as it may, it is certain that they revere and love old age and gray hairs.

It was a custom with the boatmen every morning to set aside a small portion of rice in a bamboo cup to give to the poor. Hence the beggars were generally successful in their applications; indeed, it was a most difficult matter to get rid of them otherwise, for they were most importunate and even troublesome. We were visited by so many that the boatman often complained of his inability to give more than an ounce or two of rice to each, and appealed to them on the subject. But unless the whole of the contents of the bamboo cup was emptied into the basket held out, the mendicants made a great noise, and complained that they had been deprived of their due.

Sometimes the river was so shallow and so full of stones that the only passage for boats was close in shore. The land beggars knew these places well, and always took their stations there. Each was provided with a basket suspended from the point of a bamboo pole, which he held out to the boatman and asked for alms. These landsmen were quite as importunate as their brethren in the boats, and were generally as successful in their applications.

I was not aware until now that the lower orders in China—such as these boatmen—were so charitable. Few of the beggars—and "their name was legion"—were sent away without "an alms." It might be that, ignorant and idolatrous as these boatmen were, they had yet some idea that a blessing would result from "casting their bread upon the waters."

CHAPTER IV.

City of Wae-ping — Threatened attack from boatmen — A false alarm — A border country and a border guard — Enter the district of Hwuy-chow — The tea-plant and other crops — A Chinese play — Ferry-boat and ladies — Cargo transshipped — Two coffins below my bed — A mandarin's garden — Botany of the hills — A new plant (Berberis japonica) — My servant's advice — Leave the boat — The opium-smoker outwitted — Town of Tun-che — Its importance in connection with the tea-trade — Features of country, soil, and productions — First view of Sung-lo-shan.

On the evening of the 31st of October we reached Wae-ping. It is a city of considerable size, walled and fortified, and probably contains 150,000 inhabitants. This place is just on the borders of the district of Hwuy-chow.

The dispute between Wang and the boatman had not been forgotten, and the latter considered this a fitting time to have his revenge. During the last two days he had been hinting to some of the passengers that he intended doing something at Wae-ping. These men duly reported to Wang what had been told them, and he began to be very much frightened. The rest of the Chinamen, with whom he was no favourite, seemed to enjoy his fears, and did everything in their power to exaggerate the dangers to which he had exposed himself. He had had several disputes with them also during the journey, and nearly the whole of them bore him a grudge.

Things were in this very unsatisfactory state when we reached the city of Wae-ping.

It was about eight o'clock in the evening, and quite dark, when we moored our boat close under the city walls. The boatmen went on shore, as they did every evening when we happened to stop near a town. One or two of their number, who had been left to take care of the boat, tired with the labours of the day, lay down to sleep, and the greater part of the passengers followed their example. I now observed my two men in close conversation, but as this was a matter of frequent occurrence I paid little attention to the matter. Tired with my day's rambles, I lay down upon my bed, and allowed my thoughts to wander to far distant lands.

My meditations were gradually merging into dreams when I felt a hand touch me, and a voice, which I knew to be Wang's, informed me that I must not go to sleep. When I asked the reason, he informed me that he had just discovered that the boatmen had entered into a conspiracy against us, and that we were all to be drowned that night in the river. "They have now gone into the town to get some of their friends to assist them," said he, "and they are only waiting until they think we are fast asleep."

I scarcely knew what to think of the business. We were now about three hundred miles from either Shang-hae or Ning-po, the night was very dark, and if the threatened attempt should be made we had little chance of receiving any assistance from others. But I could not allow myself to believe that in the interior of this country, where the people were generally quiet and harmless, an act of the kind could be committed with impunity.   I therefore did not get up as Wang wished, but told him that I should take care to remain awake.

The city of Wae-ping stands on the high banks of the Hwuy-chow river.   One of the gates was visible to us owing to a blaze of light thrown over it by the torches and lanterns of the Chinese.   An inclined plane, which formed the road, reached from the river up to the gate, and was visible from the boat.   As all the Chinese carry lanterns, it was easy for us to see those who came out of the city and descended towards the river.   The evening, although dark, was perfectly still, so that the slightest noise could be distinctly heard at a considerable distance.   At last the city gate opened, and about a dozen men came out, each carrying a lantern, and descended the hill towards the boat.   "Get up, get up! quick, quick!" said my servant, "for here they come."   I jumped up immediately, and waited for the threatened attack with all the composure I could command.   My two Chinamen appeared in a state of great alarm, and kept as close to me as they possibly could.   At last the foremost man in the band approached, and, jumping lightly on board, peeped in at the door of our boat. "Hilloa! what do you want?" cried both of my men at the same time.   The fellow gave a grin, said he did not want us, and jumped from our boat to another which lay alongside.   His companions also disappeared amongst the surrounding boats, and left us unmolested. "Now, do you see that?" said Wang; "you would not believe me when I told you that they intended to seize and drown us; but had we not been awake and fully prepared, it would soon have been all over with us."

I must confess I felt a little shaken in my opinion, and scarcely knew what to think of the business. The whole scene, to a looker-on who could have foreseen the result, would have been highly amusing, but it appeared to be much too serious for me to enjoy it. None of the other passengers were asleep, although they were all in bed, and they kept up a whispering conversation, which seemed ominous and suspicious. I felt quite certain that no assistance would be rendered us by them; on the contrary, it was not impossible that they would turn against us and assist the boatmen.

About half an hour after the first alarm the city gate was again opened, and some men were observed coming down the hill with lanterns, as the former ones had done. This time it proved to be the missing boatmen, who were supposed to be concocting a conspiracy with their friends inside the city. When they came on board they tried to look astonished at the state in which they found us. They laughed at Wang, and said they had no intention of drowning him. He quietly told them that he did not believe them, and, turning to me, said he was sure they still meditated an attack. The fellows now lay down to sleep, and requested us to put out our

lantern and do the same. This, however, my servants would not consent to do, as they firmly believed
that the sleep of the boatmen was only feigned.

We were in this state of excitement from eight
o'clock in the evening until three next morning.
Long before this time the boatmen seemed to be
sound asleep. The night was perfectly calm, and
the only sound which I heard was the clank of water-
wheels, similar to those of the machines I have
already described, several of which were moored on
the rapids opposite the city. The walls and ramparts
of the old town loomed black and prison-like in the
darkness, but everything was perfectly quiet, and the
whole place seemed sunk in deep sleep. I felt very
much inclined to go to sleep myself. This, however,
my men remonstrated against, and I was obliged to
keep them company for an hour longer. At the end
of that time, nothing having happened to keep up the
excitement, I felt cold and sleepy—so much so, that
no persuasion could keep me awake. Telling Wang
to call me if anything suspicious occurred, I lay down
without undressing, and was soon dreaming of robbers,
boatmen, and water-wheels.

When I awoke I found that it was daylight, and
that we were under way, and proceeding rapidly up
the stream. Fifteen of our men were on shore,
tracking the boat; the cook was busily employed
making preparation for our morning meal, and everything was going on in the usual way, as if nothing
had happened to disturb us. My own men, wearied
with watching, had fallen into a sound sleep, and

were stretched at full length on the floor of the boat. As the other passengers were also sleeping soundly, I had a little time to think quietly over the events of the preceding night, and, being anxious to see the old town by daylight, I stepped out of the cabin, and took my place on the high stern of the boat, near to the old man who stood at the helm.

The sun was just rising, and its earliest rays were playing upon the old walls and watch-towers of Wae-ping. How different the old place looked in day-light from what it had done in the darkness! Then the imagination assisted in making it appear like a dungeon, dark and gloomy, and inhabited by thieves and robbers. Now it seemed an ancient city, watered by a clear and beautiful river, surrounded by hills and romantic scenery, and defended by time-honoured walls. Such is the difference between night and morning, and such the power of imagination.

When I returned to the cabin I found my servants rubbing their eyes and scarcely awake. "Well," said I, "you see nothing has happened, and we are now under way, and some distance from Wae-ping." "Oh! that is all very well," said one of them, "but had we not been on our guard we should never have lived to see the morning."

As the river was now shallow, and in many parts very rapid, I had daily opportunities of rambling over the country, and of inspecting its productions. Soon after leaving Wae-ping one of my guides informed me that we were now on the border of another pro-vince, and that here I had better not go much out of the boat. I found that this advice was good and worth attending to. The river here is considered the highway or passage from the one district to the other, and this pass is well guarded by soldiers. Each province has its own guard-town. On the Che-kiang side we passed a long, straggling town on the river's banks, chiefly inhabited by troops, who were the guards of the pass, and under the orders of the Hang-chow mandarins. As soon as the boundary-line was crossed we came to another place of like size and appearance, also filled with soldiers, who were under the orders of the authorities of Hwuy-chow-foo, in the province of Kiang-nan. These two parties formed a sort of border guard, and bore each other, I believe, little good-will. They reminded me of our own border clans in ancient feudal times. Boats passing up and down the river were generally boarded, and had their papers examined by one of the officers.

The boatman who had the dispute with Wang now threatened to have him punished here, at which he was greatly frightened. The man, however, if he ever intended it, did not put his threat into execution, and we passed the dreaded border in safety.

When we got fairly inside the Hwuy-chow district I was able to ramble about in the country as before. The river became not only shallow, but in many parts so full of rocks and stones that it was next to impossible to pick out a passage for the boat. It still wound through a hilly and mountainous country. The hills, however, became gradually more fertile as we proceeded, and in many parts they were culti-

vated to their summits. Crops of millet and Indian
corn were growing amongst the tea-bushes, which were
now observed in large quantities on the sides of the
hills. The corn and millet, growing up in the hot
months of summer and autumn, seemed to afford a
partial shade to the tea, which was probably beneficial
to it. Another reason for the practice may be found
in the fondness of the Chinese for mixing crops—
a practice in operation all over the country. I never
saw finer crops of millet and Indian corn than those
which were growing on these hills. The crops were
just ripening (November 2nd), and the Chinese had
begun to harvest them.

This part of the country was exceedingly beautiful
and full of interest. Many of the less fertile hills
were clothed with junipers and pines, whilst on others
the patches of ripening corn afforded a striking contrast to the dark-green leaves of the tea-bushes with
which they were dotted. I had now the pleasure of
seeing many groups of the beautiful " funereal
cypress ;" it was growing on the sides of the hills,
generally near villages or amongst the graves. Everywhere it was beautiful, and produced a striking effect
in the appearance of the landscape.

In walking over the country I always, when possible, avoided entering large towns. About this
time, however, all the passengers were obliged to get
out of the boat, in order to lighten it, and allow it to
be drawn up one of the shallow rapids. We all walked
on together, and in a short time came to a town of
considerable size. It happened that the day we

arrived was a holiday, and a scene presented itself such as I had never before witnessed.

The town was on the opposite bank. Two rivers unite here, and the town was built between them just at their junction. One of the rivers was nearly dry, and its bed was now used for the purpose of giving a grand fête. The bank where we were was probably about 150 or 200 feet above the bed of the river, so that we had a capital view of what was going on below us.

The first and most prominent object which caught my eye was a fine seven-storied pagoda, forty or fifty feet high, standing on the dry bed of the river; near to it was a summer-house upon a small scale, gaudily got up, and supposed to be in a beautiful garden. Artificial figures of men and women appeared sitting in the verandahs and balconies, dressed in the richest costumes. Singing birds, such as the favourite wa-me and canaries, were whistling about the windows. Artificial lakes were formed in the bed of the river, and the favoured Nelumbium appeared floating on the water. Everything denoted that the place belonged to a person of high rank and wealth.

At some little distance a theatre was erected, in front of which stood several thousands of the natives, packed as closely as possible, and evidently highly interested in a play which was going on. Sometimes the piece appeared so pathetic that the immense multitude were perfectly still; at other times something seemed to tickle their fancies, and to afford them the greatest amusement. The actors on the stage were very gaily dressed in rich silks and satins of many colours, and evidently did their best to afford amusement to this immense audience.

Such was the scene presented to us as we approached the town. " Come," said all my fellow passengers, " come and see the play;" and they set off as fast as they could to a bridge a little higher up the river, by which they could reach the town and the place where the festivities were going on. I was quite satisfied with the view I had of the whole scene from the opposite bank, and therefore declined the invitation to go nearer. The old dwarf, whom I have already mentioned, and who had taken every opportunity in his power to show his good will, volunteered to remain with me and my two servants. We sat down on the green grass, and had an excellent view of the whole proceedings. The Chinese never seemed to tire, and would have remained there all day ; but as our boat would pass up the other branch of the river, it was necessary for us to get to it. We therefore crossed the bridge, and passed through the centre of the town. No one seemed to have the slightest idea that I was a foreigner; indeed, the poor old dwarf attracted far more attention than any of us. I did not remark anything of interest in this town, except some large tea-hongs and carpenters' shops, where tea-chests were being made.

When we had passed through this place and reached the other branch of the river, we entered a ferry-boat, and crossed over to the other side. Amongst the ferry-boat passengers were two very pretty and handsomely dressed young ladies, with whom I was greatly amused. When they came into the boat they seated themselves quietly by my side, and began chatting to each other in high spirits. I could not help contrasting their conduct with that of any of their countrywomen at the five ports where foreigners are permitted to trade. Respectably dressed females always fly from foreigners as they would do from a wild and ferocious animal. Had these pretty damsels known that a "barbarian" was seated at their side, how astonished and frightened they would have been!

About evening, just before dark, the boat arrived and lay abreast of the town during the night. All the men now applied for leave to go on shore to see the play. Some of them appeared very anxious that I should go with them, but, being quite contented with the adventures of the day, I declined the invitation. It was very late before they all came back; but this did not prevent us from getting under way at the usual time next morning and proceeding on our journey.

After we had gone some distance the head boatman came round and informed the passengers that it would be necessary to engage another boat to take part of his cargo, as the river was too shallow to allow him to get up so deeply laden as he was. Moreover, he coolly proposed that the expenses of the second boat should be defrayed by the passengers, giving as his reason that by this means they would get sooner to their destination. As the sum was not a large one, this was agreed to, and a second boat was engaged.

A circumstance now occurred which astonished me not a little at the time, although it must be a common thing in the country. When the second boat was brought alongside, and the floor of our cabin taken up to get at the cargo, I found that we had some fellow-passengers which I had never calculated upon. Two enormous coffins, each containing the body of a Chinaman, had been lying directly under my bed for the last three weeks without my having the least suspicion of the fact. It was, perhaps, just as well that this was the case, for the knowledge of the circumstance would not have added to my comfort, and might have made me sleep less soundly. These coffins were now removed to the other boat, in which they were taken onwards to their last resting-place. On inquiring, I found that the deceased were natives of Hwuy-chow-foo, and had left their native country some years before to reside at Hang-chow, where they had died. Their friends were now taking their remains back to their own land, to be buried in the graves of their ancestors.

On the following day, while walking on shore with some of the other passengers, we came to a village in which there was a celebrated garden and temple belonging to a family of high rank and influence in the country. The head of the family himself had died a short time before, but the place was still kept up in excellent style. It seemed to be open to the public, and we determined to go and see it.

The place had no pretensions to what in England would be called a fine garden; but it was evidently considered unique by the Chinese in this part of the country. Small square courts were seen here and there, ornamented with rockwork, and planted with the favourite flowers of the district. The fragrant olive, moutan, sacred bamboo (*Nandina domestica*), and other common shrubs, were met with in great abundance. Some pretty ponds were filled with the favourite water-lily. But the most interesting plant of all was a new evergreen holly, with leaves somewhat like the Portugal laurel, very handsome and ornamental.*

Amongst the buildings there was a pretty small pagoda, which we ascended, and from its top had an excellent view of the surrounding country. The whole place had evidently been laid out for the purpose of giving plays and fêtes on an extensive scale. Summer-houses, ornamental towers, balconies, and ancestral temples, were scattered over the grounds. The *tout ensemble* had an imposing appearance, and was just such as the Chinese most admire. Guides conducted us through the place in the same way as at the show-houses in England, and also expected to be paid for their services. The resemblance went a little further, for we were passed on from one guide to another, and *each* had to be paid.

On the hill sides in this part of the country I met with many plants which are rare in other parts of China, at least on the hills nearer to the sea. The fragrant Chimonanthus, which is now such a favourite

---

* Seeds of this were procured here and sent home to England.

in England (where it blooms in the open air at Christmas), was quite common. But the most interesting of these plants I found in an old garden, and it is likely to be much prized at home. I will here relate the accident by which it was discovered while we were at Tung-che. My coolie and myself were busy collecting tea-seeds on a small hill not far from the town. After collecting all the seeds we could find, I happened to get a glimpse of a very fine specimen of the funereal cypress, with which I was so charmed, that I determined to go to the spot where it was growing and enjoy a nearer view. I desired my attendant to accompany me, in case any ripe seeds might be found upon it. As we approached the village we discovered that the tree was inside a garden, which was surrounded by very high walls. Naturally supposing that there must be a gate somewhere, we walked round the walls until we came to a little cottage, which seemed to have served the purpose of a lodge. We passed in here with all the coolness of Chinamen, and soon found ourselves in a dilapidated old garden. A large house, which had formerly been the mansion, was, like the garden, in a ruinous condition. The funereal cypress which. I had seen in the distance stood in the midst of the garden, and was covered with ripe seeds, which increased the collection I had formerly obtained.

Having taken a survey of the place, we were making our way out, when an extraordinary plant, growing in a secluded part of the garden, met my eye. When I got near it I found that it was a very

fine evergreen Berberis, belonging to the section of
Mahonias, and having of course pinnated leaves.
Each leaflet was as large as the leaf of an English
holly, spiny, and of a fine dark, shining green colour.
The shrub was about eight feet high, much branched,
and far surpassed in beauty all the other known
species of Mahonia. It had but one fault, and that
was, that it was too large to move and bring away.
I secured a leaf, however, and marked the spot
where it grew, in order to secure some cuttings of it
on my return from the interior.

I had been greatly annoyed at the cowardice and
fear of Wang. He had still the most serious appre-
hensions for his safety, as his enemy, the boatman,
continued to threaten him. I tried to laugh at him
and convince him that the boatman would do him no
harm, but it was of no use. At last he came to me,
and explained a plan which he had been concocting,
and which he proposed putting into execution next
day. It was simply this:—he and I were to leave
the boat ostensibly to walk in the country as usual,
but with the intention of not returning to it. I
asked him what was to be done with our beds and
luggage, and what he proposed doing with the other
man. He replied that all must be left behind; that
if he attempted to leave the boat openly, measures
would be taken to stop him; and that, as the coolie
could not be trusted, he must be left also. He did
not intend even to pay what was due upon our passage
money! Such was the plan which, after days and
nights of deep thought, as he told me, he had at last

G

made up his mind to put into execution, and to which he now begged that I would agree.

I thought over the business for some few minutes, and then came to the determination not to adopt his suggestions. I was unwilling to leave behind me the seeds of the tea-shrub and of the other new plants which I had discovered, and I did not think the state of the case so urgent as to force me to the unworthy measure of leaving the other man behind and the boatman unpaid. " This plan of yours will not do," said I ; " if you can leave the boat in an open manner, taking your companion along with you and paying all charges, I have no objection either to go on shore or to hire another boat, but I cannot consent to go away in the manner you propose." I was very glad afterwards that I was firm enough to pursue this course.

A day or two after this I was informed in the morning that we were within thirty le of the town of Tun-che, and that we should arrive there in the evening. This was the destination of our boat, and here we should leave it. In the afternoon, about two o'clock, we were only four miles distant from this place, and as the water was very shallow, and we were making but little progress, most of the passengers determined to walk onwards to the town. We all began to pack up our luggage and make preparations for the journey. The opium-smoker, who, with all his civility, was a man I could not trust, was now very anxious to know to what part of the country we were bound. My Chinese servants, who had learned

a little wit by experience, took good care to keep all
these matters to themselves, their great object being
to cut off all connection between their *friends* in the
boat and those with whom we might have to associate
afterwards.

Our passage-money was now fully paid up, our
luggage packed, and an arrangement made between
my two men with regard to the station to which we
were bound.   When this was all arranged I left the
coolie in charge of the luggage, took Wang on shore,
and walked onwards to Tun-che, which we reached
between three and four o'clock in the afternoon.   It
is a thriving, busy town, and forms as it were the
port of Hwuy-chow-foo, from which it is distant about
twenty miles.   It is situated in lat. 29° 48′ N., and
in long. 2° 4′ E. of Peking.   All the large Hang-chow
and Yen-chow boats are moored and loaded here, the
river being too shallow to allow of their proceeding
higher up, and hence it is a place of great trade.
Nearly all the green teas which are sent down the
river to Hang-chow-foo, and thence onward to Shanghae, are shipped at this place.   The green teas destined for Canton are carried across a range of hills to
the westward, where there is a river which flows in
the direction of the Poyang lake.

This part of the country is very populous.   Nearly
the whole way from the place where we had left our
boat was covered with houses, forming a kind of
suburb to Tun-che.   This place itself is supposed to
contain about 150,000 inhabitants.   The great article
of trade is green tea.   There are here a number of

large dealers who buy this article from the farmers
and priests, refine and sort it, form it into chops, and
forward it to Shanghae or Canton, where it is sold to
the foreign merchant. Seven or eight hundred chops
are said to be sent out of this town annually. I
observed also a great number of carpenters' shops for
the manufacture of chests, a trade which of itself
must employ a large number of men. In fact, this
town and the surrounding populous district may be
said to be supported by the foreign tea-trade.

Nearly all the way from Yen-chow-foo the river
was bounded by high hills on each side. Now, however, they seemed, as it were, to fall back, and left an
extensive and beautiful valley, through the middle of
which the river flowed. Nearly all this low land is
under tea cultivation, the soil is rich and fertile, and
the bushes consequently grow most luxuriantly. I
had never before seen the tea-plant in such a flourishing condition, and this convinced me that soil had
much to do with the superiority of the Hwuy-chow
green teas.

The very sandy soil near the river yielded good
crops of the ground-nut (*Arachis hypogœa*).

After spending about an hour in the town we inquired where we could hire a chair to take us onward
about thirty le further, and were directed to an inn or
tea-house, where chairs are let on hire. A circumstance happened in this inn which gave me some
amusement at the time, and which I have often
laughed at since. When we entered this house we
found a great number of travellers of all ranks; some

were drinking tea, others smoking, and the remainder
stretched upon chairs or tables sound asleep. Seeing
strangers arrive, some of the more restless were rather
inquisitive, and began to put a number of questions
to us. My man Wang was a native of this district,
and of course understood the dialect perfectly, but he
evidently wanted to have as little to say as possible.
As for myself, I told them I did not understand what
they said. One fellow in particular, who probably
was sharp enough to detect something unusual in my
appearance, was determined not to be put off in this
way, and kept asking me a variety of questions. At
length the old innkeeper came up and said with the
utmost gravity, "It is of no use your talking to this
person, he understands the Kwan-hwa (or Court dialect) only; you do not speak that, and of course he
cannot understand you, nor you him." This seemed
to be perfectly satisfactory to all parties, and I was
left unmolested.

Our chairs being ready, we got into them, and,
passing through the town, crossed the river and took
the road for Sung-lo and Hieu-ning. We reached
our destination a little before dark, and I had the
first view of the far-famed Sung-lo-shan, the hill where
green tea is said to have been first discovered.

CHAPTER V.

Sung-lo-shan — Its priests and tea — Its height above the sea — Rock formation — Flora of the hills — Temperature and climate — Cultivation of the tea-shrub — Mode of preserving its seeds — The young plants — Method of dyeing green teas — Ingredients employed — Chinese reason for the practice — Quantity of Prussian blue and gypsum taken by a green-tea drinker — Such teas not used by the Chinese — Mr. Warrington's observations.

THE hill of Sung-lo, or Sung-lo-shan, is situated in the province of Kiang-nan and district of Hieu-ning, a town in lat. 29° 56′ N., long. 118° 15′ E. It is famous in China as being the place where the green-tea shrub was first discovered, and where green tea was first manufactured. In a book called the 'Hieu-ning-hien chy,' published A.D. 1693, and quoted by Mr. Ball, there is the following notice of this place :—

" The hill or mountain where tea is produced is Sung-lo mountain. A bonze of the sect of Fo taught a Kiang-nan man, named Ko Ty, the art of making tea, and thus it was called Sung-lo tea. The tea got speedily into great repute, so that the bonze became rich and abandoned the profession of priest. The man is gone, and only the name remains. Ye men of learning and travellers who seek Sung-lo tea may now search in vain, that which is sold in the markets is a mere counterfeit."

Sung-lo-shan appears to be between two and three

thousand feet above the level of the plains. It is
very barren, and, whatever may have formerly been
the case, it certainly produces but little tea now;
indeed, from all I could learn, the tea that grows
upon it is quite neglected, as far as cultivation is concerned, and is only gathered to supply the wants of
the priests of Fo, who have many temples amongst
these rugged wilds. Nevertheless it is a place of
great interest to every Chinaman, and has afforded a
subject to many of their writers.

The low lands of this district and those of Moo-
yuen, situated a few miles further south, produce the
greater part of the fine green teas of commerce;
hence the distinction betwixt hill-tea and garden-tea,
the latter simply applying to those teas which are
carefully cultivated in the plains. The soil here is a
rich loam, not unlike the cotton soil of Shanghae, but
more free in its texture, being mixed with a considerable portion of sand.

When forming our ideas regarding the low lands,
or plains, where the fine garden-tea is produced, it
should be kept in mind that the level country here is
not in reality low, but is a very considerable height
above the level of the sea—much higher, for example,
than the plain of Shanghae. From Hang-chow-foo to
Hwuy-chow-foo the distance is about 800 le (150 to
200 miles); and, when we take into consideration the
rapidity of the current, we see at once that the plains
about Hwuy-chow-foo must be a very considerable
height above those of Hang-chow or Shanghae, which
are only a few feet above the level of the sea.

The rocks in this part of the country are chiefly composed of Silurian slate, like that found in England, and resting upon it is a red calcareous sandstone similar to the new red sandstone of Europe. This sandstone has the effect of giving a reddish tinge to the barren hills, as it crumbles to pieces. I met with no fossil organic remains in these rocks, but my time and opportunities did not permit me to investigate them very minutely.

All these hills are very barren and wholly unsuited to the cultivation of the tea-shrub, and hence their geological formation can have little to do with the success which has attended its management on the plains. Their vegetable productions, however, depending as they do in a great measure upon climate, afford us some valuable information, and to these I paid particular attention.

The flora here has a northern character, that is, the genera common in England or in the northern parts of India are common, while those shrubs and trees which are met with only in tropical countries are entirely unknown. The only plant seen here which has any resemblance to those of the tropics is the species of palm which I have already noticed, but it seems much more hardy than any other variety of its race. A species of holly not unlike the English is common; and various species of the oak, the pine, and the juniper are also found in great abundance. The grasses, ferns, and other low-growing bushes and herbaceous plants of northern countries are here represented by various species of the same genera.

If we were to draw our conclusions from the flora of the country only, we should be apt to suppose that the tea-shrub might be successfully cultivated in some parts of Great Britain ; but this would be erroneous. We must examine the climate as well as the soil and its natural productions, and thus obtain a view of the question in all its bearings.

Shanghae is the nearest place to the green-tea country at which observations that can be relied upon regarding climate have been made to any extent.

The following table, prepared in Shanghae (lat. 31° 20' N.) from daily observations with Newman's best maximum and minimum thermometers, will give the requisite information as regards temperature :—

1844-5	THERMOMETER.			
	Mean Maximum.	Mean Minimum.	Highest during Month.	Lowest during Month.
July	90	77	100	71
August	89	77	94	74
September . . .	79	67	91	63
October	74	55	85	32
November . . .	64	52	73	40
December . . .	47	37	64	26
January	45	36	62	24
February	45	37	62	30
March	54	42	80	32
April	64	51	75	41
May	71	59	87	49
June	76	68	90	58

It is necessary to state, in connection with these observations on temperature, that the winter of

1844-5 was unusually mild. I have no doubt that in ordinary seasons the thermometer may sometimes sink as low as 10° or 12° of Fahrenheit. The winter months are not unlike those which we experience in England; sometimes heavy and continued falls of rain take place, at other times the frost is very severe, the rivers and lakes are frozen over, and the ground is covered with snow. The spring is early and pleasant. In April and May, when the monsoon changes from north-east to south-west, the weather is generally very wet; in fact, this is what is commonly called the "rainy season." From June to August it is often oppressingly hot, the sky is generally clear, little rain falls, but vegetation is often refreshed with heavy dews at night. The autumnal months are cool and agreeable, and about the end of October slight frosts are not unfrequent.

When we consider that Shanghae is 9° 30′ further south than Naples, the extremes of heat and cold will appear excessive. But in order to account for this we must bear in mind the observations made by Humboldt many years ago. "Europe," he observes, "may be considered altogether as the western part of a great continent, and therefore subject to all the influence which causes the *western* sides of continents to be warmer than the *eastern*, and at the same time more temperate, or less subject to *excesses* of both heat and cold, but principally the latter."

Shanghae is situated on the *east* side of the large continent of Asia, and is consequently liable to extremes of temperature—to excessive heat in summer and extreme cold in winter—such as are unknown in many other places in the same degree of latitude.

But Shanghae is near the sea, and the extremes of heat and cold are therefore less than in the green-tea district of Hwuy-chow. I have no doubt that the thermometer rises several degrees higher in summer in the town of Hwuy-chow-foo than it does either in Shanghae or Ning-po, and in like manner sinks much lower during the winter. If we allow eight or ten degrees each way we shall probably be very near the truth—quite near enough for all the purposes of this inquiry.

In the green-tea district of Hwuy-chow, and I believe in all other parts where the shrub is cultivated, it is multiplied by seeds. The seeds are ripe in the month of October. When gathered they are generally put into a basket, and mixed up with sand and earth in a damp state, and in this condition they are kept until the spring. If this plan is not pursued only a small portion of them will germinate. Like the seeds of the oak and chestnut, they are destroyed when exposed to sudden changes in temperature and moisture.

In the month of March the seeds are taken out of the basket and placed in the ground. They are generally sown thickly, in rows or in beds, in a nursery, or in some spare corner of the tea-farm, and sometimes the vacancies in the existing plantations are made up by sowing five or six seeds in each vacant space.

When the young plants are a year old they are in

a fit state for transplanting. This is always done at the change of the monsoon in spring, when fine warm showers are of frequent occurrence. They are planted in rows about four feet apart, and in groups of five or six plants in the row. The distance between each group or patch is generally about four feet. The first crop of leaves is taken from these plants in the third year. When under cultivation they rarely attain a greater height than three or four feet.

When the winters are very severe the natives tie straw bands round the bushes to protect them from the frost, and to prevent it and the snow from splitting them.

In my former work * I offered some remarks upon the preference which many persons in Europe and in America have for *coloured* green teas, and I will now give a " full and particular account" of the colouring process as practised in the Hwuy-chow green-tea country upon those teas which are destined for the foreign market. Having noted down the process carefully at the time, I will extract verbatim from my note-book :—

" The superintendent of the workmen managed the colouring part of the process himself. Having procured a portion of Prussian blue, he threw it into a porcelain bowl, not unlike a chemist's mortar, and crushed it into a very fine powder. At the same time a quantity of gypsum was produced and burned in the charcoal fires which were then roasting the teas. The object of this was to soften it in order

* Three Years' Wanderings in the Northern Provinces of China.

that it might be readily pounded into a very fine powder, in the same manner as the Prussian blue had been. The gypsum, having been taken out of the fire after a certain time had elapsed, readily crumbled down and was reduced to powder in the mortar. These two substances, having been thus prepared, were then mixed together in the proportion of four parts of gypsum to three parts of Prussian blue, and formed a light-blue powder, which was then ready for use.

" This colouring matter was applied to the teas during the last process of roasting. About five minutes before the tea was removed from the pans— the time being regulated by the burning of a joss-stick—the superintendent took a small porcelain spoon, and with it he scattered a portion of the colouring matter over the leaves in each pan. The workmen then turned the leaves rapidly round with both hands, in order that the colour might be equally diffused.

" During this part of the operation the hands of the workmen were quite blue. I could not help thinking that if any green-tea drinkers had been present during the operation their taste would have been corrected, and, I may be allowed to add, im-proved. It seems perfectly ridiculous that a civilised people should prefer these dyed teas to those of a natural green. No wonder that the Chinese consider the natives of the west to be a race of 'barbarians.'

" One day an English gentleman in Shanghae, being in conversation with some Chinese from the green-tea country, asked them what reasons they had for dyeing the tea, and whether it would not be better without undergoing this process. They acknowledged that tea was much better when prepared without having any such ingredients mixed with it, and that they never drank dyed teas themselves, but justly remarked that, as foreigners seemed to prefer having a mixture of Prussian blue and gypsum with their tea, to make it look uniform and pretty, and as these ingredients were cheap enough, the Chinese had no objection to supply them, especially as such teas always fetched a higher price!

" I took some trouble to ascertain precisely the quantity of colouring matter used in the process of dyeing green teas, not certainly with the view of assisting others, either at home or abroad, in the art of colouring, but simply to show green-tea drinkers in England, and more particularly in the United States of America, what quantity of Prussian blue and gypsum they imbibe in the course of one year. To 14½ lbs. of tea were applied 8 mace 2½ candareens of colouring matter, or rather more than an ounce. In every hundred pounds of coloured green tea consumed in England or America, the consumer actually drinks more than half a pound of Prussian blue and gypsum! And yet, tell the drinkers of this coloured tea that the Chinese eat cats, dogs, and rats, and they will hold up their hands in amazement, and pity the poor celestials!"

Two kinds of Prussian blue are used by the tea-manufacturers—one is the kind commonly met with, the other I have seen only in the north of China.* It is less heavy than common Prussian blue, of a bright pale tint, and very beautiful. Turmeric root is frequently employed in Canton, but I did not observe it in use in Hwuy-chow.

I procured samples of these ingredients from the Chinamen in the factory, in order that there might be no mistake as to what they really were. These were sent home to the Great Exhibition last year, and a portion of them submitted to Mr. Warrington, of Apothecaries' Hall, whose investigations in connexion with this subject are well known. In a paper read by him before the Chemical Society, and published in its 'Memoirs and Proceedings,' he says,—

" Mr. Fortune has forwarded from the north of China, for the Industrial Exhibition, specimens of these materials (tea dyes), which, from their appearance, there can be no hesitation in stating are fibrous gypsum (calcined), turmeric root, and Prussian blue; the latter of a bright pale tint, most likely from admixture with alumina or porcelain-clay, which admixture may account for the alumina and silica found as stated in my previous paper, and the presence of which was then attributed possibly to the employment of kaolin or agalmatolite."

* I formerly mistook this for a kind of indigo.

CHAPTER VI.

My reception in the house of Wang's father — A smoky Chinese
cottage — My coolie and the dwarf — The dangers to which they
had been exposed — Chinese mode of warming themselves on a
cold day — Tea-seeds, &c., obtained — Anecdote of the new
Berberis — Obtain some young plants of it — Deceitful character
of the Chinese — Leave the far-famed Sung-lo-shan — Wang tries
to cheat the chairmen — Invents a story of a " great general "—
Leave Tun-che — Mountain scenery — Pleasure of going down the
river — Gale of wind amongst the mountains — Arrive at Nechow
— Shaou-hing-foo — Tsaou-o — Pak-wan — Arrive at Ning-po.

AFTER this digression on the green-tea shrub, and
the country where it was first found, I now resume
the account of my travels.

When we reached the Sung-lo country I took up
my quarters in a house which belonged to the father
of my servant Wang. It was nearly dark before we
arrived at the house, which was situated amongst the
hills within two miles of the foot of Sung-lo. Had I
fixed upon the spot myself I could not have found
one better suited to the purposes I had in view.
Old Mr. Wang was a farmer who at one time had
been well off in the world, but, like many others, had
been unfortunate, and was now very much reduced
in circumstances. He received us in the kindest
manner, and seemed to have great affection for his
son. His wife also came to welcome us, at the same
time apologising for the poor reception they gave us,

as they were so poor. I tried not to be outdone in politeness, and we were soon on the best possible terms.

The table was soon spread with our evening meal, and, chopsticks in hand, we went to work and did ample justice to the fare set before us. Shortly afterwards, the Chinese being early in their habits, we retired to rest.

Next morning the rain was falling in torrents, so that it was impossible to stir out of doors. In these circumstances a Chinese cottage is a most uncomfortable place of confinement. Four families resided in the building in which I was now located—two in the lower and two in the upper story. Each of these families had a separate kitchen, and, as there were no chimneys, the smoke had to make its escape through the doors, windows, and roof of the house. The natives were accustomed to this, and did not greatly mind it, but to me it was almost insupportable. The smoke got into my eyes and almost drove me mad with pain. Go where I would it was all the same, for the house was quite full of it. I quite dreaded the approach of meal-time, when all the fires were lighted. There was no remedy, however, except going out into the heavy rain, so that I was obliged to suffer as patiently as I could.

On the evening of the second day my coolie and the good old dwarf arrived with my luggage, and told Wang some wonderful stories about the narrow escapes they had had from his friends the boatmen. The coolie said he had been so much alarmed that

H

he had spent the whole night in a temple, it being the only place where he considered himself safe. It was not necessary for me to believe all these things, more particularly as all the luggage had come safely to hand, which could scarcely have been the case had the boatmen been as bad as was represented.

For three days the rain fell incessantly, and it was also very cold. The Chinese tried to keep themselves warm by putting on thick clothing, and, strange to say, by reading aloud, which they did in a loud singing manner, repeating the words as fast as they could. When tired with this way of amusing themselves, nearly the whole of them went to bed, as being the most comfortable place under the circumstances, and strongly recommended me to follow their example.

Sung-lo mountain, which in ordinary weather I could have seen from the windows, was now enveloped in a cloak of mist, and every tree and bush was bent down with heavy drops of rain. At last, on the fourth day, the clouds cleared away, the sun shone out again with his usual brilliancy, and the whole face of nature wore a cheerful and smiling aspect. I was now out every day, from morning until evening, busily employed in collecting seeds, in examining the vegetation of the hills, and in obtaining information regarding the cultivation and manufacture of green tea. By this means I obtained a good collection of those tea-seeds and young plants from which the finest green teas of commerce are prepared, and much information of a useful kind,

which I have endeavoured in the last chapter to lay
before the reader.

In the mean time I had not lost sight of the beautiful new Berberis, which I have already described,
and which I was most anxious to procure, in order to
introduce it into Europe.   I had frequently desired
Wang to endeavour to procure me some young plants
of it from some garden in the neighbourhood, as I
could not believe it to be so rare as only to exist in
the old place where I had first seen it.   However,
he either could not find it, or, what was more probable, he gave himself no trouble about the matter.
Knowing the potent influence of dollars, I called
three or four of the family around me one morning,
and, showing them the leaf which I had brought
with me, promised a dollar to any one of them who
would bring me a small plant of the same shrub.
One of them went out immediately, and, to my surprise and pleasure, returned in less than five minutes
with a fresh leaf of the plant in question.   " That
will do," said I; "that is just the thing I want:
bring me a young plant with good roots, and I will
give you the promised reward."   They now held a
consultation amongst themselves in an under tone,
and at last said that the plant in question had some
peculiar medical virtues, and that the lucky possessor
would not part with it.   " Sell me this one," said I,
"and you will be able to buy a dozen others with
the money."   " No," one of them replied, " my
uncle, in whose garden it is growing, does not want
money; he is rich enough; but he requires a little

of the plant now and then when he is unwell, and
therefore he will not part with it." This was very
provoking, but the Chinese were firm, and there was
nothing for it but to go, as sailors say, " upon another
tack." This I determined to do. " Well, at all
events," said I, " let me see the plant; don't be
afraid, I shall not touch it." For some time they
refused to do even this, but through Wang's influence they were at last induced to consent, and led
the way down to a small cottage-garden, completely
covered with weeds. There the beautiful shrub was
growing apparently neglected and left to " bloom
unseen." It seemed very valuable in the uncle's
estimation, and he would not part with it, although
I tried hard to induce him to do so. It might be
that he really valued its medicinal properties, but, as
it must be common enough in that part of the country, he could easily have replaced it: it was not
unlikely, therefore, that he supposed I should offer
some very large sum to induce him to part with it.

On the following day another relation of Wang's
came to me in a secret manner, and informed me
that he was acquainted with another place where the
same plant was to be had, and that for a consideration he would go and fetch some of it for me.
I engaged him at once, merely telling him that he
must bring young plants with good roots, otherwise
they would be entirely useless to me. This he
faithfully promised to do, and he kept his word. In
the course of the day he returned with three good
plants, which he sold to me, and which I afterwards

took back to Shanghae. These are now safely in England.

I spent a week in the neighbourhood of Sung-lo, and then began to think of returning eastward with the collections I had made. My coolie was now giving Wang no little annoyance, in the hope of extorting money from him. The coolie had observed how he had been frightened by the boatmen, and doubtless thought that he too might make something out of his timidity. But Wang was now in his father's house, and consequently more bold. He refused to be " squeezed " to the amount of four dollars—a sum which the other fellow demanded. The latter, after a great deal of blustering language, left the house with the threat of bringing some countrymen of his own to force compliance with his demands. He returned, however, in the course of an hour, without any companions, and, the subject having been mentioned to me in the mean time, I sent for him, and threatened to punish him by with-holding his wages if I heard any more of the matter. After this he became more quiet, and I believe the matter was finally arranged by his accepting a loan!

In the mean time old Mr. Wang, in whose house we were staying, having occasion to go down to Tun-che on business, was desired by me to engage a boat to take us down the river again as far as a place named Nechow. He returned in due time, and brought a "chop" which had been entered into with the boatmen. I could not read the Chinese language, and therefore had to get Wang to read the

chop over to me and explain it, more particularly
that part which specified the sum I was to pay.
The chop stated where we were to be taken to; the
number of men we were to have in the boat; the
charges for good rice, which they were to supply
three times a day, and the hire of the boat. With
regard to the last item, Wang informed me that it
stated I was to pay the sum of twenty-four dollars,
part before we started, and the remainder at the end
of the journey.

The sum which I had brought with me was
reduced to about thirty dollars. I had been obliged
to pay very high prices for everything during the
journey, and felt convinced that the Chinese system
of *squeezing* had been in full operation. Up to the
present time I had submitted to it with a good grace,
knowing that this was the only way by which I was
likely to attain the object I had in view. But now
it was absolutely necessary for me to rebel. The
place to which we were to be taken by this boat was
at least one hundred miles from any of the ports
where the English resided, and where money could
be procured, and I had every reason to expect that a
sum equal to this would be demanded for taking me
on from Nechow to Ning-po—and this latter demand
I should not have been able to pay. Besides, I knew
very well, or at least I had every reason to suspect,
that the sum stated to me by Wang was much more
than his father had agreed for with the boatmen.
I therefore said to him that I was quite sure the
chop was not correct, and that, whether it was or not,

I could not pay such a large sum, and must devise some other means of proceeding down the country. He pretended to be highly indignant at my even suspecting his veracity, and was entering into a long explanation, when I cut the matter short by saying that my mind was made up upon the subject, and that, as the sum he named was out of the question, I should endeavour to engage another boat myself or through the coolie. Moreover I hinted that, if things could not be managed in that way, I would call upon the mandarin of Tun-che, and ask his assistance to enable me to engage a boat at a fair and proper price. I then desired him to say no more to me on this subject, and walked away.

This treatment produced exactly the effect which I intended it should do, and in a few minutes old Wang returned, and coolly asked me what sum I was willing to give for the hire of the boat. "What is the use of your asking that question?" I replied: "you tell me you have engaged a boat at twenty-four dollars; if I take the boat I must of course pay this sum; if not, I only forfeit the bargain-money which you say you have paid." "Never mind that," said he; "tell me what sum you can give for the hire of this boat, and then we shall see whether it is sufficient or not." "Well," said I, "I must reach Ning-po for twenty dollars, and I know that sum is quite sufficient for the journey." "Very well," he replied with the greatest coolness, "give fifteen for this boat from Tun-che to Nechow, and I will guarantee that the other five shall take you on to Ning-po." This was agreed to on my part, and the business was apparently arranged to Mr. Wang's satisfaction; and no wonder; for, having kept the chop, which I afterwards got translated at Ning-po, I found that five dollars, instead of twenty-four, was the sum charged for the boat to Nechow; so that the Wangs had, after all, made ten by the transaction.

Such is the character of the Chinese. They have no idea of telling the truth unless it suits their interests to do so; in fact I used often to think that they rather preferred lying unless it was against their interests.

All our arrangements being complete, the seeds put up, and the plants packed, I hired a chair, and on the afternoon of the 20th of November bade adieu to Wang's family, and to the country of the far-famed Sung-lo-shan. The day was wet and stormy, and I had a most disagreeable ride to Tun-che. Towards evening the gale increased, and the rain fell in torrents. I had procured some oil-paper to protect my feet and knees from the rain, which was blown in upon me in front, and my men who accompanied me also covered themselves with the same material, but it was of very little use to us, and long before we reached our destination we were drenched to the skin. To make matters worse, it became quite dark before we reached Tun-che, and it was with great difficulty that my chairbearers could keep on the narrow road, and prevent themselves from slipping and falling down. Our road led along the high bank of the river, and was rather dangerous to travel on in such a night. Once the foremost man came down, and I was all but blown over the bank into the river; indeed, had the second man not held on firmly by the chair, I believe I must have fallen over the precipice, chair and all.

The lights of the town at last came in sight, and, as we entered its narrow streets, I ordered the chairmen to set me down and wait until my servants came up. The bearers accordingly stopped in front of a tea-house, into which they entered and called for some refreshment. While they were inside the house I was looking out for my men, as it was just possible that they might pass us in the dark. In a few minutes Wang came up to me in a state of great excitement, and almost pulled me out of the chair. "Come away—be quick!" said he; "leave the chair where it is, and let us hurry onwards." I got out, thinking that something very serious was about to happen, and plunged onwards through the mud and rain. We had not gone many yards when the chairmen gave chase, and, coming up with us, collared Wang and demanded their fare. "What is the meaning of this proceeding?" said I: "you received money from me to pay these men before we started, and now you want to run off without paying them at all." "Do not make any noise," he replied; "I will account for the money afterwards, but give me some more now to get rid of these men." I did so, and we then went on.

When the chairmen left us I was bringing Wang to task for dishonesty. He then told me that, as he was coming up behind my chair, he had observed another chair, in which there was a great general, closely following mine, and that he suspected that this man had some intention of seizing us and making us prisoners.

We plunged onwards, and saw no more of the " great general," who was probably all the time thinking much more of getting indoors from the pelting storm than of molesting us. Indeed I strongly suspected that the whole affair was only a trick of Wang's to get rid of the chairbearers, and to rob them of their money, which ought to have been paid to them on starting.

We were now in the town of Tun-che, and, having crossed the river by a bridge, soon reached our boat. My bed and all my clothes were soaked with rain, and I spent a most uncomfortable night. Early on the following morning the boat was pushed out into the stream, and we proceeded rapidly down the river.

The storm of the previous night had entirely passed away, and never had I seen a more beautiful morning. The sun shone gaily, the atmosphere was clear and bracing, and everything wore a cheerful and smiling aspect. With little exertion on the part of our crew, we floated rapidly down the stream, passing in quick succession the woods, towns, and villages which lined its banks. Sometimes, as we looked onwards, our course seemed to be stopped by mountain-barriers, but as we approached them a way opened out, and we glided rapidly through, between mountains which frequently rose to a height of at least three thousand feet.

The moon was just past the full, and the scenery by moonlight was striking and grand. Sometimes the moon rose in all her grandeur above the tops of the mountains, and threw a flood of mellowed light upon the clear and shining river, which made it appear to sparkle as if covered with a thousand bright gems. Again, as we approached the eastern shore, the moon appeared to sink behind the mountains, and set where she rose, and we were left in the shade; and so, as we floated onwards, she rose and set many times, until she was so high in the sky that the mountains could no longer intercept her rays.

On our way up the river I had marked the spot where the beautiful *Berberis* grew, and I now paid it another visit, and procured some good cuttings of it from an old woman who seemed to be in charge of the place. I would gladly have bought the plant itself, but it was too large to move with any chance of success. A goodly number of tea-seeds were also collected on our way down, as well as more of the seeds of the Funereal cypress. The boat being wholly engaged by myself, I was able to stop when and where I chose.

The river being rapid, and in many parts studded with rocks and large stones most dangerous to navigation, we were often obliged, when evening came, to drive a bamboo pole into the bank, and fasten our boat up for the night. On one occasion a sudden change of weather took place, an event common amongst these mountains. When we went to bed the evening was calm and serene, and there was no appearance of any change in the weather. Before midnight, however, two or three sudden gusts of wind followed each other in quick succession; and in the short space of a quarter of an hour it was blowing a gale. I was awakened by a sudden gust which blew the door open, and then nearly swept the roof off. At the same time the boat was torn from her moorings, and driven out into the stream. We were now in a dangerous position, for this part of the river was full of rocks. All the men were up, and with two large sculls and bamboo poles tried to get the boat inshore. Some of them were lashing the roof firmly down to the hull with ropes, and I thought it would have been carried away before it could have been secured. Chinamen-like, our crew were making a great noise; all were giving orders, and none obeying them. In the mean time we were flying down before the wind, and with a rapid current. I expected every moment that the boat would strike upon the rocks, and be dashed to pieces. Luckily, however, they managed to get her inshore, and ran upon a bank of sand, where she was made fast again.

At daylight the wind had abated considerably, but it still blew too strong for us to get under way. We were therefore obliged to remain where we were during the greater part of the day. Our boatmen invited some of their friends, who were detained by the same cause as ourselves, to come on board to dine and

play cards; and in this way they amused themselves
until the afternoon, when the weather had moderated,
and we proceeded on our voyage.

In three days we arrived at the city of Yen-chow-
foo—a journey which occupied twelve days in going
up; and in three days more, that is on the sixth day
after leaving Tun-che, we arrived at the town of
Nechow.

Nechow is a small but busy town, a few miles
higher up the river than the city of Hang-chow-foo.
It is a place of some importance, as it stands on the
main road between Hwuy-chow and Ning-po. Large
numbers of river boats were at anchor abreast of the
town, some from Hwuy-chow, Yen-chow, and the
other towns up the river, and many from the city of
Hang-chow. I suppose the population of the town
and boats may amount to twenty or thirty thousand.

I had frequently heard of the rapidity of the tides
in the river, but had never seen anything remarkable
about them until this evening. We were all seated
at dinner, or rather supper, for it was the third and
last meal of the day, when I heard a rush of water
and a great noise amongst the boats with which
we were moored. "Jan-shui! jan-shui!" (the flood-
tide! the flood-tide!) exclaimed a hundred voices;
and two or three of our men jumped up, and ran out
to guide the boat. I went out also to see what was
going on, and observed a large wave coming rolling
up towards us. Taking boat after boat in its progress,
it whirled it round in an instant, until the whole fleet
were "riding to the flood." I can only compare the

scene to that presented by some highland river, which, swelled after a storm by many mountain streams, comes rolling down to the lowlands, flooding the country in its course, and bearing everything before it.

Having discharged our Hwuy-chow boat, we proceeded through the town to the terminus of a small canal, where another boat was engaged to take us on to a town called Shang-o, or Tsaou-o, a place not very far from the source of the Ning-po River. The canal was narrow, and led us through a beautiful hilly country. All the low land was evidently very wet, and only fit for the cultivation of rice and vegetables.

A few miles below Nechow we passed a small town where there are Government salt warehouses. About this part of the canal, boats are not allowed to go on by night, in order, I suppose, to prevent smuggling. We were therefore stopped about nine o'clock in the evening, and informed that we must not proceed until daylight. I thought this was quite settled, when Wang came and asked me whether I wanted to go on or not. He said, if I wished to proceed, it was only necessary to pay the soldier who had stopped us about twenty cash (one penny), and then I might do as I pleased. This is the way these things are managed in China. We of course paid the cash and went on.

Next morning we arrived at a town of considerable size, named Shaou-hing-foo. It is situated in latitude 30° 6' N., and in longitude 120° 29' E. It seems densely populated, and probably contains nearly as many inhabitants as Shanghae (270,000). The city is walled and fortified, in the same manner as all other places of this class.

The canal passes round the city walls, and forms a sort of moat. A branch of it goes straight through the city itself. Being anxious to visit this place, I directed my boatmen to go through the city, and we entered it by an arch in the ramparts.

The walls of Shaou-hing-foo are between three and four miles in circumference, but, like most Chinese cities, the space enclosed is not all built over. On the sides of the canal the houses have a somewhat mean and poor appearance, but they are better in other parts of the town. A great trade seems to be carried on in all the common necessaries of life ; and as the town is as it were a half-way station between Hang-chow and Ning-po, it is visited by a great number of travellers. A considerable quantity of tea is grown on the hills not far from here. It is, I believe, of a very fair quality, and second only to that of Hwuy-chow.

Amongst the sights here which the Chinese point out, and are proud of, is a fine Buddhist temple standing on a pretty little hill just outside the city walls. I saw many ornamental gates in the town, erected to the memory of virtuous women, who, judging from the number of these structures, must have been unusually numerous in the place ; but its chief fame results from the number of literary men which it has produced, and who are scattered over the whole of the empire. Wherever you meet them, it is their pride and boast to have received their education in the city of Shaou-hing.

The surrounding country here is flat, and in every direction intersected by canals. The hills, which are seen at no great distance, have a barren appearance—at least they are far from being so fertile as those in the green-tea country, from which I had just come. Rice appeared to be the staple production, as it is on all low wet lands in this part of China. Tallow-trees were abundant, both in the plains and on the lower sides of the hills.

About three o'clock in the afternoon we arrived at the town of Tsaou-o. Here we left the Nechow boat, and walked about a mile across the country to another small town named Pak-wan. This town stands on the banks of a river which falls into the bay of Hang-chow. When I first saw this river I imagined it to be the one which flows down to the city of Ning-po, but I soon found that this was not the case.

Pak-wan is a long straggling town, full of pack-houses, eating-houses, and tea-shops for the accommo-dation of travellers and their goods. I found that several foreigners had been here before, and conse-quently the inhabitants were well acquainted with their features. I was recognised as a foreigner im-mediately on my entering the town, but was most civilly treated, and had no difficulty in engaging a boat to take me onwards. For this purpose I entered the Hong-le, or boat-inn, and procured a chop, by which the innkeeper bound himself to send me on to Ning-po for the sum of three dollars.

During the night we passed over two embank-ments, which, for small vessels, answer the same pur-poses as the locks on our canals at home. We were drawn over the embankment by means of a windlass and an inclined plane. This mode of getting from a higher to a lower level, or *vice versâ*, is common in China, where locks, such as those seen in Europe, do not seem to be used. As our boat glided swiftly down the inclined plane at midnight, amidst the lanterns of the Chinese, the effect was curious enough to a person like myself who had never seen anything of the kind before. The second launch brought us upon the waters of the Ning-po river.

During the night we passed a large city named Yu-eou, and next morning I found we were sailing down a wide and beautiful stream, which I knew passed by the city of Ning-po, and entered the sea at Chinhae. The country in its general features was hilly, but a plain of some extent was seen on each side of the river. This low ground was wet and marshy, and only fit for the cultivation of rice.

An immense number of tombs were seen covering the sides of the hills, and plainly betokened that we were approaching a large and populous city. Juniper and pine trees were grouped about the graves, and gave a sombre yet pleasing aspect to the last resting-places of the dead. The tallow-tree still occupied a prominent place on the edges of the fields and canals, as well as on the hill-sides; and showed, by the extent to which it is cultivated, that it must be a most im-portant tree to the Chinese.

I

Nothing worthy of note occurred until I reached the town of Ning-po. It was as welcome a sight as I had seen for many a day, when the old town, with its pagoda, temples, and ramparts, came in view. It was well known to me in former years, and I felt myself "quite at home," after a long and somewhat perilous, although in many respects a pleasant journey.

CHAPTER VII.

Kintang or Silver Island — Its inhabitants and productions — Bay of
   Chapoo — Advantages of an inland route — New year at Shanghae
   — Flower-shops and flowers — Sacred bamboo — The Chrysanthemum — Mode of cultivating it — Weather-prophets — Sail for
   Hong-kong — A game-ship — The Enkianthus — Canton seeds,
   and mode of packing them — False notion regarding their being
   poisoned.

On my arrival at Ning-po I engaged a Chinese boat
to take me to Kintang.   Kintang or Silver Island is
one of the islands of the Chusan archipelago, situated
between Chusan and the mouth of the Ning-po river,
in about the 30th degree of north latitude.   It is about
seven miles in length, and from two to three in
breadth at its widest part.   I found two opium vessels
at anchor in the little harbour of Leh-kong, and was
kindly received by Captain Priestman, who gave me
quarters on board his ship.

Silver Island, although near Chusan, was rarely
visited by the English during the time they held
that place.   All sorts of stories used to be told about
it.   It was said to be a place of banishment for
mandarins who had offended the Government ; and
this circumstance, taken in connexion with its name,
led us to believe that it was a place of wealth and
luxury.   Moreover, the Chinese Government had
requested that none of our officers or soldiers might

be allowed to go there, as it was full of Chinese troops, who might be exasperated if they came in contact with those who had vanquished them during the late war.   Having all these matters in my mind, I naturally expected to find this a very important place; but my ideas with regard to its soldiers and riches were not realized.   Small villages are scattered over the valleys, but there is no town of importance, and judging from appearances the inhabitants generally are very poor.   No fierce soldiers were met with in any part of the island : these, however, might have been withdrawn since 1844.

The inhabitants, like those of Chusan and Ning-po, are quiet and inoffensive.   They were very civil to me, and often treated me with great kindness.   They had little to offer but their good will; and this they showed by asking me to sit down in their houses, or, what was often preferable, under the awning in front of the door.   Here they never failed to offer a draught of the national beverage—tea.   I do not know anything half so refreshing on a hot summer's day as a cup of tea : I mean pure and genuine as the Chinese drink it, without sugar and milk.   It is far better and much more refreshing than either wine or beer.   It quenches thirst, is a gentle stimulant, and wards off many of the fevers incident to such a climate.

If Silver Island is not inhabited by rich men and brave soldiers, nature at least has been most bountiful, for it is one of the most beautiful of the group to which it belongs.   On paying it a visit at this time

I was particularly struck with the scenery.   Passing through the small town or village of Leh-kong, I soon came to the foot of the first range of hills, and ascended the pass which led over them into the interior of the island.   On the sides of the road and scattered over the hills I observed large quantities of the tallow-tree.   Its seeds are carefully gathered by the natives, and are valuable for the oil and tallow which they contain.   A few patches of tea were seen dotted on the lower parts of the hills.   When I reached the top of the first ridge of hills, and looked down on the other side, a most charming view presented itself.   A quiet and beautiful valley lay below, here and there studded with small farm-houses, and apparently bounded on all sides by hills richly clothed with shrubs and trees.   It was a fine autumnal day, and many of the leaves had assumed their red and yellow tints before falling to the ground.   Those of the tallow-tree and a species of maple had become of a clear blood-red colour—others were nearly white; and the contrast between these colours and the deep green foliage of the pines was most striking.   Clumps of fine bamboos, and the *sung*—the species of palm already noticed—gave a tropical appearance to the scenery.

The green-tea shrub is cultivated very extensively in the interior of the island; and my chief object in coming here was to procure a quantity of its seeds. For this purpose I took my two servants with me, and examined all the tea-farms on our way.   Chinamen generally have a great aversion to long walks,

and my men were no exception to the rule. From
the way in which they lagged behind I suspected they
had some intention of turning back when I was far
enough advanced to be out of sight. This they
contrived to do, and when they got home reported
that they had lost me amongst the hills. I felt
rather annoyed, as I expected to have secured a
considerable quantity of tea-seeds, but contented myself with a determination to look better after them the
next day. On the following morning I procured a
pony, and with my two defaulters set off for the tea-
farms situated in the middle of the island. Captain
Priestman accompanied me; and as he had seen the
conduct of my two men on the day previous, he
assisted me to look after them with hearty good will.
When we had crossed the first range of hills and were
descending into the valley on the opposite side, the
two Chinese disappeared just as they had done the
day before. Riding back some distance, we found
them lingering behind, and evidently intending to
lose us again and return home. This time, however,
it would not do; so calling them to come on, and
placing them between us on the narrow road, we
moved forwards. I fear, I must confess, that we
did not take the nearest road to our destination, which
we reached at last, having been between three and
four hours on the way. We gathered a good supply
of tea-seeds from various farms on the hill-sides; and
when we had finished the day's operations rode quietly
homewards, leaving the Chinamen to bring the collections which had been made. The same plan was

adopted daily until nearly all the farms were visited, and a large supply of tea-seeds was obtained.

Silver Island consists of a succession of hills and valleys not unlike those of Chusan, but even more rich in appearance. Passing over the first hill and descending into the valley, the traveller at first imagines that he is surrounded on every side by hills; but proceeding onwards, the road gradually winds round the base of the hills, and another valley as pretty as the last opens up to view. Thus, like a splendid panorama, picture after picture is presented to the eye, painted by the hand of nature beautiful and perfect.

There is more tea grown on Silver Island than on any of the other islands in the Chusan archipelago. The greater part of what is not consumed by the natives is sent over to Ning-po and Chapoo for home consumption or for exportation to the Straits. Although good tea, it is not prepared in a manner to suit the English or American markets. The tallow-tree (*Stillingia sebifera*) and the " Tung-eau " (*Dryandra cordata*, Thunberg) both produce articles of export. The former is well known to produce the tallow and oil so much in use in China: the latter furnishes a valuable oil which is used in mixing with the celebrated varnish of the country, and hence this tree is often called the varnish-tree.

Having procured a collection of the seeds of these useful trees, as well as a large quantity of tea-seeds, I had the whole of them carefully packed, and left Silver Island for Shanghae, *viâ* Chapoo. This route,

which I opened some years ago, is now commonly
used by foreigners travelling between the two northern
ports, and, although not provided for in the " treaty,"
is not objected to by the Chinese authorities. The
consuls of different nations and their families, merchants, and missionaries, all avail themselves of it;
and when we consider the number of foreigners in
Shanghae, an outlet such as this seems absolutely
necessary. All acknowledge the powerful influence
of change of air in cases of fever, and I have no doubt
that the lives of some have been saved by being able
to get down quickly to the islands in the Chusan
archipelago. But had there been no route *viâ*
Chapoo, this would oftentimes have been very difficult, as the only other way is by sea. While I
mention this to show the folly of the treaty we made
with the Chinese—a treaty, by-the-by, which is observed neither by the Chinese nor by ourselves—it
also shows how much may be done by quietly and
peaceably breaking down those barriers which have
been erected by prejudice and ignorance.

The bay of Chapoo abounds with pirates, and
unless one's boat is well armed the passage across is
rather dangerous. It was here poor Mr. Lowrie, the
American missionary, was murdered in 1845 or 1846.
He was a man of great promise, and was much regretted. My boat was well armed, and having moreover two Lascars on board, I had little to fear. We
crossed the bay in safety. I then engaged a canal boat,
and jogged quietly onwards to Shanghae, which place
we reached without any adventure worth recording.

It was now the middle of January, and the depth of winter in the north of China. The Chinese new year was approaching; it fell on the 24th, and all the natives were busily employed in collecting their debts and arranging their books. It is considered a great disgrace to have outstanding debts at the beginning of the year. Merchants and shopkeepers will often make considerable sacrifices in order to raise money at this season, and hence foreigners generally consider this a good time to make cheap purchases. These purchases must all be made before new year's day, as then the shops are closed, and little or no business is transacted for a week; after which trade begins again as before. At this festive season flowers are as much sought after here for the purposes of decoration as they are at home at Christmas time. On visiting some of the flower-shops in Shanghae, in the middle of January, I was surprised to find a great many flowers which had been forced into bloom and were now exposed for sale. I was not previously aware that the practice of forcing flowers was common in China. Many plants of *Magnolia purpurea* were in full flower; as were also many kinds of double-blossomed peaches, the pretty little *Prunus sinensis alba*, and a variety of camellias. But what struck me as most remarkable was the facility with which the Moutan Pæony had been brought into full bloom. Several varieties of this plant were in full flower; and at this season of the year, when everything out of doors was cold and dreary, they had a most lively effect. Their blooms were tied up, to keep them from expanding too rapidly. All these things had been brought from the celebrated city of Soo-chow-foo, the great emporium of Chinese fashion and luxury.

It may be thought that the Chinese have glass houses, hot-water pipes, and all those fine things which assist gardeners and amateurs in Europe. Nothing of the kind; they do all these things in their houses and sheds, with common charcoal fires, and a quantity of straw to stop up the crevices in the doors and windows.

At this season of the year the "Kum-quat" (*Citrus japonica*), which is extensively grown in pots, is literally covered with its small, oval, orange-coloured fruit. This as well as various other species of the orange is mixed with the forced flowers, and together produce an excellent effect. I think if the "Kum-quat" was better known at home it would be highly prized for decorative purposes during the winter months. It is much more hardy than any other of its tribe; it produces its flowers and fruit in great abundance, and it would doubtless prove a plant of easy cultivation. In order, however, to succeed with it as well as the Chinese do, one little fact should be kept in view, namely, that all the plants of the orange-tribe which bear fruit in a small state are grafted. There is also a plant, with red berries, which takes the place of our English holly. It is the *Nandina domestica*, and is called by the Chinese the "Tein-chok," or Sacred Bamboo. Large quantities of its branches are brought in at this time from

the country and hawked about the streets. Each
of these branches is crowned with a large bunch of
red berries, not very unlike those of the common
holly, and, when contrasted with the dark, shining
leaves, are singularly ornamental. It is used chiefly
in the decoration of altars, not only in the temple,
but also in private dwellings and in boats—for here
every house and boat has its altar—and hence the
name of " Sacred Bamboo " which it bears.

The Nandina is found in English gardens, but,
judging from the specimens which I have seen at
home, no idea can be formed of its beauty. It does
not appear to produce its fruit so freely in England
as it does in China, probably owing to the temperature
of our summers being lower than those of its native
country. But the chrysanthemum is the Chinese
gardener's favourite winter flower, although it is generally past its full beauty at the Chinese new year.
There is no other plant with which he takes so much
pains, or which he cultivates so well. His camellias,
azaleas, and roses are well grown and well bloomed,
but in all these we excel him in England; in the
cultivation of the chrysanthemum, however, he stands
unrivalled. The plants themselves seem, as it were,
to meet him half way and grow just as he pleases;
sometimes I found them trained in the form of animals, such as horses and deer, and at other times
they were made to resemble the pagodas, so common
in the country. Whether they were trained into
these fanciful forms, or merely grown as simple
bushes, they were always in high health, full of fresh

green leaves, and never failed to bloom most profusely in the autumn and winter.

The method of cultivating the chrysanthemum in
China is as follows. Cuttings are struck every year
from the young shoots, in the same manner as we do
in England. When they are rooted they are potted
off at once into the pots in which they are to grow
and bloom ; that is, they are grown upon what would
be called by our gardeners " the one-shift system."

The soil used in potting is of a very rich description. About Canton it is generally obtained, in the
first instance, from the bottom of lakes or ponds,
where the Nelumbium or water-lily grows. It is
then laid up to dry and pulverise for some months,
when it is mixed with old night-soil taken from the
manure-tanks found in every garden. A heap of this
kind, after being laid up for some time and frequently
turned over, is in a fit state for potting the chrysanthemum. Manure-water, taken also from the tanks,
is liberally supplied during the growing season, and
its effects are visible in the luxuriant dark-green
leaves which cover the plants.

In forming the plants into nice compact bushes,
which, with due deference to Chinese taste, I think
much prettier than animals and " seven-storied pagodas," their system is as follows:—The plants are
trained each with a single stem ; this is forced to
send out numerous laterals near its base, and these
are tied down in a neat and regular manner with
strings of silk-thread. By having the plants clothed
with branches in this way, and by keeping the leaves

in a green and healthy state, the specimens never have that bare and broom-headed appearance which they often present in England when they are taken into the greenhouse in winter.

About Shanghae and Ning-po the chrysanthemum is still better managed than it is near Canton; but the success which attends it may be attributed, partly at least, to the more favourable nature of the climate, the plant being indigenous to the central or more northern parts of the empire. The system of cultivation is nearly the same—the main points attended to being those which have been noticed, namely, choosing a rich soil, planting at once into large pots, training to a single stem, and inducing it to send out numerous laterals, and giving liberal supplies of manure-water during the growing season. The Chinese are fond of having very large blooms, and, in order to obtain these, they generally pick off all the small flower-buds.

In China, as in England, the chrysanthemum flowers during the winter months. When in bloom it is in great request among the people, and is used in the decoration of court-yards, halls, and temples. It is everybody's plant, and blooms alike in the garden of the lowly Chinese cottager and in that of the red-buttoned mandarin.

Although we are indebted to China for the parents of those varieties of chrysanthemums which now enliven our gardens during the dull months of winter, yet, strange to say, the progeny is more numerous in Europe than in China itself. Some of those beautiful

kinds raised by Mr. Salter in France would be much admired even by the Chinese florist. It is a curious fact,
however, that many of those kinds, such as *formosum*
and *lucidum*, which were originally raised from seed
in Europe, are also met with in the north of China.

The Chinese, like ourselves, have their weather-
prophets and cold winters. It had been predicted that
this winter (1848-9) was to be very severe. The
thermometer was now down to 17° Fahr., and there
was every appearance of the prediction being fulfilled.
This degree of cold is felt much more in Shanghae
than in England, owing to the piercing nature of the
wind, which seems to find its way through every pore
of the skin.

Since my return to Shanghae I had been engaged
in getting the tea-plants carefully planted in Ward's
cases, in order to send them to India. As there was
no vessel in Shanghae bound for Calcutta direct, I
determined to take the collection to Hong-kong, and
to ship them thence to India.

At the time we sailed game of all kinds was most
abundant in Shanghae, and the merchants took the
opportunity of sending a large quantity down to their
friends in Hong-kong and Canton. The poop of our
good ship looked like a row of poulterers' shops at
Christmas. Pheasants, woodcocks, hares, ducks,
geese, and teal were hanging about in all directions.
Every airy place, such as the davits, boats, poop-
rail, &c., was covered with them, besides which there
were a number of baskets filled with living pheasants
stowed away in the hold. Many of these birds were

very beautiful, particularly the white-necked pheasants, and the ducks and teal with feathers of every hue.

All cargo of this kind is taken down freight free; but, as it is of a perishable nature, there is generally a tacit understanding between the sender and the master of the vessel that, if any of it show signs of becoming bad, it should either be eaten or thrown overboard. Some masters of vessels, and passengers who are perhaps a little sea-sick, cannot endure the smell of game in this state, however agreeable it may be to those for whom it is intended.

It may easily be believed, then, that we did not fare badly on our passage to Hong-kong. We were lucky in having a medical man on board of high character, and I can honestly say that no plump wood-cock, wild duck, or pheasant was condemned without being examined by him and pronounced in imminent danger: on the other hand, it must be confessed that none, so far as I knew, were ever thrown overboard.

As soon as we got out to sea all sail was crowded on our vessel, and we ran merrily on before the wind. In four days after leaving the Yang-tse-kiang river we were safely at anchor in the bay of Hong-kong, having run fully one thousand miles.

The tea-plants having reached Hong-kong in good order, I lost no time in getting them transshipped to vessels bound for India, where they afterwards arrived in excellent condition.

All my spare time in Hong-kong was spent in rambling about the hills. I was frequently accompanied by Captain Champion, one of the best botanists

I met with in China, and the discoverer of the beautiful *Rhodoleia Championi* figured by Sir William Hooker in the ' Botanical Magazine.'

At this season of the year the well-known Enkianthus was just coming into bloom. This is one of those few Chinese plants which will scarcely submit to cultivation in England, or perhaps it would be more correct to say that its proper management is not understood there. A description of its habits, as observed on its native mountains in Hong-kong, will probably assist those who are trying to cultivate this beautiful plant in England. The island of Hong-kong has often been called a barren rock, an expression which, in our days at least, is not quite correct. When it was formed by some convulsion of nature, in the earlier periods of the world's history, it was no doubt a barren chain of rocks of very irregular outline. Gradually, however, like those islands in the eastern seas which are every day forming by the agency of animals, a great portion of the surface of these rocks became partially covered with soil and vegetation, although many of their peaks are still uncovered, remaining as barren as they were when first formed, and appearing to bid defiance to time and change.

On these mountains, from 1000 to 2000 feet above the level of the sea, the Enkianthus is found growing abundantly, and in great luxuriance. It is never seen in the valleys or low lands, unless when brought down by the natives. The soil is loamy, not unlike what we see at Shirley or Wimbledon, and mixed

with stones and large pieces of granite which have
become detached from the rocks. The plant delights
in fixing itself in the crevices of the rock, and is often
found in such situations with very little soil about its
roots.   About the end of April or beginning of May,
at the change of the monsoon, the wet season begins.
The Enkianthus then grows most luxuriantly, and all
the leaves, buds, and shoots are then fully formed.
In the autumn, with the exception of a week or two
in September, the weather is dry and very hot.   At
this period the branches and buds of the plants get
perfectly ripened, many of the leaves fall off, and the
plant, having formed its secretions for the following
year, remains in a dormant condition during the
winter, which in Hong-kong is cool and dry.   In the
hottest months in the year, namely, June, July, and
August, the maximum temperature in the shade
rarely exceeds 90° Fahr., but on a clear day one of
my thermometers indicated 140° in the sun.   In
winter, although the north winds are cold and piercing,
frost and snow are almost unknown in this part of
China.   When the first impulse is given to vegetation
by spring the Enkianthus bursts into bloom, and the
sides of the barren hills become gay with its number-
less flowers.

This is the way in which Nature treats this charming plant, and we must follow her example before we
can hope to see it half so beautiful as it is on its
native mountains.   There are, however, two circumstances connected with its success in its natural
state which are difficult if not impossible to imitate.

K

The one is the bright sunshine which ripens the wood in autumn, and the other is the peculiar nature of the mountains on which the plant grows. In the hottest weather, even when no rain has fallen for months, and, when the valleys are parched and burnt up for want of it, these mountain-sides are always moist a few inches below the surface, and teem in all directions with cool and refreshing springs.

The Enkianthus is always in blossom at the time of the Chinese new year, when its flowers are in great request in the south of China for the decoration of the houses, boats, and temples, just as those of the Nandina are in the north. It is brought in large quantities from the hills, and sold in the streets, or sent about in presents, after the same fashion as the holly and mistletoe in England. If the branches are cut and placed in a jar of water before the flowers are fully expanded, the latter will remain in perfection for a fortnight or three weeks. The pretty wax-looking globular flowers are very handsome, and are held in high esteem amongst the natives.

Having a few days to spare before commencing my second campaign in the north, I determined on paying a visit to the Fa-tee gardens near Canton. I was curious to obtain some information concerning the process of preparing and packing those seeds which are usually sold to foreigners to be sent home to friends in Europe and America. I had been accustomed to believe, with all good charitable people, that these seeds were boiled or poisoned in some way by the Chinese before they were sold to our merchants, in order that the floral beauties of China should not find their way into other countries, and the trade in seeds be injured.

The Chinese are certainly bad enough, but, like other rogues, they are sometimes painted worse than they really are. " Come, Aching," said I to the old man who generally supplied these seeds, and in whose good graces I stood pretty high, from having made him a present of a rare and curious plant, " I want to see your method of packing seeds for foreigners. Take me to your seed-room and show me the whole process from beginning to end." The old man led me up to the middle of his garden, where he had an ornamental shed or seed-room. It was nicely fitted up with shelves, on which were arranged a great number of small porcelain bottles, such as I had often seen in London with seeds from China. " Sit down," said he, " and I will explain the business to you. I first gather the seeds from the plants. I then put each kind, separately, into one of these small bottles, and then pack the whole into a little box, ready for being shipped to Europe or America." " I understand that part of the business," said I ; " but what is the substance which you put into the bottles along with the seeds ?" This was a white ashy-looking matter, which we supposed in England might be burnt bones, and some conjectured that it was mixed with the seeds for the purpose of manure. " Burnt lice," said Aching. " Burnt what ?" I asked, with a smile which I could not conceal. He repeated the assertion with all the gravity of a judge. The reader may probably be ignorant of the Chinese language, and I must therefore explain that a Chinese cannot pronounce our letter *r*; he has not such a sound in his language. In trying to pronounce any word in which the letter occurs, he invariably substitutes the sound of *l* for that of *r*. It was therefore burnt rice, or the husks of rice reduced to ashes, that he meant. I then asked him the reason why he used this substance in packing seeds, and he replied, in Canton English, " *S'pose my no mixie this seed, worms makie chow-chow he.*" Although the Chinese in Canton would consider this excellent English, it may be as well to explain that his meaning was, " Suppose I did not mix ashes with the seeds, worms would eat them." He alluded to a little maggot which would come out during the voyage. " Don't be angry," said I, "but we English fancy you do something to destroy the vitality of the seeds, instead of endeavouring to preserve it." " I know," said the old man, " you fancy I boil them!"

It is a most difficult matter to preserve the seeds of trees and shrubs in the south of China, owing to the attacks of maggots. This is, without doubt, one of the reasons why Canton seeds so seldom grow when they are received in England; another reason is the age of the seeds. Old ones, gathered in former years, are generally mixed up with the fresh ones, and are all sent together. Most assuredly, however, poor Aching does not boil them nor poison them in any way.

CHAPTER VIII.

Foo-chow-foo — Jealousy of the mandarins — A polite way of getting
rid of a spy — Scenery amongst the mountains — Temple of Koo-
shan — Its priests and idols — Buddha's tooth and other relics —
Trees and shrubs — City of Foo-chow-foo — Chinese mode of getting out when the gates are shut — Journey up the Min — Chinese
sportsmen and their dogs — A deer-hunt — Scenery about Tein-
tung — Wild flowers — Roadside temples — The bamboo — A
priest and siphon — Lakes of Tung-hoo.

THE vessel in which I had taken a passage for the
north being now ready for sea, my luggage was put
on board, and we sailed for Foo-chow-foo, the capital
of the province of Fokien. This port was opened to
foreigners by the treaty, but it has hitherto proved
of little value as a place of trade. The English
consular staff has been greatly reduced, and there is
only one merchant at the port. Many missionaries,
both English and American, have been stationed in
the city and suburbs, and are labouring patiently, but I
fear with little success, amongst an ungrateful people.

The mandarins at Foo-chow, and the people generally, resemble their brethren at Canton. They
are jealous of foreigners, and would gladly see them
turned out of the province. A strict watch is kept
upon all their actions, which are duly reported to the
authorities.

On my arrival I had my luggage conveyed to an

empty house, rented by Captain Hely, who had
kindly offered me the use of it during my stay. I
had just entered the house, and had gone up stairs to
look for a room in which I could have my bed placed,
when I heard a person below putting various questions to my servants. I paid little attention to this
at first, as I knew the Chinese to be very inquisitive;
but as the examination continued longer than was
agreeable, I went down stairs to see what was the
matter. There I found an ill-looking fellow with a
brass button in his hat, and evidently belonging to
the lowest class of mandarins, standing over my servants, and putting questions to them in a most autho-
ritative manner, and in the Fokien dialect, which, as
they were both northern men, they did not understand. For ten minutes they had been going on in
this way, and neither party was any wiser than when
they began. Turning to my servants, I asked them
who the man was, and what he wanted. They
replied that he was a mandarin, that he had been
putting some questions to them concerning me; but
as he spoke in the Fokien dialect they could not
understand him.

The Chinese generally stand in great dread of
their Government officers, and on this occasion my
servants thought they had given me a good and sufficient reason for their having been detained so long.
But I had not forgotten the annoyances which I had
formerly endured at this place from Government
spies, and at once ordered my servants to leave their
interrogator, and attend to their duties. The officer

looked rather disconcerted, and walked out of the house.

Having completed my arrangements in the house, I went out to call upon Mr. Morrison, interpreter to the British Consulate, who was very unwell, and had got as far as this place on his way to Hong-kong. The house in which he had taken up his quarters was only about two or three hundred yards from mine. As I was walking thither, some one came trudging behind me, and on looking round I discovered my old friend the mandarin at my heels. When I turned round he stopped for an instant, and, as I looked intently at him, he seemed inclined to pass on. I stopped him, and asked him, as politely as I could, where he was bound for. He said he was going to some place on the river side, with which I was unacquainted. " Could you not go there to-morrow?" said I; "pray do, for I am going there to-day, and company is disagreeable to me." With that I put my hand on his arm, turned him gently round, and made him a very polite bow. The fellow looked rather confused, grinned, and walked away, and I never saw him again. I was afterwards informed that all foreigners are dodged in this way, and all their operations duly reported to the authorities.

I had often heard of a celebrated Buddhist temple, not very far from Foo-chow, so I determined to pay it a visit. It is called the Temple of Koo-shan, and is situate amongst the mountains, a few miles to the eastward of the city. This temple seems to be the Jerusalem of this part of China, to which all good

Buddhists repair at stated seasons to worship and pay their vows. Having reached the foot of the mountain, I passed through a spacious porch or gateway, and began the ascent. The hill of Koo-shan is fully 3000 feet above the level of the river Min, and the temple is about 2000 feet up, or 1000 feet below the summit. A well-paved path, about six feet in width, has been made the whole way up to the temple. As the traveller ascends by this winding causeway, he gets now and then the most charming view that can be imagined, which well repays him for his toil in the ascent. Now, he looks down amongst rocks and trees into some retired and rugged valley, where the soil is so barren that it will not repay the industry even of the Chinese:—a corner is turned, and he reaches one of those resting-places which are built at regular distances for the accommodation of the weary pilgrim, where a glorious view is spread before him. It is the wide and fertile valley of the Min, intersected everywhere by rivers and canals, and teeming with a numerous and industrious population.

In about an hour I reached the porch of the temple. Some idle-looking priests were lounging about the steps which led up to the first range of buildings. As soon as I was observed, one of them ran off and informed the superior or abbot, who came down and received me with great politeness. I told him I had come to see the temple, of which I had often heard, and requested he would send some one to conduct me over it. An old priest clothed in a yellow gown now presented himself to conduct me through the various parts of this extensive edifice and over the grounds.

This temple is built upon the same plan as that at Tein-tung, near Ning-po; indeed, a description of one would nearly do for the other. It consists of three principal buildings, one behind the other, on the side of the hill; the second being built on a higher foundation than the first, and the third in like manner higher than the second. At right angles with the three large temples on each side are the dwellings of the priests. The "three precious Buddhas," past, present, and future, the deity with numerous arms, and many other images crowd· these temples. In one I observed upwards of a hundred cushions on which the devotees kneel in front of the idols, and candles and incense were burning in all directions.

Having seen the principal temples, I was led to the kitchen and dining-room. When it is remembered that upwards of a hundred priests take their meals here daily, it may easily be imagined that these places are worthy of a visit. The dining-room is a large square building, having a number of tables placed across it at which the priests eat their frugal meals. At the time of my visit they had just sat down to dinner, so that I had an opportunity of seeing a greater number of them together than I had ever seen before. They appeared a strange and motley assembly. Most of them had a stupid and unintellectual appearance—these were generally the lower orders of the priesthood. The abbot and those who ranked highest were intelligent and active-looking men; but all had a kind of swarthy paleness of countenance, which was not agreeable to look upon. Many of them rose as I entered their dining-hall, and politely asked me to sit down and eat rice. I thanked them, but declined the invitation, and proceeded with an inspection of the place. In the kitchen the wonders shown to the visitors are some enormously large coppers in which the rice is boiled.

I was now taken to the library, which contains an extensive assortment of religious books, carefully locked up in presses, and apparently seldom perused. I had heard that in this part of the building there was a precious relic, nothing less than one of Buddha's teeth, and other things, which were sometimes shown

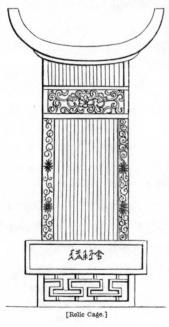

[Relic Cage.]

to visitors with a great deal of ceremony. Having requested the priest to show me these, he led me to a small temple adjoining, where he said they were kept. " Have you any money in your pocket?" said he with great gravity, "for before the precious box can be opened I must burn incense on this altar." I gave him a small piece of money, but told him that as I did not worship

Buddha I could not burn incense upon the altar, and that the money I gave him was a reward for his civility. "Do you not worship Buddha in your country?" he asked. I replied that we did not. "Then whom do you worship?" I pointed upwards, and said that we worshipped the great God, who made the heavens and the earth. "Oh, yes," said he, "his name is *Ye-su*, is it not?" They had known something of the Catholic religion, it appeared, there being in this part of China a number of converts to that faith. While this conversation was going on, one of the priests had lighted two candles, and was burning incense on the altar. "Now," said he, "come and see the precious tooth."

[Buddha's Tooth.]

I stepped up to the altar; and the front of a large case being removed, the relics were exposed to view, protected by a grating of iron bars. On a flat bason in front lay the so-called tooth, a large whitish substance about six inches square, and much more like a stone than a tooth. Behind this was another relic which appeared to me much more curious than the first. It appeared to be a small piece of crystal cut in the form of a little vase, with a curious-looking substance inside. I was afterwards informed that

[Crystal Vase.]

this was only a crystal bottle, with the relic suspended in some way from its mouth; but being inside the bars, I could not examine it very minutely. "Now," said the priest, "look from this side, and tell me what you see in the vase." I looked from the side indicated, and saw what appeared very like a man's head with the eyes staring at me. I was informed, however, that this was a something which had grown on Buddha's forehead; and that, whenever the same thing was observed upon the heads of mortals, it was a sign of their having arrived at a very high state of perfection, approaching to the gods. "Now turn to the other corner, and tell me what colour the relic appears to you." I did so, and the substance, whatever it was, presented a reddish hue. "Ah! that is very good," said the priest, "that is a good omen,—for it appears of that colour only to the most favoured persons. It appears of different colours to different individuals; but that which you have seen is the best."*

The old priest now led me to a different part of the grounds, to see a famous spring. This was in one of the most romantic looking dells or ravines that I had ever beheld. We descended to it by a flight of stone steps, crossed a bridge which spanned the ravine, and found ourselves in front of a small temple. On one side of it the water was gushing down, clear and cool, from the mountain, into a small cistern placed there to receive it; while on the other a caldron or large kettle was always boiling during the day, in order that tea might readily be made for visitors. Here a number of priests were lounging about, apparently attached to this temple. They received me with great kindness, and begged me to be seated at a table in the porch. One of them took a cup and filled it with water at the spring, and brought it to me to taste. They all praised its virtues; and it certainly was excellent water. I told them it was the best I had ever tasted, and they then brought me a cup of tea made with water from the same spring.

---

* The grating prevented me from having a closer examination of these curiosities, and I was obliged to be contented with the information I had obtained respecting them from the priests. When I returned to Foo-chow-foo, however, I requested Mr. Morrison (a son of the well-known Dr. Morrison, one of the earliest and best of Chinese scholars) to send for his teacher, in order, if possible, to get further information. This old gentleman was a native of the city of Shaou-hing-foo, a place famed in China for its literary men. He, too, had visited the temple of Koo-shan, and had seen the precious relics. Upon questioning him, he gave us the same account as I had already received from the priests.

After drinking the tea I wandered away along a paved path that led me round the side of the mountain, amidst vegetation which had been planted and reared by the hand of nature alone. The Chinese fir (*Pinus sinensis*) and a noble species of Abies were the only trees of any size; but the path was lined with many beautiful shrubs, among which the Azalea was most conspicuous. It was spring-time, and these charming flowers were just bursting into bloom. I have often seen them highly cultivated in England, and they certainly produce a most gorgeous effect in our greenhouses and at our flower-shows; but my taste leads me to admire them more when growing wild and free on the mountain side, peeping out from amongst the brushwood, or mingling their glowing colours with other flowers and gaining additional beauty by the contrast.

My progress onwards was at last arrested by a steep precipice where the walk ended, and on the top of which a summer-house had been erected. I entered the house, and sat down upon one of the benches placed there for visitors. The view which I now obtained was one of the grandest I had seen for many a day. Above me, towering in majestic grandeur, was the celebrated peak of Koo-shan, 1000 feet higher than where I stood. Below, I looked down upon rugged and rocky ravines, in many places barren, and in others clothed with trees and brush-wood, but perfectly wild. To afford, as it were, a striking contrast to this scenery, my eye next rested on the beautiful valley of the Min, in which the

town of Foo-chow-foo stands.   The river was winding through it, and had its surface studded with boats
and junks sailing to and fro, and all engaged in active
business.   Its fields were green, and were watered by
numerous canals; while in the background to this
beautiful picture were hills nearly as high as Koo-
shan, from amongst which the river runs, and where
it is lost to the eye.

A sight which is much prized by the Chinese is
the view of the sunrise from the peak of Koo-shan.
Many sleep in the temple, and by torchlight reach
the summit of the mountain in time to see the rising
sun.   I can easily imagine what a striking effect
would be produced upon the mind of a Chinaman—
particularly if a native of an inland province—when
he saw for the first time the sun rising apparently out
of the ocean.

Pleased with what I had seen, I lingered for a
long time amongst this beautiful scenery.   At last
my servants reminded me that it was time to take
our departure for Foo-chow, so, bidding adieu to the
priests, we descended to the plains.   When we
reached the foot of the mountain we found our boat
waiting for us, and with a fair tide we soon sculled
up to the bridge of Foo-chow.

Being engaged to dine with my friend Mr. Compton, who resided inside the city, and between two
and three miles from the bridge near which I was
staying, I lost no time in securing a sedan-chair,
and hurried to his house.   These chairs are the cabs
of Foo-chow: every one who can afford it goes about

in them, just as we in England do in the hackney
cabs of our large towns.

The gates of the city are always locked soon after
dark, and the keys taken to the house of one of the
high mandarins. When I had been in the city on
former occasions, I had always hurried out before
nightfall, for fear of·being locked in, for here the
gates, when once closed, are never opened until
morning, come who may. In other cities of less
note—such, for example, as Shanghae or Ning-po—
a few cash will always get them opened, at least
until a very late hour.

The Chinese, however, have always some way
of evading any very stringent regulation. Here they
had a mode of getting in and out of the city which
was rather amusing, and, strange to say, they were
assisted in it by the officers of Government, and no
doubt the system was well known to the magistrates
of the city.

When dinner was over Mr. Compton and myself
walked leisurely down to the city gate, and found it
closed for the night. The Chinese, seeing what had
happened, good-naturedly pointed to the ramparts on
one side, and informed us that if we went there
we should find a way to get out. Following their
directions we were soon on the ramparts, where a
most curious and amusing scene presented itself. A
ladder was placed at the foot of the wall opposite one
of the embrasures, by which numerous men were
ascending and descending like a hive of bees. One
of the guards was evidently reaping a rich harvest,

for each man had to pay a few cash for the use of the ladder. Following in the train of the Chinamen, I descended the ladder, greatly to the astonishment of the celestial guardsman, who little expected a " quang-yang"* by this convenient route.

After spending a few days more in Foo-chow, and procuring some tea-plants from the hills in the vicinity, I was anxious to proceed onwards to Ning-po and Shanghae. There were three routes which might be taken; one was by sea, another was a land road which led along the coast by the city of Wan-chow, and the third was up the river Min to Kein-ning-foo and across the Bohea mountains. The latter was much the longest way, as it leads far to the westward, in the direction of the far-famed Woo-e-shan. For many reasons I was most anxious to reach this place, and so determined on the Min route.

Having finished my business in the district, I collected my things together, and went down to the mouth of the Min. Here I engaged a boat and set out on my journey. A few miles above the town of Foo-chow the river divides into two streams, one of which passes the city, while the other takes a more southerly course for some distance; they, however, reunite about ten miles from the sea. I took the southern passage, and thus avoided the city of Foo-chow altogether. Both wind and tide being fair, my boat glided up the river with great rapidity, and the first night I had the satisfaction of getting as far as the second bridge, three or four miles above the town.

* The name given to foreigners here.

Here we sculled the boat in-shore, and rested for the night. On the following morning at daybreak we got under way again, and proceeded up the river. Numerous boats accompanied us, being on their way for the large towns of Suiy-kow, Yen-ping-foo, and Kien-ning-foo, all on the banks of the Min. As I was dressed in the costume of the country, no one took the slightest notice of me, and I considered myself in a fair way to accomplish the object I had in view.

The boatmen, who had been engaged at the mouth of the Min, were perfectly ignorant of my intentions. They now began to inquire how far I intended to go in their boat, and whether it was my intention to return with them. I told them I intended to take their boat as far as Suiy-kow, a town said to be about 240 le from Foo-chow-foo. They held up their hands in astonishment, and declared it was perfectly impossible for their boat to go so far. " Oh, very well," I replied; " then I shall engage another boat, and you may return." Thereupon they held a consultation amongst themselves for a minute or two, and at last came to the conclusion that such a thing *was* possible, and agreed to take me to Suiy-kow.

Hitherto we had been passing through what is commonly called the valley of the Min. It is rich and fertile to an extraordinary degree. Groves of leechee, longan, peach and plum trees, are seen over all the plain. The sweet-scented *Aglaia odorata* is largely cultivated for mixing with and perfuming tobacco, and the *Chloranthus* for scenting the finer kinds of tea. Sugar-cane and tobacco are extensively grown in all the fields, and, besides the usual quantity of vegetables, I observed a large number of sweet-scented flowers, amongst which the Italian tuberose and the jasmine (*Jasminum Sambac*) occupied a prominent place. The latter are sold in the markets, and eagerly bought by the ladies for the purpose of ornamenting their hair.

When we got a few miles above Foo-chow we seemed to leave the valley, and the scenery began to change and assume quite a different aspect. The hills in many places were close to the water's edge. Many of them were rugged and barren, while others appeared more fertile and were cultivated a considerable way up their sides; a third class were richly clothed with trees and brushwood. The fruit-trees already named were frequently seen growing on little level spots near villages. The forest-trees consisted chiefly of the common Chinese pine and *Cunninghamia lanceolata*. Altogether the scenery was most striking in its character, and richly repaid me for the inconveniences attending the journey.

A large trade in wood is carried on here—indeed, it is the principal trade of Foo-chow—and we were constantly meeting large rafts floating down the stream on their way to the city. I observed small houses built on some of these rafts for the accommodation of the persons who had charge of them. Their occupation seemed to me a most delightful one, and as they glided gently down the stream, having on all sides the most beautiful and romantic scenery, I almost envied them their happy lot.

The country on the banks of the Min at this part

did not appear to be very thickly populated. I saw no towns of any size from Foo-chow to Suiy-kow; even villages and small farm-houses were few and far between. Whenever I landed—and I did so every day during the ebb tide—I had a good opportunity of forming an opinion on the character of the natives. Most of them seemed miserably poor, but all were quiet and harmless, and very different from those at the mouth of the river and on the islands near the coast. The latter are a dangerous set; they live by robbery and piracy, and often set the Government itself at defiance.

On the morning of the fourth day we arrived at Suiy-kow. Travellers bound for the towns north of this place generally leave the river here, and go on by chair, as the rapids are numerous, and boats make slow progress against the stream.

This place is most pleasantly situated on the left bank of the river. It is but a small town, and I suppose does not contain more than 5000 or 6000 inhabitants. A very large number of boats, for the size of the place, were moored along the banks of the river. The principal trade of the town seems to be in furnishing supplies for the boatmen and their passengers, as they pass on their way either to the interior or down towards the coast.

My servants were now despatched to engage another boat, while I took a stroll through the town and its suburbs. In the course of two hours we met again at the landing-place, when I found they had not been successful, and were now most anxious for me to proceed by chair, which they said was the usual way for travellers. As the journey was a long one, I was afraid I had not brought money enough to defray the expenses of travelling in that way, and was obliged, from prudential motives, to defer this interesting journey for a time.

I now considered that the best plan I could adopt, under the circumstances, was to send my servants onwards by themselves to the fine black-tea country of Woo-e-shan. Were I to take them with me by sea to Ning-po, and then send them back across the Bohea mountains, what guarantee had I that they would go there at all? They would be much more likely to provide themselves with plants in a country nearer home, and return, pretending they had been in Woo-e. But by sending them up the Min they were necessarily obliged to pass through the black-tea country in question on their route, and could have no inducement to deceive me. If they brought me any tea-plants at all I should be able to judge, from various circumstances, whether they were from the black-tea country.

Having arranged this matter in my own mind, I gave them a sufficient number of dollars to pay the expenses of their journey, and to make the purchases I had directed, besides which I promised them a liberal reward if they performed their mission to my satisfaction. I then left them to prosecute their journey, and returned alone to the mouth of the Min. Here I found a Portuguese lorcha ready to sail for Ning-po, in which I took a passage, and reached that city in twelve days.

Three weeks afterwards one of my men arrived, bringing with him a fine collection of young tea-plants, which were no doubt obtained in the fine black-tea district of Woo-e-shan. It appeared from his account that he and his companion had fallen out by the way, and had parted company at Kein-ning-foo, soon after I left them.

Wang had directions to proceed northwards from Fokien into the district of Hwuy-chow, and to make a further collection of tea-plants in the green-tea country. He had been there with me in the previous autumn. It would of course be much easier for him to get his collections in the Bohea hills than in Hwuy-chow; and he would have had no difficulty in telling me he had been in a country where he had not been, but I had the following check upon him, which proved useful more than once, and with others besides Wang:—It may be recollected that, during my visit to the green-tea country in the autumn before, I discovered a beautiful evergreen shrub, the *Berberis japonica*, and that was the only place in which I had met with it. Wang was therefore told that he must bring me some plants of this as well as the tea-plants, and that if he did not do so he would have no claim to the promised reward. He returned to Ning-po about five weeks after the other servant, bringing me only a few plants and a very long bill. However, he had really been in Hwuy-chow, and what he brought me were valuable.

Whilst waiting for these men at Ning-po I determined to pay a visit to my old quarters, the temple of Tein-tung, situated amongst the hills about twenty

miles from this town. On my way there I fell in
with an old friend (Mr. Wills, of Shanghae), who
was enjoying a few days' sport amongst the Tein-tung
hills. During his rambles he had accidentally met
with a band of Chinese sportsmen, and had made an
engagement with them for the following day. I gladly
agreed to join the party, being most anxious to witness the manœuvres of the natives in this character.

We started early the next morning for the ap-
pointed rendezvous, where we found the Chinamen,
with their guns and dogs, already waiting for us. The
group was a most striking one, as may easily be imagined. The leader of the band was one of the best
specimens of a Chinaman I had ever seen. He was
tall, well made, and had a fine high forehead and
open expression of countenance. Here he is, with

[Mo-ze the Chinese Sportsman.]

his gun and dogs, taken to the life by the pencil of Mr. Scarth, a gentleman to whom I am indebted for several of the sketches in this work.

All the others seemed to look up to Mo-ze, for that was his name, and were guided entirely by him. Their guns were all of the same description : they were long matchlocks, very slender in their make, and apparently not very safe when English powder was used instead of Chinese. All who had guns now came and begged from me a supply of powder and shot, which they seemed to think much superior to their own. They then lighted the cord-matches which each carried on his arm, called the beaters and dogs together, and started in pursuit of deer.

It was a lovely spring morning, and spring is really lovely amongst these northern hills. The dew was on the grass, the little birds were chanting their morning song of praise, and the Chinese labourer was already at work in the fields. Many grass-cutters were working in the woods or on the borders of the dense un-cultivated jungle, and to these our companions applied for information regarding the haunts of the wild deer. They succeeded at last in obtaining some specific information, and determined on beating an adjoining hill covered with coppice and jungle.

Those who had guns were now stationed at different places on the edge of the wood, and the beaters and dogs were sent into the jungle. I had never seen Chinese dogs hunting before, and was highly amused with their performance. They seem to have little or no scent, but they have a quick eye and a swift foot, and a wounded animal rarely gets away from them. They are clever beaters, when taught as these dogs were, and at all events make noise enough. They are not, however, to be compared for a moment with our English dogs.

In a few minutes after the beating began, a deer was seen bounding over the brushwood across the side of the hill. One of the dogs pursued it, and all eyes were turned to the place, watching the point where it was likely to emerge from the coppice. At last it came within the range of our sportsmen's guns. Mr. Wills and a Chinaman both fired at the same instant. One of the shots broke the animal's hind leg, and the dogs soon hunted him down. Coppice after coppice was afterwards beat in the same manner with varied success, and when evening came we had no reason to be dissatisfied with our day's sport.

Returning to our boat, weary and ravenously hungry, we enjoyed our dinner, fought our battles o'er again, and enjoyed a sound and refreshing sleep. Next morning I rose early, and walked across the hills to the ancient temple of Tein-tung, a distance of five or six miles. When I reached the top of the first pass, where there is a small temple and a ruined pagoda, the view was grand indeed. Behind me lay the wide valley of Ning-po, watered by a network of rivers and canals, and exceedingly fertile. Before me lay a quiet and lovely valley, bounded apparently on all sides by hills. Rice was growing in the valley, and patches of tea were seen dotted on the lower sides of the hills; but all above this was in a state of nature, untouched by the hand of man.

All around wild flowers grew in great profusion. The yellow *Azalea chinensis* seemed to paint the hill-sides, so large were its flowers and vivid the colours. There was another shrub which is new to botanists, and scarcely yet known in Europe, called *Amelanchier racemosa*, not less beautiful than the azalea, and rivalling it in its masses of flowers of the purest snowy white.

As I descended the hill I passed a small and unassuming temple, erected, as the tablet states, to the " honoured gods of the soil." The accompanying sketch by Captain Cräcroft gives a good idea of it.

Small temples, or " tablets," of this description are often met with on the roadsides, particularly in the vicinity of monastic buildings. Idolatrous as they are, they show a spirit of thankfulness to the Supreme Being for the " showers that usher in the spring, and cheer the thirsty ground."

[Roadside Altar.]

Having visited many places on my route to the temple, it was past midday ere I reached its sacred precincts. The large bronze bell in the belfry was tolling, and the priests were hurrying to the great hall, where their devotions were about to commence, for " it was the hour of prayer."

The hills in the vicinity of the temple are richly wooded. Indeed the priests of this sect seem to preserve, in a most scrupulous manner, the trees which grow in the neighbourhood of their temples, and thus contribute greatly to the beauty of the scenery. Some fine trees of *Cryptomeria japonica* adorn the approaches to the temple; and the largest specimens of the Chinese pine (*Pinus sinensis*) which I have met with in the country stand near it. There are also some fine bamboo woods here, which deserve more than a passing glance. The stems of this variety are sometimes a foot in circumference, clean, straight, and from thirty to fifty feet in height. Those rough branching kinds which I have seen in India, and in other parts of the world, are not to be compared to the northern Chinese variety. It ought by all means to be introduced into our Indian possessions in the Himalayas, where it would be as useful to the natives as it is to the Chinese.

The bamboo is one of the most valuable trees in China, and is used for almost every conceivable purpose. It is employed in making soldiers' hats and shields, umbrellas, soles of shoes, scaffolding poles, measures, baskets, ropes, paper, pencil-holders, brooms, sedan-chairs, pipes, flower-stakes and trellis-work in

gardens; pillows are made of the shavings; a kind
of rush cloak for wet weather is made from the leaves,
and is called a *So-e,* or "garment of leaves." On the
water it is used in making sails and covers for boats,
for fishing-rods and fish-baskets, fishing-stakes and
buoys; catamarans are rude boats, or rather floats,
formed of a few logs of bamboo lashed firmly together.
In agriculture the bamboo is used in making aque-
ducts for conveying water to the land; it forms part
of the celebrated water-wheel, as well as of the plough,
the harrow, and other implements of husbandry. Excellent water-pipes are made of it for conveying
springs from the hills, to supply houses and temples
in the valleys with pure water. Its roots are often
cut into the most grotesque figures, and its stems
finely carved into ornaments for the curious, or into
incense-burners for the temples. The Ning-po furniture, the most beautiful in China, is often inlaid with
figures of people, houses, temples, and pagodas in
bamboo, which form most correct and striking pic-
tures of China and the Chinese. The young shoots
are boiled and eaten, and sweetmeats are also made
of them. A substance found in the joints, called
tabasheer, is used in medicine. In the manufacture
of tea it helps to form the rolling-tables, drying-
baskets, and sieves; and last, though not least, the
celebrated chop-sticks—the most important articles in
domestic use—are made of it.

However incredulous the reader may be, I must
still carry him a step further, and tell him that I have
not enumerated one-half of the uses to which the

bamboo is applied in China.   Indeed it would be
nearly as difficult to say what it is *not* used for as
what it is.   It is in universal demand, in the houses
and in the fields, on water and on land, in peace and
in war.   Through life the Chinaman is almost de-
pendent upon it for his support, nor does it leave
him until it carries him to his last resting-place on the
hill-side, and even then, in company with the cypress,
juniper, and pine, it waves over and marks his tomb.

At the time of the last war, when the Emperor of
China, very considerately no doubt, wanted to con-
quer the English by withholding the usual supplies
of tea and rhubarb, without which, he supposed, they
could not continue to exist for any length of time, we
might have returned the compliment, had it been possible for us to have destroyed all his bamboos.   With
all deference to the opinion of his celestial Majesty,
the English *might* have survived the loss of tea and
rhubarb, but we cannot conceive the Chinese existing
as a nation, or indeed at all, without the bamboo.

When I had reached my old rooms in the priest's
house, I found two of my Shanghae friends — Mr.
Bowman and Dr. Kirk — domiciled there.   The
Doctor had been trying to astonish and instruct the
priests by showing them a siphon, and by emptying
one of their troughs with it; but it is difficult to astonish a Chinaman, or to convince him that there is
anything he does not understand!   The man looked
on in silence for a second or two, and then, with a
triumphant smile on his countenance, pointed to his
bamboo tubes, which are here used for conveying

water to the priests' houses. " Did not the water rise perpendicularly in them, and to any height he pleased?" It did, but not on the siphon principle, for the source of the spring which supplied these pipes was high up on the hill-side.

In a day or two I left the temple, in company with my two friends, for the lakes of Tung-hoo. Having engaged boats, we sailed over the lakes and visited all their shores. When it was known that one of my companions was a medical man, he had many applications from " the sick, the maimed, and the blind," who fancied he could heal all manner of diseases. During an interview which the Doctor had with one old man, a laughable incident occurred. My friend supposed, from what the man said, that he wished to tender a fee; but upon inquiry it turned out, on the contrary, that he was trying to make the Doctor understand that his advice and assistance could only be taken if they were given gratis!

During the three days we were here I had my hands full enough in collecting objects of natural history. The shores of the lakes were rich in plants, and richer still in insects. Many of the latter are perfectly new to entomologists, but my collections are not yet arranged and examined.

I could have lingered much longer in this part of the country, but my servants had returned from the Bohea mountains, and my holidays, for the present, had terminated. I therefore returned to Ning-po, and made preparations for another and perhaps still more important journey.

CHAPTER IX.

Leave Ning-po for the Bohea mountains — My guides — A flag and its
   history — The Green River again — Spring scenery on its banks —
   Yen-chow and Tā-yang — A storm in a creek — Boatwomen — A
   Chinese Mrs. Caudle and a curtain lecture — Natural productions
   — Funereal cypress and other trees — Our boat seized for debt and
   the sail taken away — A Chinese creditor — Town of Nán-che —
   Its houses, gardens, and trade — Vale of Nán-che — Productions
   and fertility — City of Chu-chu-foo — Moschetoes and Moscheto
   " tobacco " — Arrive at Chang-shan.

I WAS not quite satisfied with the result of my journey
up the river Min.   Although one of my men had
brought me a fine collection of tea-plants and seeds
from the celebrated black-tea country, and although
the expedition was planned so that he could scarcely
have procured them elsewhere, had he wished to
deceive me, I confess I felt that it would be much
more satisfactory if I could visit the district myself.
I did not like the idea of returning to Europe without being perfectly certain that I had introduced the
tea-plant from the best black-tea districts of China
into the Government plantations in the North-western
Provinces of India.   There may also have been a
lingering desire to cross the Bohea mountains and to
visit the far-famed Woo-e-shan.   At all events I
made up my mind to make another attempt, and determined to start from Ning-po, where the people are
not so greatly prejudiced against foreigners as they
are farther to the south, about Foo-chow and Canton.

The man who had just returned from that country expressed his willingness to accompany me, and as he was well acquainted with the road I could not have found a better guide. He showed me a small triangular flag which he had in his possession, and which he had obtained from a mandarin with whom he formerly travelled to Peking, and told me that with this in our hands no one would dare to interfere with us. I confess I was rather sceptical as to the power of this flag, but allowed him to have his own way.

Having hired a boat, we left Ning-po on the evening of the 15th of May. The tide and wind being both in our favour, we swept rapidly up the river, passing in quick succession the British consulate and the houses of the missionaries, which stand on the river's banks. It was a dull and dreary evening, and the rain began to fall heavily as the darkness closed in around us. I felt rather low-spirited; I could not conceal from my mind that the journey I had undertaken was a long one, and perhaps full of danger. My road lay through countries almost unknown, and the guide I had with me was not fully to be depended upon. But the die was cast, and, committing myself to the care of Him who can preserve us alike in all places, I resolved to encounter the difficulties and dangers of the road with a good heart.

My servant now presented himself, and reminded me that it was time to make a change in my "outward man," and adopt the costume of the country.

When this operation was finished I doubt whether my nearest friends would have known me. Indeed, when I looked into the glass I scarcely recognised myself. "You will do very well," said my servant; "and when we reach the town of Nan-che I shall buy a summer hat, which will make the dress more perfect."

The next morning at daylight we found ourselves passing a town of considerable size, named Yu-yeou, which had been visited by our troops during the war. This is a walled city. The walls and ramparts enclose a hill of considerable extent, on whose summit many Buddhist temples have been erected. The suburbs stretch along the banks of the river, and form the principal part of the town. A few miles beyond this the river becomes narrow, and seems to be lost in a network of canals, showing that we were near its source. Soon after this we arrived at the drawbridge, or inclined plane, which I have noticed in a former chapter.

A curious circumstance happened whilst we, with about fifty other boats, were waiting for our turn of the windlass. Most of these boats had come from Ning-po with the same tide as ourselves, and were going to the little town or village of Pak-wan. We had to wait about an hour until our turn came. During this time a strong noisy fellow of a boatman, evidently a bully, who was astern of us all, began to get impatient, and came pushing past the other boats, thinking to get over before his turn came. Amidst a great deal of clamour and threats he succeeded in

M

passing many of the boats ahead of him, and at last got as far as mine. As we had been waiting for some time, I did not like the idea of this man getting past us, but, not wishing to have any disturbance, I determined not to interfere between him and my boatmen. My servant, however, who was a spirited and powerful man, had evidently made up his mind upon the subject, and was determined that the fellow should not pass us. When he came up he began pushing our boat aside as he had done the others, and in a blustering manner desired us to allow him to get on, as he was in a great hurry. "You cannot pass this boat," said one of our crew, and at the same time pushed the bow of our boat against the bank of the canal so as to shut up the passage. "Oh, but I will," replied he, and, notwithstanding the angry remonstrances of our boat's crew, continued pushing us aside, and endeavouring to get past. Sing-Hoo, for that was my servant's name, now went out, and in an angry manner asked the fellow what he meant. "Do you know," said he, "that there is a mandarin in this boat? you had better take care what you are about." "I don't care for mandarins," said the man; "I must get on." "Oh, very well," replied Hoo, "we shall see;" and he walked into the boat. Taking the small triangular flag already noticed, he walked quietly out and fastened it to the mast of our boat. "There," said he to the other, "will you pass now?" Greatly to my astonishment our blustering friend became all at once as meek as a lamb, stammered out some excuses for his conduct, and sat quietly down on the stern of his boat to wait his turn like the rest, while the different boats' crews, who had witnessed the circumstance, had a good laugh at his expense.

Sing-Hoo now came to me with a smile on his countenance, and said, "You see the effects which may be produced by this little flag." I acknowledged it had astonished me, and asked him to tell me more about it. He said that some years before he had been in the service of a mandarin connected with the imperial family, and had travelled with him and his family to Shantung and Peking. The fl g now in his possession had been carried by them in all their travels, and had always protected them from insult. On his return to his own province the old gentleman had made him a present of it—so he told me—and he had often used it on occasions like the present. He spoke with great pride of serving in the imperial family; he had seen the old emperor Taou-kwang, and had worn the yellow livery, which he still had in his possession.

Two ropes, connected with the windlass, were now fastened to the stern of our boat, and we were drawn up the inclined plane, and launched on the higher canal. A few miles further on we came to another canal still higher, and were drawn up and launched in the same way. The second canal leads to and terminates at the small town of Pak-wan, which I have already noticed. Leaving our boat here, we walked across to the canal which leads to Shaou-hing-foo and Nechow, where we engaged another

M 2

boat, and proceeded on our journey. But as I came down this way before, and have fully described the route in a former chapter, I need not say much regarding it here.

We arrived at the small town of Nechow on the following day. Here we took our passage in a large boat, and proceeded up the Hwuy-chow, or Green River. I may remind the reader that this river falls into the sea a little below Hang-chow-foo. Being, as it were, the highway or chief road from the northern parts of Fokien, as well as from Kiang-see and Hwuy-chow, to the large towns of Hang-chow-foo, Soo-chow-foo, and Shanghae, on the eastern coast, nearly all the black and green teas of commerce, which are exported from northern China, come down this way. As this subject may prove of some interest to the merchant, I shall take a survey of the whole route in a subsequent chapter.

When we got upon the Green River, having a fair wind, we sailed rapidly onwards. There were several passengers on board our boat besides ourselves. They were all country people from the westward, knew little of foreigners, and seemed to have no idea that I was one. My servant, I believe, told them that I came from some far distant province beyond the great wall, and with this information, indefinite as it was, they seemed to be perfectly satisfied. Besides, I was now well acquainted with their habits and manners, I could eat with the chopsticks as well as any of them, and my dress was, I believe, scrupulously correct, even to the glossy black tail, which had

been grafted on my own hair, and which hung gracefully down nearly to my heels.

I have already described the scenery on this beautiful river as it appeared to me on a former occasion.
It was autumn then, and vegetation was tinged with
many different hues.   Now it was spring-time; the
rains had begun to fall, and hill and valley were
clothed in the liveliest green.   The hill-streams were
gushing down the ravines, and forming hundreds of
beautiful waterfalls.   This is a striking part of the
country at all times, and it is difficult to say whether
it is most beautiful in autumn or in spring.

On the evening of the third day after leaving
Nechow the old city of Yen-chow-foo came in sight.
The river here flows through a fine and fertile valley,
in which the city is situated.   " *This beautiful vale
abounds with camphor and tallow trees.*"   So it is
written in a map which the learned Jesuits made
many years ago; and such I found to be the case.
A little below the town two rivers unite.   One, as
I have already noticed, comes from the north-west,
and rises amongst the hills of Hwuy-chow, and it was
this one which I ascended the previous autumn.
The other flows from the south-west, and has its
sources amongst the mountains bordering on Fokien,
and partly amongst some hills north-west of the town
of Chang-shan, where the three provinces of Chekiang, Gnan-hoei, and Kiang-see meet.

My route lay up the latter and largest river.   I
was now about to enter upon new ground which
I had never trodden before.   Knowing that if I

accomplished the object I had in view it would be
necessary to travel upwards of 200 miles by land,
and that too over a mountainous country, I had
determined upon taking with me as little luggage of
any kind as possible. My servant, however, had a
strange propensity of accumulating as we went along.
If we started with ever so little, his portion was sure
to increase to an inconvenient size in a very short
time. As he had relations in Yen-chow-foo, I warned
him to leave everything with them, except a few
necessary clothes and a mat to sleep upon. This he
was the more readily inclined to do, as he had been
obliged to dispose of, at a loss, a fine new trunk
which he had bought in Foo-chow, when he started
on his former expedition up the river Min. Having
seen him pack up everything, except the indispensable
articles already specified, I sent him on shore to
leave the package at the house of his relation.

We got under way early next morning, and about
midday arrived at a small town named Tā-yang,
situated on the left bank of the river, near one of the
rapids, which were now becoming frequent on this
part of the river, which is beyond the influence of
the tide. By great exertion we succeeded in getting
our boat up the rapid, and, as the men were very
tired, we decided on remaining at Tā-yang for the
remainder of the day. This gave me an opportunity
of examining at my leisure the natural productions
of this part of the country.

When I returned from my rambles, I found that
our boat had been removed from her station abreast

of the town, and drawn up into a small creek, where
she was made fast for the night. The sky had been
black and threatening for some hours, and there was
now every indication of a severe thunder-storm.
After dark a great number of small boats came into
the creek where we were, in order to be safe from
the flood which the people expected to come down
the river. I shall never forget the confusion and
noise which took place as the last boats came hurrying in. Each person seemed perfectly indifferent as
to what might befal his neighbour, provided he was
only safe himself. Our boat came in for a share of ill
usage, and got many a bump as the others rushed past.

All the Yen-chow and Nan-che boats are what
we may call family boats, that is, the captain or proprietor carries his wife and family along with him,
while the Hwuy-chow people, who go up the other
branch of this river, leave their families at home.
The women always take a prominent part in the
management of the boat, sculling and poling as well
as the men. If they equal their better halves in
these laborious duties, they far exceed them when
any disturbance takes place in which the tongue has
to play a leading part. In the evening in question,
as the numerous boats came in to anchor in the
creek, they drove each other about in great confusion. The main stream being very rapid, the boats
coming down it shot into the creek with great velo-
city. The night was very dark, and heavy drops of
rain began to fall. The thunder-storm, which had
been threatening for some time, came gradually up

against the wind, and now and then bright flashes of
fire lighted up the creek, and showed us the motley
groups by which we were surrounded. The boatmen
were shouting in angry tones as the different boats
came rudely in contact; children were screaming,
and the shrill voices of the women were heard in all
directions, giving orders to the men and scolding
each other. A person unacquainted with the habits
of these people would have thought that something
very dreadful was about to happen. I had seen such
scenes too often, however, to feel any alarm, and,
although the rain came through the roof of my boat
and soaked my bed, I confess I was rather amused
than otherwise.

The Chinese had good reasons for the precautions
they had taken. In two hours the river came down
sweeping everything before it. Had any of our
boats been in the stream they would have been torn
from their anchors and probably dashed to pieces.
Such mountain-floods are not unfrequent on these
rivers, and the boatmen, who know them well, take
great care to be out of the stream before they come
down, particularly if this is likely to happen at night.

We were all safely moored at last, and the conflict
of tongues, as well as of the elements, gradually
ceased. Now and then a remark was made upon
what had taken place, and the good-humoured laugh
which followed showed that the person bore no ill-will
against those with whom he had had a war of words
a few minutes before.

In our boat the good lady was the only one who

seemed ill at ease. Her husband, who had gone on shore before dark, had not returned, and she was evidently a little jealous of his proceedings when out of her sight. The result proved that she had good reasons for her uneasiness, for when the man returned, about three o'clock in the morning, he was in a state of intoxication. The good lady—a Mrs. Caudle in her way—did not spare him, and at the same time gave me an opportunity of hearing a Chinese curtain lecture. Mrs. Amee was not a whit behind her great prototype, for she soon put her husband to sleep, and as she talked till a late hour I followed his example.

When I awoke the next morning the storm and all its effects had passed away. The sun was just tinging the tops of the hills, and every tree and bush was glistening with heavy drops of rain and dew. The river had fallen considerably, but the stream was still too rapid for our progress upwards, so I had an early breakfast and went on shore.

The low lands through which this river flows were now much broader—the hills appeared to fall back, and a beautiful rich valley was disclosed to view. The soil of this valley is a deep sandy loam, resting on a bed of gravel. I observed some patches of the mulberry and tea plants under cultivation; but the tallow-tree (*Stillingia sebifera*) is evidently the staple production of the district. The number of these trees cultivated in the province of Chekiang is immense, and shows that the tallow and oil expressed from their seeds must be considered articles of great importance and value. Groups of pine-trees were observed scattered over the country. They marked the last resting-places of the dead, and had a pleasing and pretty effect. Amongst these pines I frequently observed the beautiful weeping cypress (*Cupressus funebris*) which I had discovered in the green-tea country the autumn before. It is certainly a handsome and striking tree.

The camphor-tree is also common in this valley, and so is the tung-eau or oil-tree, which I have already described. Amongst grains, rice is cultivated in the low lands, whilst wheat, barley, millet, and Indian corn are grown on higher elevations, where the land is comparatively dry.

About three o'clock in the afternoon, the stream having become less rapid, we proceeded on our journey. Between Tā-yang and Nan-che we had many rapids to pass, but the wind being fair we made good progress. The next day, about two o'clock, we were within 30 le of Nan-che, and had every prospect of being able to reach it the same evening. A circumstance happened, however, which detained us by the way. We had been sailing quickly up the right side of the river for some time, and, as we had reached a rapid, it was necessary to cross to the other side to pass it "close in-shore." As soon as we got across, four men, who had been concealed behind a bank, suddenly jumped up and seized our boat. A noisy altercation now took place between our crew and the strangers in a dialect which was perfectly unknown to me. I called Sing-Hoo, who, Chinaman like, was

already in the midst of the fray, and asked him what
was the matter. He told me that the captain of our
boat on a former voyage had bought some rice, for
which he had not paid, and that the creditor and
some of his friends had come with the determination
of getting the money, or, if not, they intended to
carry off our sail. This was tantamount to stopping
our boat, for we could not stem the current, which
was still very strong, if our sail was taken away
from us.

When I went out I found two men already on the
roof of the boat, unbending and hauling down the
sail. The old creditor was standing in the bows,
coolly looking on, and watching the progress of his
men. Our captain had retired to the stern, where
he was quietly smoking his pipe. His wife, however,
was not taking things so tranquilly. She was stamp-
ing about—I beg her pardon, I ought to say skipping
—with her little feet, in a towering rage, now running
to the creditor, and now to her husband. At one
time she tried to coax, at another to storm, but all
was of no avail. " Pay me the debt," said the
obdurate creditor, " or I must take the sail." She
begged him to allow the boat to proceed to Nan-che
and deliver the cargo, when the debt should be paid.
" Ah," said he, " I did that once before, and, instead
of paying me, you got a fresh cargo, and ran down
to Hang-chow-foo. No, no, you must pay me here,
and while I have your sail there is no great danger
of your running away." Threats, promises, and
coaxing were alike useless, the old man was inex-

orable. The sail was unbent, one of the men got it on his shoulders, and our visitors walked away.

This was a serious mishap to me, as I could see no means of getting on to Nan-che. At last Sing-Hoo proposed to walk to the town, and bring down a small boat for me and the luggage. This appeared to be the best plan under the circumstances, so I consented, and he took his departure. The people in the boat did not seem to give themselves much uneasiness about the business. With the exception of the captain and his wife, they all lay down in their berths, and were soon fast asleep.

At daylight on the following morning I was awakened by a noise in the boat, and on opening my eyes I observed the captain standing on the bows and threatening to drown himself in the river. He was held back by his wife and one of his men, who were both entreating him to desist from his purpose and to come inside. He struggled with great violence until he shook them both off, when he commenced deliberately to throw off his clothes. The others looked on in silence, and as he was still intoxicated I fully expected to see him plunge into the stream. When left to himself, however, he seemed to change his mind, and, after looking moodily on the river for a few seconds, he walked quietly into the boat, called for his pipe and began to smoke. Soon afterwards he started for Nan-che to try and raise some money to satisfy his creditor.

About mid-day my servant arrived with a small boat which he had brought to take me on to Nan-

che. A dispute now arose between him and the
captain's wife about four hundred cash—one shilling
and sixpence—which he had agreed to pay for the
small boat. According to his ideas of justice the
proprietors of the large boat were bound either to
take us on to Nan-che themselves, or to pay for our
conveyance thither. As they did not do the former,
he determined to deduct the charge for the small
boat from the amount of the bill which was presented
for the food with which they had supplied us on our
way up. I saw plainly enough we should have a
great disturbance if the money was not paid, and
advised him to pay it at once. This, however, he
strongly protested against, and began getting our
luggage out into the small boat. In the mean time
the woman declared she would rather go with us than
lose her four hundred cash. As good as her word,
she scrambled into the small boat, and called to one
of her people to hand in her child, a young thing
about a year old. The whole scene, to one not concerned, must have been highly amusing. It would
have been very inconvenient for me to travel with
such baggage, so, to cut the matter short and stop all
further proceedings, I ordered Sing-Hoo to pay the
money. Our luggage being removed into the small
boat, we shoved her off, and by dint of sculling and
tracking got up to Nan-che about six o'clock the
same evening.

Nan-che, or, as it is sometimes called in the maps,
Lanchee, is about 120 le westward from Yen-chow-
foo. It is one of the prettiest Chinese towns which

I have seen, and reminded me of an English place more than a Chinese one. The houses are generally two-storied and have a clean and neat appearance. It is built along the banks of the river, and has a picturesque hill behind it: an old tower or pagoda in ruins heightens the general effect of the scene. The town is about two and a half or three miles round, and probably contains about 200,000 inhabitants. The river in front of it is covered with boats, which are constantly plying between it and Yen-chow, Hang-chow, and many other towns both to the east and west.

Sing-Hoo was anxious to make a great many purchases in this town. He told me that everything was good which came out of Nan-che, and advised me to lay in a large stock of provisions for the remainder of our journey by water. In the mean time we had engaged another boat to take us to the town of Chang-shan, a city situated near the source of this river, or as far up as it is navigable. By the time this business was settled and our purchases on board it was nearly dark. Having had little to eat during the day, we were hungry and weary enough. Our new boatmen, however, were very kind and attentive to all our wants. An excellent dinner was soon ready, consisting of rice, fish, eggs, and vegetables, added to which we had some of the good things of Nan-che, such as cakes and wine, which had been highly recommended by Sing-Hoo.

The next morning I went on shore to see the town, and also to inspect some gardens in which plants are kept for sale. I had been informed that Nan-che boasted of three or four nurseries; and as it is a central place, and at a great distance from Shanghae, Ning-po, and the other coast towns, I was not without hope of finding some new and valuable plants worthy of being sent to England.

I passed through some crowded streets of the same description as those at Shanghae. All Chinese towns have a striking resemblance to each other; the shops are built and arranged in the same way, they contain the same kinds of articles, and everything about them seems alike. A person, therefore, who has seen one large Chinese city can form a good idea of all the rest in the empire.

I found the nursery-gardens in the suburbs of the town. I examined three of them, but could find nothing new or worth taking away. They contained large quantities of jasmines (*Jasminum Sambac*), clerodendrons, roses, azaleas, camellias, and nelumbiums, but nothing that was new to me, or that I had not found in abundance nearer the coast. The gardeners were extremely civil, and did not seem to have the slightest idea that a foreigner stood before them. The only thing which surprised them was the information that their gardens did not contain the flowers which I wanted. They inquired the names of the plants I was looking for, and I told them that I wanted new ones, such as were not to be found in the gardens at Soo-chow, Hang-chow, and places nearer the coast. "Ah," said they, "you cannot expect to find in Nan-che anything which is not in Soo-chow." My visit being fruitless, I returned to my boat, when we got under way and proceeded on our journey.

The vale of Nan-che is even more beautiful than that in which the city of Yen-chow stands. It is surrounded by hills, dotted over with clumps of pine, cypress, and camphor-trees, traversed by a branching and winding river, and extremely fertile. The tallow-tree is cultivated in great abundance; in many places, indeed, the lowland is nearly covered with it. At the time of my visit its fresh green leaves contrasted finely with the dark and sombre cypress and pine. The whole valley seems, as it were, one vast and beautiful garden surrounded and apparently hemmed in by hills; but as we sailed up the river to the westward the hills gradually opened and the valley became much broader. I found afterwards that it extended from Tā-yang, a little above Yen-chow-foo, to Chang-shan on the borders of the province of Kiang-see. The distant hills seemed rugged and barren, and, even with Chinese industry, quite unfitted for agricultural purposes.

Ninety le from Nan-che I arrived at a small place named Long-yeou, also on the banks of the river. Three pretty pagodas were seen here, all placed on the most picturesque spots that could be found. The camphor-tree is very numerous and attains a large size. It was the time of the summer harvest when I was there, and the people were busily employed in cutting and threshing out their crops of wheat and barley. Hemp was largely cultivated for making ropes and other articles much in demand amongst the boat-people. I also observed large quantities of buckwheat, Indian corn, millet, and soy growing in the fields. A species of berberis, apparently a variety of our English one, was cultivated rather extensively, but for what purpose I could not learn, probably for medicine or as a dye.

Above Long-yeou the river became in many places narrow and very rapid. Several old water-wheels were observed half sanded up and completely useless. Trees and bushes dipped their branches into the stream, and reminded me of the country rivers in England. We passed a great number of small villages, but saw no place of any size or importance until we reached Chu-chu-foo, a large city 90 le west from Long-yeou and 180 from Nan-che.

Soon after daylight on the 1st of June two pagodas came in sight, and indicated, as they always do, our near approach to some important town. This was Chu-chu-foo, which was then only three or four miles distant. As we approached nearer to it, groves of orange-trees became common. The tea-plant was also extensively cultivated, but the produce is not considered first-rate. Earth-nuts (*Arachis hypogæa*) and soy are plentiful, both of these crops delighting in a light sandy soil. A great number of low hills are seen in the midst of the plain. Th soil of these hills or hillocks is generally perfectly barren, and of a brick-red—the colour of the calcae reous sandstone of the district. The Chinese do not make many attempts to cultivate them.

At Chu-chu-foo there is a pretty bridge of boats,

N

through which we passed. This bridge is taken
away when the river is likely to become much
swollen by heavy rains. Although this city ranks
in the second class, it is not a very important one, at
least in a mercantile point of view. It is not large,
its walls are scarcely more than two miles in circumference, and there are many large spaces inside on
which there are no buildings. Politically it ranks
higher than Nan-che, but it is far from being such
an important place. We remained here for a few
hours to procure some necessaries, and then proceeded
onwards.

About a mile above the city two rivers unite their
waters: one comes from the south-west, and has its
source on the northern side of the Fokien mountains;
the other flows from the west, and rises a few miles
above Chang-shan, the town to which I was now
bound. We went up the left branch, which was very
narrow, shallow, and oftentimes rapid.

In the evening we stopped with some other boats
like our own near a small village, where we proposed
to pass the night. The day had been very warm,
and the moschetoes were now becoming very troublesome. The night before this, neither my servant nor
myself had been able to close our eyes, and I now
saw with dread these pests actually swarming around
us, and anticipated another sleepless night. Our
boatmen, who heard us talking about them, asked
Sing-Hoo why he did not go and buy some moscheto
tobacco, which they said might be had in the village,
and which would drive all the moschetoes out of the

boat. I immediately despatched him to procure some of this invaluable substance. In a few minutes he returned with four long sticks in his hand, not unlike those commonly used for burning incense in the temples, only somewhat longer and coarser in appearance. He informed me they cost only two cash each—certainly cheap enough if they answered the purpose.

Two of these sticks were now lighted and suspended from the roof of the boat. They had not been burning five minutes when every moscheto in the boat sought other quarters. We were quite delighted, and enjoyed a sound and refreshing sleep, for which we were most thankful. I had always dreaded these insects during this journey, as I did not carry curtains with me on account of their bulk. I now found, however, that there was no need of them wherever we could procure the moscheto tobacco.

Various substances are employed by the Chinese to drive away moschetoes. This which we had just purchased was made with the sawings of resinous woods—I believe procured from juniper-trees—and mixed with some combustible matter to make it burn. A piece of split bamboo, three or four feet in length, is then covered all over with this substance. When finished it is as thick as a rattan or small cane. The upper end of the bamboo has a slit in it for hooking on to any nail in the wall, or to the roof of a boat. When once lighted, it goes on burning upwards until within six inches of the hook, beyond which there is no combustible matter, and it then dies out. A somewhat fragrant smell is given out during combustion, which, at a distance, is not disagreeable. Sometimes the sawdust is put up in coils of paper, and is then burned on the floors of the houses. Various species of wormwood are likewise employed for the same purpose. The stems and leaves of these plants are twisted and dried, and probably dipped in some preparation to make them burn.

The moscheto has a mortal aversion to all these substances, and wherever they are burning there the little tormentors will not come. I procured the sticks in question, and burnt them daily, after this; and although the insects were often swarming when I entered the boat or an inn, the moment *their* "tobacco" was lighted they quickly disappeared, and left me to sit at my ease, or to enjoy a refreshing sleep. Whoever discovered this precious tobacco was a benefactor to his country, and should have been honoured with the blue button and peacock's feather at the least. But I suppose, like all other Chinese discoveries, it is so old that the name of its original discoverer cannot now be traced.

We were now evidently approaching the head of the Vale of Nan-che, and one of the sources of the Green River. The hill from which the town of Chang-shan takes its name was pointed out to me, and in a short time afterwards the masts of the boats and the town itself came into view. Having a strong fair wind, we sailed rapidly over the current, and were soon moored in safety amongst a great number of other boats within a short distance of the town.

The river being no longer navigable, it was necessary for me to prosecute my journey by land. I
determined therefore to remain at Chang-shan for
the night, in order to make arrangements for the
change of conveyance.

CHAPTER X.

City of Chang-shan and its trade — Land journey — My chair and
chair-bearers — Description of the road — Trains of tea coolies —
Roadside inns — Boundary of two provinces — Dinner at a Chinese
inn — Value of the chopsticks — Adventure with two Canton men
— City of Yuk-shan — Its trade and importance — Quan-sin-foo —
My servant speculates in grass-cloth — A Chinese test of respecta-
bility — Description of the country and its productions — Arrive at
the town of Hokow.

CHANG-SHAN is a city of the third class, and is said
to be 140 le from Chu-chu-foo. Judging from the
population of other towns in China, I estimated the
population of this place at from twenty to thirty
thousand. It is built at the base of a hill about a
mile from the river, but its suburbs extend down to
the water's edge. The streets are narrow, and the
shops have a mean appearance when compared with
those of Hang-chow-foo or Ning-po. It has no trade
of its own, but, as it is situated on the principal road
which leads from the towns on the coast to the great
black-tea country of Fokien, to the large towns of
Yuk-shan, Quan-sin-foo, Hokow, to the Poyang Lake,
and even to Canton, it is necessarily a place of considerable importance. Hence the town is full of
hongs, inns, tea-shops, and warehouses for the accommodation of travellers, coolies, and merchandise, the
latter being chiefly the black teas of Fokien and
Moning.

On the morning after our arrival we bade adieu
to our boat and our obliging boatmen, and proceeded
on foot to one of the inns in the city, in order to hire
chairs for the next stage of our journey. We did
not attract the slightest notice as we passed along the
streets, and, as popularity in my present circumstances
was not desirable, I confess I felt much pleased at
this. When we reached the inn the landlord received
us with great politeness, asked us to be seated, and
brought us some tea. In reply to our inquiries
respecting a chair, he said that those he had were
uncovered, and pointed to some of them which were
standing in the entrance-hall. I observed that they
were exactly like those mountain-chairs which I had
frequently used amongst the hills near Ning-po, and
informed him that one of them would answer my
purpose. This chair is a most simple contrivance,
and consists of two long poles of bamboo, with an
open seat in the middle and a small crossbar slung
from the poles on which the feet can rest. The
coverlet on which I slept was thrown over the seat,
and my primitive carriage was ready for the journey.

After breakfast the chair-bearers arrived, and we
started. A number of other travellers were going
and returning by the same road as ourselves. Some
of them had chairs like mine, while others had a
light framework of bamboo erected over the seat, and
covered with oil-paper, to afford some protection from
the sun and rain. I found when too late that it
would have been much better for me to have had
one of these chairs instead of the one I was in. It

was no use, however, now to indulge in vain regrets;
so with a Chinese umbrella over my head I jogged
along, consoling myself with the thought that, at
least, I enjoyed a better view of town and country in
this chair than if I had been shut up in a more
comfortable one.

I had now passed through the crowded street of
Chang-shan, and was already in the open country.
It had rained heavily during the night, but, as the
morning was fine, the late showers had only tended to
increase the natural beauty of the country. There
was a coolness in the atmosphere too which was most
agreeable. The grass on the hill-sides and the
young rice in the valleys were of the liveliest green.
Every bush and tree was loaded with heavy drops of
rain which glistened in the sunshine. Altogether the
scenery was delightful, and, with the freshness of the
morning air, put me in the highest spirits.

The road on which we were travelling was one of
the broadest and best I had met with in the country.
It was well paved with granite, about twelve feet in
width, and perfectly free from weeds, which proved,
if other proof had been wanting, that there was a
great traffic upon it. The general aspect of the
country was hilly, but there was abundance of good
land in the valleys amongst the hills. It reminded
me of some of the pretty islands in the Chusan
archipelago. No mountain-passes had to be crossed
on our way, for the little hills seemed, as it were, to
open up a passage for the road as we went along.

For the first few miles after leaving Chang-shan

we met with few people by the way. I was indulging
in the hope that my day's journey would be through
a quiet country district like what one sees on some
of the country roads at home; but, in so far as a
quiet country road was concerned, I was soon unde-
ceived. Long trains of coolies were now met, loaded
with tea which was destined for Hang-chow-foo, and
thence for Shanghae, to be sold to the English and
American merchants. As my chair-bearers walked
very fast, we likewise passed great numbers on the
road going the same way as ourselves. These were
hands returning after having got rid of their loads at
Chang-shan; but they were not returning empty-
handed; they were loaded with raw cotton, cotton
goods, lead, and various other articles, which had
either been imported from foreign parts, or produced
in countries nearer the sea. At nearly every le of
the road as we went along we found inns and tea-
shops. The road in front of these houses was generally thatched over, in order that those who stopped
for refreshment might be protected from the sun and
rain.

When we had journeyed in this way about thirty
le, my chair-bearers said they must rest awhile, and
have some refreshment. I readily agreed to this
proposition, as I was rather thirsty myself, and desired them to set me down at the first house we came
to, which they accordingly did. We walked into
the house, and I took a seat at one table, while my
servant and the chair-bearers seated themselves at
another. The good lady of the house set down a

teacup before each of us, into which she put some tea, and then filled each cup up with boiling water. I need scarcely say she did not offer us any sugar or milk. Other tables were crowded with people, most of whom were coolies going to Chang-shan with tea, and whose chests nearly blocked up the road in front of the door. We drank our tea, which I found most refreshing, in its pure state without sugar and milk. Now and then some one connected with the house came round and filled our basins again with boiling water. This is usually repeated two or three times, or until all the strength is drawn out of the leaves.

Having smoked our pipes and paid two cash each for our tea, I got into my chair and resumed my journey. The road now led us up between two hills, and a huge stone gateway and pass showed me that I was on the outskirts of the province of Chekiang, and about to pass into Kiang-see. A strong wall, not unlike the ramparts of a city, connected the two hills, the gateway being of course in the centre of the pass. The whole place had a warlike appearance, and there was a military station on each side, so that each province might be duly represented and duly guarded. These stations were in a ruinous condition, and I observed only women and children about the houses. In peaceful times the soldiers are, no doubt, permitted to convert the sword into the ploughshare, and engage in the cultivation of the land.

Although small villages and houses for refreshment extended, at short intervals, along the whole

line of road, we rarely passed any town even of moderate size. About mid-day, however, we came to a
place considerably larger than any we had passed—
I forget its name—and before I knew where I was,
I was set down at the door of a large inn. Numerous
chairs were standing at the door which belonged to
travellers who were either going the same road as
myself, or returning from the west to Chang-shan and
the other towns in the east.

The moment I got out of my chair the innkeeper presented himself, and my chair-bearers very
officiously informed him that it was my intention to
dine there. I felt rather annoyed, but thought it
best to put a good face on the matter, and ordered
dinner accordingly. I had given Sing-Hoo strict
injunctions never to stop at the inns much frequented
by merchants, as I had no wish to meet men who
were in the habit of seeing foreigners both at Shanghae and Canton. I had the greatest objection to
meeting Canton men, who are continually travelling
to and from the tea country, and who, with the same
knowledge of foreigners as the Shanghae people, are
much more prejudiced against us. Sing-Hoo had
fallen behind, however, and was not aware of what
the chair-bearers had done until it was too late. It
appeared afterwards that the men had a good and
substantial reason for their conduct, inasmuch as they
got their own dinner free as a reward for bringing a
customer to the house.

The inn was a large and commodious building extending backwards from the main street of the town.

Its front was composed of a number of boards or
shutters which could be removed at pleasure. The
whole of these were taken down in the morning and
put up again at night. The floor of the building was
divided into three principal compartments, the first
facing the street, the second being behind it, and the
third at the furthest end. Some small rooms which
were formed on each side were the bedrooms.

Coolies and chair-bearers crowded that part of the
building next to the street, in which they had their
meals and smoked their pipes. The second and
third divisions were destined for travellers, but, as
there were large doors between each which stood wide
open, it was easy to see through from the front to the
back part of the premises.

When I got out of my chair I followed "mine
host" into the second compartment, in which I observed a table at each side of the room. One of
them being unoccupied, I sat down at it, and with
becoming gravity lighted my Chinese pipe and began
to smoke. The host set a cup of tea before me
and left me to attend upon some one else. I had
now leisure to take a survey of the strange scene
round me. At the opposite table sat two merchants, who a single glance told me were from the
province of Canton. They were evidently eyeing me
with great interest, and doubtless knew me to be a
foreigner the moment I entered the room. One of
them I had frequently seen at Shanghae. This
person looked as if he wished me to recognise him,
but in this he was disappointed, for I returned his

inquiring look as if I had never seen him before. I
now observed him whispering to his companion, and
thought I heard the word Fankwei used. In the
mean time Sing-Hoo, who had just arrived, came in
and began to bustle about and get in the dinner,
which was soon ready. The host was a civil sort of
man, but very inquisitive, and as he set down the
dinner he put various questions to me. With Chinese politeness, he asked me my name, my age,
where I had come from, and whither I was bound,
and to all such questions he received most satisfactory answers. For example, when asked where I
had come from, I replied, " From Chang-shan ;" and
to the question as to whither I was bound I answered,
" To Fokien." These answers were perfectly true,
although not very definite. The Canton merchants
were all eyes and ears while this conversation was
going on, and one of them quietly prompted the innkeeper to ask a few more questions.

These gentlemen wanted to know the starting-point
of my journey, the particular part of Fokien to which
I was bound, and the objects I had in view. As I
could not see that answers to these questions concerned them very much, or could be of any use, I
judged it better to keep them in the dark.

Several dishes being now set before me, and a cup
of wine poured out by the host, I took a sip of it,
and taking up my chopsticks went on with my
dinner. Having had great experience in the use of
the chopsticks, I could handle them now nearly as
well as the Chinese themselves ; and as I had been

often accustomed to all the formalities of a Chinese dinner, I went on with the most perfect confidence.

On my former journey in the interior, as well as on this, I had discarded all European habits and luxuries. Chopsticks were substituted for knives and forks, tea and light wines for stronger drinks, and a long bamboo Chinese pipe for Manilla cheroots. By these means I had arrived at a high state of civilization and politeness. In eating my dinner, such rude things as knives and forks were never thought of. The cutting up of meat and vegetables was done by servants in the kitchen, before the food was cooked or brought to table. When the various dishes, prepared in this manner, were brought to table, the chopsticks—those ancient and useful articles—answered every purpose. Talk of knives and forks indeed! One cannot eat rice with them, and how very awkward it would be to pick out all those dainty little morsels from the different dishes with a fork! In the first place, it would be necessary to push them to the bottom of the basin before the fork would take a proper hold; and in many instances we should do what the novice in the art of using chopsticks frequently does—drop the food on its way from the dish to the mouth. There is no such difficulty or danger with the chopsticks when properly used. The smallest morsel, even to a single grain of rice, can be picked up with perfect ease. In sober truth, they are most useful and sensible things, whatever people may say to the contrary; and I know of no article in use amongst ourselves which could supply their place.

Excepting the fingers, nature's own invention, nothing is so convenient as the chopsticks.

When I had finished dinner, a wooden basin containing warm water and a wet cloth were placed before me, in order that I might wash my hands and face. Wringing the wet cloth, I rubbed my face, neck, and hands well over with it in Chinese style. Having finished my ablution, I returned again to the table. The dinner and dishes having in the mean time been removed, tea was again set before me.

The Canton men still remained at the opposite table, but the greater part of the others, who, at their instigation, had been taking sly peeps at me, had gone away. I suppose, when they saw that I ate and drank just like the rest, they must have felt some little surprise, and had their original opinion strengthened, namely, that after all I was only one of themselves.

My chair-bearers having dined as well as myself, they sent a message by Sing-Hoo to say that they were ready to proceed. Making a slight bow to mine host, and a slighter one to the Canton gentlemen, in Chinese style, I got into my chair and went my way. As soon as I had left the house, Sing-Hoo, who was paying our bill, was closely questioned about me. According to his account he had completely mystified them, by informing them, as he had done others before, that I came from some far country beyond the great wall, a statement which those who knew best would not have called in question.

Our road was still crowded with coolies: indeed

nearly the whole way across from Chang-shan to Yuk-shan they formed one unbroken line.   Yuk-shan was the name of the town to which we were now bound. As we proceeded, we began to get more extensive views of the country.   We had passed the line or ridge which divides the streams which flow to the eastward from those which flow westward.   The country appeared to open up, and we were evidently approaching some river of considerable size.   At last a hill, richly wooded, came into view, and was pointed out to me as that from which the town of Yuk-shan had taken its name, and which was situated in its vicinity.   We reached the town about four o'clock in the afternoon, having travelled about thirty miles since the morning.

Yuk-shan is a walled town of considerable size, and I should imagine contains from thirty to forty thousand inhabitants.   It appears to be a larger place than Chang-shan; and, like that town, it stands at the head of a navigable river.   All the merchandise of the Bohea mountains, and of the countries east of the Poyang lake, which is destined for Hang-chow-foo, Shanghae, and other towns in that district, is landed here, to be carried across to Chang-shan by coolies. Hence these two towns appear to be the connecting links between two most important rivers, as well as between the richest countries of China.   One of them is connected with the great black-tea country, and the other with the green-tea districts, and also with those rich silk and cotton lands near the coast; and the importance of these two towns and rivers will be further appreciated when I state that through their agency large quantities of our manufactures find their way into the heart of the country.

Passing over a fine stone bridge, we were soon at the walls of the city. Having entered the gates, we proceeded along one of the principal streets. It was crowded with people, all hurrying to and fro, and apparently engaged in active business. The shops were of the same kind as I have frequently described, and I am not aware of any particular kind of manufacture being carried on in the place. Like their neighbours at the head of the other river, the inhabitants seem to be busy enough in housing and carrying the merchandise brought here to be sent onwards. The western suburb is very extensive, and adjoins the river. To this part of the town we bent our steps, and soon reached the Hong-le, or inn, recommended by our chairmen, and with which they were connected.

I had no object in remaining long in this town. When we reached the Hong-le, therefore, I sent my servant to engage a boat to take us on ; and so quickly did he manage the business, that in half an hour we had left Yuk-shan, and with a fair wind were sailing rapidly down the river to the westward.

Our boat was engaged to take us as far as the city of Quan-sin-foo, a distance of ninety or a hundred le ; and as the stream was very rapid, we arrived abreast of that place early the next morning. It appeared to be a fine large city, but a place of little trade. Its walls and ramparts seemed in excellent order, and there is a pretty bridge of boats across the river ; but I was only a short time here, and had no time for minute examination.

Sing-Hoo was now despatched to engage another boat, and to lay in the necessary supplies for our journey.　He remained absent a long time, and when he returned excused himself by saying that he had called upon a friend and countryman of his own, to get information regarding our route.　I was obliged to content myself with this explanation, but was rather surprised to see a person come into our boat shortly afterwards, carrying two large packages of grass-cloth.　These weighed at least forty pounds. " To whom does this cloth belong ? " I asked.　" Oh, it is mine," replied Sing-Hoo ; " this cloth is very cheap here, and I want to take it back with me to a friend in Shanghae."　This was very provoking : here was the old accumulating propensity at work again. I knew we had still a long journey before us, over many steep and rugged mountains, where our baggage had to be carried on the backs of coolies.　I had reduced my own baggage as much as possible, and had already obliged Sing-Hoo to leave all his superfluous things at Yen-chow-foo, and now he brought a package larger than all we had, and expected me to hire coolies to carry it twice across the Bohea mountains, because this grass-cloth was a few cash cheaper at Quan-sin-foo than at Shanghae or Ning-po !　I really believe such a project would never have entered the brain of any one except a Chinaman.

I attempted to reason with him on the folly and impropriety of his conduct, but his excuse was plausible enough. "You see," said he, "it will be necessary to have a coolie to carry our baggage, but we have reduced it so much that he will not have half a load. Now the carriage of this cloth will not add anything to the expenses, and the man's load will be properly balanced. And," added he, with great gravity, "travellers in my country who have a goodly portion of luggage are always considered more respectable than those who have little."

While this conversation was going on we were sailing rapidly down the stream in the direction of Hokow, a large town about ninety or a hundred le westward from the city of Quan-sin-foo. The valley through which the river flows is thickly studded with little hills, and far away to the right and left lofty mountains were seen rising in all their grandeur. I observed many curious rocks, shaped like little hills, but without a vestige of vegetation of any kind upon them. They stood in the midst of the plain like rude monuments, and had a curious and strange appearance.

The country through which I passed is an extensive rice district. No very large trees were observed; and the tallow-tree, which forms such an important branch of agriculture in the countries nearer the sea, is scarcely ever met with, or only seen here and there. Camphor-trees are common, but they do not attain the size they do in many other parts of the country. Nevertheless, on passing down the river, we came sometimes to pretty and romantic spots, where the trees and brushwood were overhanging the banks, and dipping their branches into the clear stream ; and these strange monumental-looking rocks were objects of striking interest in themselves.

In the afternoon of the day on which I left Quan-sin-foo, we arrived at the town of Hokow. I had now got as far to the west as was necessary, and intended from this point to journey southwards to one of the passes in the Bohea mountains, across which I had to go on my way to Woo-e-shan. This part of my journey had to be done in chairs.

CHAPTER XI.

Town of Hokow — Its situation, trade, and great importance — Bohea
mountain chair — Mountain road — Beggars by the wayside —
Beautiful scenery — The priest and his bell — Town of Yuen-shan
— Appearance of the road — Tea coolies — Different modes of
carrying the tea-chests — Large tea-growing country — Soil and
plantations — My first night in a Chinese inn — Reception — Dirty
bed-rooms — I console myself, and go to dinner.

Hokow, or Hohow, as it is called by the southern
Chinese, is one of the most important inland towns
in the empire. It is situated in latitude 29° 54'
north, and in longitude 116° 18' east, on the left
bank of the river Kin-keang, down which I had come.
Judging from its size, and comparing it with other
towns, I imagine it contains about 300,000 inhabitants. It is the great emporium of the black-tea
trade. Merchants from all parts of China come here,
either to buy teas, or to get them conveyed to other
parts of the country.

Large inns, tea-hongs, and warehouses, are met
with in every part of the town, and particularly
along the banks of the river. The boats moored
abreast of the town are very numerous. There are
small ones for single passengers, large passage-boats
for the public, and mandarins' boats gaily decorated
with flags. Besides these there are large cargo-boats,
for conveying tea and other merchandise either eastward to Yuk-shan, or westward to the Poyang lake.

Hokow is to the inland countries of the west what Shanghae and Soo-chow are to places nearer the sea.

On the day after our arrival I proceeded to a hong, or inn, in the town, and engaged a chair and coolies to take me across the Bohea mountains to the town of Tsong-gan-hien, near Woo-e-shan. One of the men was to carry our luggage, including the large package of grass-cloth. When we were making our agreement with the innkeeper for the men and chair, he informed us that the distance between Hokow and Woo-e-shan was 320 le, and that, as the road was very hilly in many parts, we should require four days at least for the journey. As I had been frequently consulting my map and measuring the distances, I was surprised to hear that we had so far to go, but when I gave the matter a little consideration I had reason to believe that the innkeeper was perfectly correct. In calculating my distances I had not taken into consideration the many hills and mountains we had to cross on our way, which not only impeded our progress, but made the road much longer than it appeared on the map.

It is no child's play to cross these mountains, and therefore, before we started, the chair had to be examined and made as strong as possible. Chairs used for long journeys of this kind are constructed in a different manner from those seen in towns and in the level districts of the country. The common mountain-chair, which consists of little more than two stout bamboo poles and a cross-bar to sit upon, is very well for a short journey, but it would be rather inconvenient to travel in one for 300 or 400 le, exposed to a fierce sun, and oftentimes to heavy rain.

The Bohea-mountain chair is constructed with more attention to the comforts of the traveller. It has above the seat a light bamboo frame covered with oiled paper or glazed cloth. The seat has a back to it formed at an angle of 45 degrees, and as the chair itself, foot-board and all, is generally about four feet long, the traveller can recline and sleep if he chooses to do so. Some soft article, such as the wadded bed-cover in common use, is generally spread over the bottom and back of the chair, which makes it very comfortable.

Having made all our arrangements, I got into my chair, and we left Hokow, travelling in a southerly direction across the valley, which I have already noticed. A small river, which rises on the north side of the Bohea mountains, and which falls into the Kin-keang near Hokow, comes winding down this valley, and was crossed several times on our way.

Leaving the valley of Hokow we gradually began to enter a hilly country, and now and then our road led us up hill-passes of considerable steepness. In going over one of these passes my chair was besieged by a host of beggars, the most importunate I ever met with. Another traveller, who was a few yards in advance of me, had them all about him for some time. I could hear him protesting that he had no cash in his pockets, and beseeching them to go away, but this seemed only to render them more importunate. Whether he gave them anything or not

I cannot tell, but they left him and came to me. I had not a single cash in my pocket, and, Sing-Hoo being far behind, I did not know what to do. I, however, closed my eyes, and feigned to be fast asleep. When they held out their baskets for alms I was of course sleeping most soundly. "Loi-ya, loi-ya,"* they bawled in my ear, and did their best to awake me; but finding the tongue of no avail, they beat the sides of the chair with their hands, and at last got hold of my clothes. I have a great horror of being touched by a Chinese beggar, who is generally filthy beyond description. Starting up, I nearly capsized the chair, greatly to the annoyance of my bearers, who immediately forced the beggars to desist and to go away. When we reached the top of the pass I desired my bearers to put me down and to rest themselves. There was a pretty little house, or traveller's resting-place, just on the summit, from which I obtained an excellent view of the country.

In the valley beyond me lay a small town, named Yuen-shan. At first sight it appears to be completely encircled by hills; but this is not the case, for the mountain stream which I have just noticed passes the town, and winds round the hills on its way to Hokow.

Descending the hill on our way to Yuen-shan I had another encounter with beggars, but having provided myself with a few cash I easily got rid of them. Many of them were lame and blind, but somehow or other all managed to get close to my chair.

We now came to an archway erected over the

* A term applied to a mandarin or government officer.

road near the base of the hill. As I was passing
through this archway an old man, a priest, came out
and struck a bell three times. Whether this was
done in my honour, or to propitiate the gods for my
safety and success, I cannot tell, but it was evident
the priest expected something for his trouble, and
Sing-Hoo, who pretended to be a good Buddhist,
gave him a few cash as we passed under the arch.

We now entered the town of Yuen-shan. It is
about 60 le distant from Hokow, and stands on the
banks of the mountain stream. Though not large, it
seems a flourishing place. It is on the highway from
the black-tea country of Fokien, and nearly all the teas
brought thence on the backs of coolies are here put
in small boats and conveyed to Hokow. Owing to
there being a water-communication between these
towns, I did not observe much traffic on the road.
I was now, however, about to enter upon a crowded
and bustling thoroughfare, like that between the
sources of the two rivers described in the last chapter.

As it was mid-day when we entered Yuen-shan, I
went to an inn, and had some refreshment, while the
coolies had their dinner. When we resumed our
journey, we found many travellers on the road, going
and returning from the tea-country in chairs. All of
them seemed to be sound asleep. This is a common
practice amongst the mountain travellers, the chairs
being constructed so as to enable them to do so com-
fortably.

Coolies were now met in great numbers, loaded
with tea-chests. Many of them carried only one

chest. These I was told were the finer teas; the chest was never allowed to touch the ground during the journey, and hence these teas generally arrive at their destination in much better order than the coarser kinds. The single chests were carried in the following manner. Two bamboos, each about seven feet long, had their ends lashed firmly to the chest, one on each side. The other ends were brought together, so as to form a triangle. By this means a man could carry the chest upon his shoulders, with his head between the bamboos in the centre of the triangle. A small piece of wood was lashed under the chest, to give it an easy seat upon the shoulders. The accompanying sketch will give a better idea of this curious mode of carrying tea than any description.

When the coolie who carried his burden in this way wanted to rest, he placed the end of the bam-

boos upon the ground, and raised them to the perpendicular.   The whole weight now rested upon the

ground, and could be kept in this position without
any exertion.   This was very convenient in coming
up the steep passes amongst the mountains, for in
some of them the coolies can only proceed a few
yards at a time without resting, and if they had not
a contrivance of this description the loads would have
to be frequently put down upon the ground.   When
stopping at inns or tea-shops for refreshment, the
chests carried in this way are set up against a wall,
and rest upon the ends of the bamboos.

All the low-priced teas are carried across in the
common way ; that is, each coolie, with a bamboo
across his shoulders, carries two chests, one being
slung from each end of the bamboo.   Whenever he
rests, either on the road or at the inn, the chests are
set down upon the ground, and consequently get soiled,

and do not arrive at their destination in as good order
as those carried in the other way.

The route we pursued was now in all respects
a highland road. At one time we were passing
through a beautiful valley, at another our road wound
round the mountain side, and frequently it boldly
breasted the hill, and led us over into another valley
beyond. As we went over the passes we always
rested while on the highest point, from which we
obtained a view, not only of the valley through which
we had come, but also of that to which we were
going. The long trains of coolies laden with chests
of tea and other produce, and with the mountain
chairs of travellers, presented a busy and curious
scene, as they toiled up the mountain side, or were
seen winding their way through the valleys. These
were views of "China and the Chinese" as they are
seen in everyday life.

After leaving the town of Yuen-shan we entered a
large tea-growing country. The shrubs were dotted
on the lower sides of all the fertile hills. Sometimes they were growing on level land, but that was
invariably dry, well drained by its position, and much
higher than rice-ground. The soil of these plantations consisted of a red-coloured loam mixed with a
considerable portion of gravel and sand. Many of
the tea-farms had been but lately formed, and the
cultivation of the shrub in this district is evidently
on the increase. Tea grown and manufactured here
can of course be conveyed to the great export marts
of Shanghae and Canton much quicker and more

cheaply than those from the southern side of the Bohea mountains.

We were now approaching the end of our first day's journey from Hokow. The day was far advanced, and we intended to put up for the night at Chu-chu, a small town near the foot of the Bohea mountains properly so called. During all my wanderings in China I had never yet slept in a Chinese inn, and could not help indulging in various speculations respecting it. Calling Sing-Hoo, I desired him and the coolie with the luggage to go before, and look out for a respectable place in which we could pass the night.

The town of Chu-chu is built on the two sides of a mountain stream. It is a small, poor place, supported by travellers and coolies passing to and from the Bohea mountains, and by the trade in the tea which is grown and manufactured in the surrounding districts.

My chairmen followed Sing-Hoo down the main street of the town for some distance. He had been making many inquiries by the way, and at last entered one of the numerous inns which abound in the place. Having hastily inspected it, and seeing it would suit our purpose, he returned to the door to give me this information. After being received in due form by the landlord, I walked through the outer part of the premises into the reception-hall.

This inn, although somewhat smaller than the one formerly described, was built upon the same plan. The part fronting the street was perfectly open, being entirely composed of pillars and shutters. Mine host,

with a cloth in his hand, hastily wiped a table and
chair, and, bowing politely, asked me to be seated.
He then placed a cup of tea before me, and brought
a joss-stick to light my pipe, and, having done so, he
retired and left me to my own reflections.

I had now time to take a survey of my quarters.
In the front part of the building a number of persons
were dining at tables placed there for the accommodation of travellers. I had given them a slight
glance as I passed through, but was now able to
examine the groups with more leisure. My chair-
bearers and coolie were already seated at one of those
tables, evidently enjoying their evening meal after
the fatigues of the day. Sing-Hoo was bustling about
with the landlord, making himself quite at home, and
ordering the materials for my dinner. Perhaps this
had a tendency to turn the landlord's attention more
to his own business than to that of his guests; but
be this as it may, he never appeared to have the
slightest idea that he had a foreigner under his roof,
and asked no troublesome questions.

On each side of the hall in which I sat there were
a number of small sleeping apartments—I can scarcely
call them bedrooms—and in one of them my luggage
had been placed. It was about twelve feet square,
and had two beds and a table in it. It had no
window, nor any aperture of the kind for the admission of light, but the front boarding was not carried
so high as the roof, and hence an imperfect light
streamed in from the top, or through the doorway
when that was open. Add to this an uneven earthen

floor, and the walls besmeared with the remains of
tallow and dirt, and a fair idea may be formed of the
place in which I was about to pass the night.

In ordinary circumstances these appearances would
have been very discouraging. But I had "counted
the cost" of all these things before I began to travel
in China. I never expected to find my way strewed
with luxuries; I knew the people were not very
remarkable for cleanliness in their dwellings, and
I was therefore in some measure prepared for all the
inconveniences to which I was subjected. The only
way was to make myself as comfortable as the circumstances would admit of.

I therefore called Sing-Hoo, and desired him to
sweep my bedplace before he unpacked my sleeping
mat and other articles for the night. Whilst this
was going on the host informed me that dinner was
ready and placed on the table in the centre of the
hall. The fare was plain and homely. There was
a large basin full of boiled rice, with other smaller
ones containing fish, eggs, and pork. The vegetables
consisted of cabbages and bamboo. The latter I
thought extremely good, and always ordered it during
the remainder of our journey.

I did full justice to the rice, eggs, fish, and bamboo, and left the other articles for Sing-Hoo, who
seemed to enjoy them with equal relish. Dinner
being over, the dishes were removed, and tea set
upon the table. Our labours for the day being over,
pipes were lighted, and the smoke rose in wavy curls
to the roof of the inn.

CHAPTER XII.

First view of the Bohea mountains — Mountain pass — A noble fir-
    tree — Its name and history — Flora of the mountains — New plants
    — Source of the river Min — Entertainment for man and beast —
    A rugged road and another pass — A gale amongst the mountains
    — An amusing old China-woman — Sugar and tea-spoons — A kind
    landlord — The Tein-sin — Arrive at the city of Tsong-gan-hien —
    Its situation, size, and trade — Tea-farms.

Nothing occurred during the night to disturb our
slumbers, and mine were as sound and peaceful as if
I had been in "the old house at home." When
morning dawned we had an early breakfast and proceeded on our journey. One of the grandest sights
I had ever beheld was now awaiting me. For some
time past I had been, as it were, amongst a sea of
mountains, but now the far-famed Bohea ranges lay
before me in all their grandeur, with their tops
piercing through the lower clouds, and showing themselves far above them. They seemed to be broken
up into thousands of fragments, some of which had
most remarkable and striking outlines. It is difficult
to form an estimate of their height, but, comparing
them with other mountains known to me, the highest
here may be six or eight thousand feet above the
level of the sea. There are some spots on the sides
of the lower hills under cultivation, but all above
these is rugged and wild.

I always like to look on scenery of this kind early in the morning.   I do not know whether it is that there is a freshness and beauty about it then which it loses when the day is further advanced, or whether the mind is more susceptible of impressions then than at other times ; it may be that both these combine to render morning views most delightful and pleasing to the eye.   Had I chosen the time for my first view of the Bohea mountains, I could not have been more fortunate.   The morning was clear, the air cool, and the sun was just shining on their eastern sides.   As its rays shone on the rugged peaks, they gave a rich and golden tint to some, while those in the shade looked gloomy and frowning.   Strange rocks, like gigantic statues of men or various animals, appeared to crown the heights, and made the view most remarkable.

Our road had been of an undulating character all the way from Hokow, and, although we had ascended a great number of hills, yet we generally descended again into valleys on the opposite side, but, on the whole, we were gradually attaining a higher elevation above the level of the sea.   We had now, however, arrived at the foot of the central and highest range, and began the ascent towards the mountain pass. The road here is about six feet in width, and paved with granite.   It led us round the sides of the mountains, and gradually carried us higher and higher, and at last, when we had rounded one of the upper windings, a view of the pass itself, in the highest range, was presented.   This pass is much lower than

P

any other part of the range, and consequently has the mountains rising high on each side of it. Just before we arrived at the top the road was so steep that even Chinese travellers get out of their chairs and walk, a proceeding unusual with them on ordinary occasions. From the foot of the range to the pass at which we had now arrived the distance was twenty le, or about five miles.

This pass is a busy thoroughfare. It connects the countries of Fokien with those of Kiang-see, and is the highway, through the mountains, from the black-tea districts to the central and northern provinces of the Chinese empire. Long trains of coolies were met or overtaken at every turning of the road. Those going northward were laden with chests of tea, and those going south carried lead and other products for which there is a demand in the tea country. Travellers in chairs were also numerous, some going to, and others returning from, the towns of Tsong-gan-hien and Tsing-tsun, and the surrounding country· Whether I looked up towards the pass, or down on the winding pathway by which I had come, a strange and busy scene presented itself. However numerous the coolies, or however good the road, I never observed any two of them walking abreast, as people do in other countries; each one followed his neighbour, and in the distance they resembled a colony of ants on the move.

At every quarter of a mile, or sometimes less, there is a tea-shop, for the refreshment of those who are toiling up or down the mountain. We frequently stopped at these places on our way, and refreshed ourselves with a cup of the pure bohea on its native mountains. During the ascent I walked nearly all the way, being anxious to inspect the natural productions of the mountains. My chair-bearers were delighted with this arrangement, the more so as they are not accustomed to anything of the kind from their countrymen.

We arrived at last at the celebrated gates or huge doors which divide the provinces of Fokien and Kiang-see. The pillars of these gates have been formed by nature, and are nothing less than the "everlasting hills" themselves. The arched doorways of the place bore a great resemblance to the gates of a Chinese city. As we passed through the archway I observed a guard of soldiers lounging about, but they did not take any notice of us, or attempt to examine our baggage. We were soon through the pass, and in another province. The province of Kiang-see had been shut out and left behind us, and our view now opened on Fokien. Never in my life had I seen such a view as this, so grand, so sublime. High ranges of mountains were towering on my right and on my left, while before me, as far as the eye could reach, the whole country seemed broken up into mountains and hills of all heights, with peaks of every form.

While gazing with wonder and admiration on the scene, my attention was arrested by a solitary pine-tree of great size, standing about a hundred yards from the gateway. No other trees of any size were near it. Its solitary position near the pass, and its great height and beautiful symmetry, made it appear a most striking object. "What could it be? was it new, or did we already possess it in England?" I must confess that for a few seconds I had eyes for nothing else. Chairs, coolies, and mountains were all forgotten, and I believe, had the guard of Celestials attempted to prevent me from going into Fokien, the only boon I should have asked at their hands would have been to be allowed to go and inspect this noble pine.

The Chinese guard, however, had not the slightest intention of interfering with my movements, and, as the tree was on the roadside, I soon came up to it, and found it to be the Japan cedar (*Cryptomeria japonica*), a tree which I had already introduced into England, and which, even in a young state, had been greatly admired there. I had never before seen such a noble specimen, and, although I would rather it had been something new, I yet felt proud of having been the means of introducing into Europe a tree of such size, symmetry, and beauty. It was at least one hundred and twenty feet in height,—it might be much more,—as straight as a larch, and had its lower branches drooping to the ground. It had not been "lopped," like other Chinese trees, and was evidently preserved with great care. My Chinamen looked upon it with great admiration, and informed me it was the only specimen of the kind in this part of the country, and that it had been planted by some former emperor when he crossed the mountains.

The indigenous plants of these mountains are of great interest. The ravines were rich in bamboos, many of which were of great beauty. The Chinese pine (*Pinus sinensis*) was abundant everywhere, but did not attain a large size. Higher up various species of oak were met with, and a thistle, not unlike the common English thistle, was abundant. Very few trees were to be seen near the top of the highest mountains, which were covered with low-growing shrubs, grasses, and other herbaceous plants.

I met with one or two new plants, which deserve particular notice. One of them was a very beautiful species of *Hydrangea*; another was a species of *Spiræa*, with red flowers, not unlike the *S. bella* in colour, but having a different habit. A fine species of *Abelia* was also met with on the Fokien side of the mountains, which will probably be a favourite in English gardens. Its flowers are as large as those of the *Weigela rosea*, of a blueish tinge, and bloom in great profusion for a long time. When I first saw this plant I took it to be the *Abelia chinensis* of Brown, but I observe that Dr. Lindley, to whom the plant was sent for examination, calls it *A. uniflora*. It is a curious circumstance that Dr. Abel, after whom the genus was named, discovered his plant on the same mountains, about a hundred miles to the north-west of the spot where the *Abelia uniflora* was found. He was then on his way with the embassy from Peking to Canton.

I dug up, from time to time, living plants of all these species, and took them on with me. Many a time I thought I should be obliged to leave them behind me, for the Chinamen could not see the propriety of being burdened with what they considered weeds, and of no value; however, by dint of determination and perseverance, by sometimes using promises and sometimes threats, I got them carried several hundred miles in safety, and at last deposited them in the garden of my friend Mr. Beale, at Shanghae. They are now in Europe, and are, perhaps, the first plants which have been brought direct from the Bohea mountains.

The streams which flowed from the sides of the hills now ran to the southward, towards the town of Tsong-gan-hien, and I was doubtless at one of the many sources of the river Min. After travelling about thirty le from the pass, we approached a small town named Ching-hu, where we intended to remain for the night. We were now about seventy le from where we stopped the night before, and, as our road had been a steep and rugged one during the day, w were tired enough, and glad of rest.

Ching-hu is a small town on the banks of the stream, which gradually swells as it glides onward until it becomes the noble river we see at Foo-chow-foo. The town is built in a ravine, and high, steep hills rise on each side of it. As we passed down the main street I observed three Canton men taking an evening stroll, and apparently admiring the beauty of the situation. Calling Sing-Hoo, I desired him to take care not to go to the inn where these men were staying, as I was not desirous of having any more

encounters with natives who had been in the towns
where foreigners reside.

It was nearly dark when we reached our inn, a
building with accommodation for man and beast.
The latter title refers not to horses, but to pigs,
which are great favourites with the Chinese, particularly in Fokien. The arrangements of the inn were
exactly like those of the last one, and therefore I
need not describe them. Tired with the fatigues of
the day, I retired early, and slept more soundly than
if I had been on a bed of down.

The next day we had to cross another mountain pass,
not so high as the last, but presenting scenery equally
beautiful. Being at a lower elevation, the hill-sides
were clothed with trees and brushwood, and reminded
me of the rich tropical scenery which I had seen near
Batavia and Singapore. Here were some beautiful
forests of the lance-leaved pine (*Cunninghamia
lanceolata*), the finest I had ever met with in China.

The making of the road over this pass must have
been a gigantic undertaking. The sides of the
mountain, both above and below the road, were steep
and rugged. So dangerous had the Chinese considered this road, even after it was made, that they
had fixed in many places a massive stone rail on the
lower side to prevent people from falling over. Far
below, in a beautiful dell, a little stream was gushing
down amongst the rocks and trees, which was fed by
many waterfalls from the sides of the mountain. In
some places the height was so great that it made me
giddy to look down.

When we crossed this pass it was blowing a gale of wind, and I was obliged to have the cover taken off my chair. Had I not done so there would have been some danger of my being blown over the rocks; indeed after the covering was removed the danger seemed so great that I considered it safest to get out and walk. Stopping at one of the tea-houses on our way, which was kept by a very talkative old woman, she contributed not a little to our amusement. "Hai-yah," said the chair-bearers, as we entered the house, "what a stormy day; how high the wind is!" "Pooh, pooh!" said the old dame, "this is nothing; you must not call this a high wind; it is plain enough you know nothing about the wind amongst these mountains. Our houses are often unroofed, and sometimes it is not possible for us to stand on the public road without support. You could not have brought that chair over the pass on a really windy day, I can tell you. Ah, you should see one of these gales, and you would not call this a high wind."

Having drunk the tea which she had set before us, Sing-Hoo asked one of our men what ought to be paid in this part of the country. The man replied, "A cash each cup, of course; tea is cheap here." The sum was thrown down upon the tray, and the old woman was called to receive it. When she came she refused to take anything, telling us that "her house was not a tea-shop; that when it was one,—which was not likely though,—she would then receive our money." This was the first instance of a Chinese refusing money which had come under my observa-

tion.   The old lady did not lose anything by it, however, for I bought some cakes and other things which
were not below her dignity to sell, and we parted the
best of friends.   We had many a good joke and hearty
laugh at her expense as we pursued our journey.

The sky had been overcast during the morning,
and, the wind having died away, the rain came down
in torrents.   We were obliged to take shelter in
another tea-house, and remained there for some
hours.   It continued to rain, however, and we were
glad to proceed a little further on to a small village,
where there was an inn, in which we took up our
quarters for the night.   The landlord paid me the
most marked attention.   When I entered the hall
tea was set before me as usual, but in this instance a
curiously shaped tea-spoon was in the cup, and the
tea was sweetened with sugar.   I had never seen the
Chinese use either sugar or tea-spoons before, and
was rather surprised; and it is still a question with
me whether we are not indebted to them for our
mode of *making* tea, as well as for the tea itself.   It
was only on our first entering that this was done, for
when tea was brought afterwards it was always made
in the usual way, that is, the leaves were put into a
cup and boiling water poured over them.

To the question usually put to Sing-Hoo, of "who
his master was," he invariably returned the same
answer, "A Loi-ya from a far country beyond the
great wall."   I much doubt whether he had himself
a clearer idea of the position of England than this
answer conveyed to his interrogator.   In the present

case, however, this being in a small village, and our host himself a simple countryman, the information that his guest was a Loi-ya produced a marked effect, and his attentions were redoubled, until they became quite irksome. He made a great many excuses for the poorness of the fare which he set before me. " Had I only sent him notice of the honour I intended doing him by coming to his house, he would have been better prepared," and so on. I praised the house and fare, and tried not to be outdone in politeness by my kind-hearted landlord.

In the course of the evening a little boy, the landlord's son, came to me and asked me whether I should like to smoke opium, as they had some in the house of good quality. I thanked him, but, of course, declined the offer. Upon inquiry I found that opium is kept in all these inns, where it is retailed in small quantities, just as a London innkeeper retails tobacco. It is very disagreeable, and I afterwards found it so, to be in one of these places when you have a number of opium-smokers for fellow-travellers.

Between nine and ten o'clock at night, and just as I was retiring to rest, Sing-Hoo came and informed me that the landlord wished me to partake of a fine supper which he had prepared. I think he called it the Tein-sin. I believe this is not an unusual proceeding on the part of Chinese landlords when they have any one in their houses whom they " delight to honour." Being perfectly ignorant of the existence of such a custom, I desired my servant to beg the landlord to excuse me, as I had had my dinner, and did not feel inclined to eat anything more that night. Sing-Hoo, however, said it was a most unusual proceeding to refuse the Tein-sin, and, thinking it better to conform to the customs of the country, I followed him into the hall. Here I found a table covered with many Chinese dishes. Our host had killed some fowls for the occasion, which had been cut up into small pieces, and were served up with, or rather in, some excellent soup. Had I been at all hungry I might have made an excellent meal, but in the present circumstances I could not be expected to enjoy it with much relish. The landlord waited upon me himself, and pressed me to eat. He kept constantly pointing to the different dishes, saying " Eat this, eat this," in his most pressing manner. I tasted the different dishes, eating more or less of each as they took my fancy, and at last, considering I had gone quite as far as even Chinese politeness required, I laid down my chopsticks, and expressed my delight at the manner in which the Tein-sin had been served. But he pressed me more and more by putting the different dishes near me and praising their quality. At last he finished his part of the play by removing the viands from the table and setting tea before me. I was now free again, and retired to rest, afraid of night-mare and all the evils of not taking supper sparingly.

Early the next morning our host appeared, and informed me that the Tein-sin was ready. I partook of it in the same manner as I had done the night before, but with much greater relish. To my sur-

prise, however, a few minutes afterwards my breakfast was placed upon the table, as if I had eaten
nothing. Sing-Hoo now presented himself, and
asked what he was to give the landlord for the treatment we had received, observing at the same time
that he would make no charge. Of course I was
obliged to give the man a handsome present. Half
suspecting that Sing-Hoo or the coolies had been at
the bottom of the Tein-sin affair, I desired him to
take care and discourage everything of the kind for
the future. I knew that I had still a long journey
before me and many expenses, and it would not do
for me to run short of money by the way.

I was now on the outskirts of the great black-tea
country of Fokien. I observed large quantities of
tea-plants under cultivation. They were generally
to be found on the lower sides of the hills, and also
in the gardens of the villagers. About ten o'clock in
the forenoon we arrived at Tsong-gan-hien, a large
town in the midst of the black-tea country, where
nearly all the teas of this district are packed and
prepared for exportation. Tsong-gan-hien, according
to observations made by the Jesuits many years ago,
is situated in latitude 27° 47' 38" north. It stands
in the midst of a fertile plain of small extent, surrounded by hills, and is in the district of Kein-ning-
foo, a city to which I have already alluded in my
journey up the river Min.

The walls of the city are about three miles in circumference. Both these and the ramparts are in
many parts ruinous and overgrown with weeds.

They seem hoary with age, and were doubtless built in more warlike times than the present. The population may amount to one hundred thousand inhabitants, but I have no means of forming a correct estimate. The suburbs, which I include in this calculation, are very large and populous, and extend a considerable way down the sides of the river.

This city abounds in large tea-hongs, in which the black teas are sorted and packed for the foreign markets. All those coolies whom I had met on my journey across the mountains were loaded here. Tea merchants from all parts of China where teas are consumed or exported come to this place to make their purchases of tea and the necessary arrangements for its transport. Canton men in particular come in great numbers, as they carry on a large trade with foreigners both at Canton and Shanghae. I saw many of them walking about in the streets, but for obvious reasons avoided them as much as possible. They are easily distinguished by their features from the natives of Fokien, as well as from the more northern Chinese.

The plain in which the town of Tsong-gan-hien is situated is not of great extent. Hills are seen apparently surrounding it on all sides, on some of which the tea-shrub is extensively cultivated. Many of these hills have a most barren appearance, although there are here and there very fertile spots on their sloping sides. Tea is also cultivated extensively in the lowlands, but these are invariably well raised above the banks of the river. It will be better, how-

ever, to collect into one chapter the remarks I have
to make upon the tea cultivation in this important
part of the country.

As I arrived at Tsong-gan-hien early in the day, I
stopped there only three hours. This was sufficient
to enable me to take a survey of the town, and to
obtain some refreshment both for myself and my
men. At the end of that time I got into my chair
and took the road for Woo-e-shan, which was only
forty or fifty le further on. As soon as we were
clear of the town the road seemed entirely different
from that which we had been travelling on before.
The fact is we had left the great tea highway,—that
had ended at the town we just passed. Our road
was now more narrow and less frequented. The
travellers in chairs, the coolies with tea-chests on
their shoulders, and all that motley band which we
had seen on our journey across the mountains, had
disappeared, and we were now journeying alone.

CHAPTER XIII.

Woo-e-shan — Ascent of the hill — Arrive at a Buddhist temple — Description of the temple and the scenery — Strange rocks — My reception — Our dinner and its ceremonies — An interesting conversation — An evening stroll — Formation of the rocks — Soil — View from the top of Woo-e-shan — A priest's grave — A view by moonlight — Chinese wine — Cultivation of the tea-shrub — Chains and monkeys used in gathering it — Tea-merchants — Happiness and contentment of the peasantry.

As soon as I was fairly out of the suburbs of Tsong-gan-hien I had my first glimpse of the far-famed Woo-e-shan. It stands in the midst of the plain which I have noticed in the previous chapter, and is a collection of little hills, none of which appear to be more than a thousand feet high. They have a singular appearance. Their faces are nearly all perpendicular rock. It appears as if they had been thrown up by some great convulsion of nature to a certain height, and as if some other force had then dra. n the tops of the whole mass slightly backwards, break ing it up into a thousand hills. By some agency of this kind it might have assumed the strange forms which were now before me.

Woo-e-shan is considered by the Chinese to be one of the most wonderful, as well as one of the most sacred, spots in the empire. One of their manuscripts, quoted by Mr. Ball, thus describes it:

" Of all the mountains of Fokien those of Woo-e are the finest, and its water the best.   They are awfully high and rugged, surrounded by water, and seem as if excavated by spirits ; nothing more wonderful can be seen.   From the dynasty of Csin and Han, down to the present time, a succession of hermits and priests, of the sects of Tao-cze and Fo, have here risen up like the clouds of the air and the grass of the field, too numerous to enumerate.   Its chief renown, however, is derived from its productions, and of these tea is the most celebrated."

I stood for some time on a point of rising ground midway between Tsong-gan-hien and Woo-e-shan, and surveyed the strange scene which lay before me. I had expected to see a wonderful sight when I reached this place, but I must confess the scene far surpassed any ideas I had formed respecting it.   There had been no exaggeration in the description given by the Jesuits, or in the writings of the Chinese, excepting as to the height of the hills.   They are not " awfully high ;" indeed, they are lower than most of the hills in this part of the country, and far below the height of the mountain ranges which I had just crossed.   The men who were with me pointed to the spot with great pride, and said, " Look, that is Woo-e-shan! have you anything in your country to be compared with it ?"

The day was fine, and the sun's rays being very powerful I had taken up my position under the spreading branches of a large camphor-tree which grew by the roadside.   Here I could willingly have remained until night had shut out the scene from my view, but my chairbearers, who were now near the end of their journey, intimated that they were ready to proceed, so we went onwards.

The distance from Tsong-gan-hien to Woo-e-shan is only about 40 or 50 le. This is, however, only to the bottom of the hills, and we intended to take up our quarters in one of the principal temples near the top. The distance we had to travel was therefore much greater than this. When we arrived at the foot of the hill we inquired our way to the temple. "Which temple do you wish to go to?" was the answer; "there are nearly a thousand temples on Woo-e-shan." Sing-Hoo explained that we were unacquainted with the names of the different temples, but our object was to reach one of the largest. We were directed, at last, to the foot of some perpendicular rocks. When we reached the spot I expected to get a glimpse of the temple we were in search of somewhere on the hill side above us, but there was nothing of the kind. A small footpath, cut out of the rock, and leading over almost inaccessible places, was all I could see. It was now necessary for me to get out of my chair, and to scramble up the pathway —often on my hands and knees. Several times the coolies stopped, and declared that it was impossible to get the chair any further. I pressed on, however, and they were obliged to scramble after me with it.

It was now about two o'clock in the afternoon; there was scarcely a cloud in the sky, and the day was fearfully hot. As I climbed up the rugged steep,

Q

the perspiration streaming from every pore, I began to think of fever and ague, and all those ills which the traveller is subject to in this unhealthy climate. We reached the top of the hill at last, and our eyes were gladdened with the sight of a rich luxuriant spot, which I knew at once to be near a Buddhist temple. Being a considerable way in advance of my chairbearers and coolies, I sat down under the shade of a tree to rest and get cool before I entered its sacred precincts. In a few minutes my people arrived with smiling countenances, for they had got a glimpse of the temple through the trees, and knew that rest and refreshment awaited them.

The Buddhist priesthood seem always to have selected the most beautiful spots for the erection of their temples and dwellings. Many of these places owe their chief beauty to the protection and cultivation of trees. The wood near a Buddhist temple in China is carefully protected, and hence a traveller can always distinguish their situation, even when some miles distant. In this respect these priests resemble the enlightened monks and abbots of the olden time, to whose taste and care we owe some of the richest and most beautiful sylvan scenery in Europe.

The temple, or collection of temples, which we now approached, was situated on the sloping side of a small valley, or basin, on the top of Woo-e-shan, which seemed as if it had been scooped out for the purpose. At the bottom of this basin a small lake was seen glistening through the trees, and covered with the famous lien-wha, or *Nelumbium*—a plant held in high esteem and veneration by the Chinese, and always met with in the vicinity of Buddhist temples.   All the ground from the lake to the temples was covered with the tea-shrub, which was evidently cultivated with great care, while on the opposite banks, facing the buildings, was a dense forest of trees and brushwood.

On one side—that on which the temples were built—there were some strange rocks standing like huge monuments which had a peculiar and striking appearance.   They stood near each other, and were each from 80 to 100 feet in height.   These no doubt had attracted, by their strange appearance, the priests who first selected this place as a site for their temples.   The high-priest had his house built at the base of one of these huge rocks, and to it we bent our steps.   Ascending a flight of steps, and passing through a doorway, we found ourselves in front of the building.   A little boy, who was amusing himself under the porch, ran off immediately and informed the priest that strangers had come to pay him a visit.   Being very tired, I entered the reception hall, and sat down to wait his arrival.   In a very short time the priest came in and received me with great politeness.   Sing-Hoo now explained to him that I had determined to spend a day or two on Woo-e-shan, whose fame had reached even the far-distant country to which I belonged ; and begged that we might be accommodated with food and lodgings during our stay.

While the high-priest was listening to Sing-Hoo he drew out of his tobacco-pouch a small quantity of Chinese tobacco, rolled it for a moment between his finger and thumb, and then presented it to me to fill my pipe with. This practice is a common one amongst the inhabitants of these hills, and indicates, I suppose, that the person to whom it is presented is welcome. It was evidently kindly meant, so, taking it in the same kind spirit, I lighted my pipe and began to smoke.

In the mean time our host led me into his best room, and, desiring me to take a seat, he called the boy, and ordered him to bring us some tea. And now I drank the fragrant herb, pure and unadulterated, on its native hills. It had never been half so grateful before, or I had never been so much in need of it; for I was hot, thirsty, and weary, after ascending the hill under a burning sun. The tea soon quenched my thirst and revived my spirits, and called to my mind the words of a Chinese author, who says, "Tea is exceedingly useful; cultivate it, and the benefit will be widely spread; drink it, and the animal spirits will be lively and clear."

Although I can speak enough of the Chinese language to make myself understood in several districts of the country, I judged it prudent not to enter into a lengthened conversation with the priests at this temple. I left the talking part of the business to be done by my servant, who was quite competent to speak for us both. They were therefore told that I could not speak the language of the district, and that I came from a far country "beyond the great wall."

The little boy whom I have already noticed now presented himself, and announced that dinner was on the table. The old priest bowed to me, and asked me to walk into the room in which the dinner was served. I did not fail to ask him to precede me, which of course he "couldn't think of doing," but followed me, and placed me at his left hand in the "seat of honour." Three other priests took their seats at the same table. One of them had a most unprepossessing appearance; his forehead was low, he had a bold and impudent-looking eye, and was badly marked with the smallpox. In short, he was one of those men that one would rather avoid than have anything to do with. The old high-priest was quite a different-looking man from his subordinate. He was about sixty years of age, and appeared to be very intelligent. His countenance was such as one likes to look upon; meekness, honesty, and truth were stamped unmistakeably upon it.

Having seated ourselves at table, a cup of wine was poured out to each of us, and the old priest said, " Che-sue, che-sue"—Drink wine, drink wine. Each lifted up his cup, and brought it in contact with those of the others. As the cups touched we bowed to each other, and said, " Drink wine, drink wine." The chopsticks which were before each of us were now taken up, and dinner commenced. Our table was crowded with small basins, each containing a different article of food. I was surprised to see in

one of them some small fish, for I had always understood that the Buddhist priesthood were prohibited
from eating any kinds of animal food. The other
dishes were all composed of vegetables. There were
young bamboo shoots, cabbages of various kinds
both fresh and pickled, turnips, beans, peas, and
various other articles, served up in a manner which
made them very palatable. Besides these there was
a fungus of the mushroom tribe, which was really
excellent. Some of these vegetables were prepared
in such a manner as made it difficult to believe that
they were really vegetables. All the dishes, however, were of this description, except the fish already
noticed. Rice was also set before each of us, and
formed the principal part of our dinner.

While the meal was going on the priests continually pressed me to eat. They praised the different
dishes, and, as they pointed them out, said, "Eat
fish, eat cabbage," or, "eat rice," as the case might
be. Not unfrequently their politeness, in my humble
opinion, was carried rather too far; for they not only
pointed out the dishes which they recommended, but
plunged their own chopsticks into them, and drew to
the surface such delicate morsels as they thought
I should prefer, saying, "Eat this, eat this." This
was far from agreeable, but I took it all as it was
intended, and we were the best of friends.

An interesting conversation was carried on during
dinner between Sing-Hoo and the priests. Sing-Hoo
had been a great traveller in his time, and gave them
a good deal of information concerning many of the

provinces both in the north and in the south, of which they knew little or nothing themselves.   He told them of his visit to Pekin, described the Emperor, and proudly pointed to the livery he wore.   This immediately stamped him, in their opinions, as a person of great importance.   They expressed their opinions freely upon the natives of different provinces, and spoke of them as if they belonged to different nations, just as we would do of the natives of France, Holland, or Denmark.   The Canton men they did not like; the Tartars were good—the Emperor was a Tartar.   All the outside nations were bad, particularly the Kwei-tszes, a name signifying Devil's children, which they charitably apply to the nations of the western world.

Having finished dinner, we rose from the table and returned to the hall.   Warm water and a wet cloth were now set before each of us, to wash with after our meal.   The Chinese always wash with warm water, both in summer and winter, and rarely use soap or any substance of a similar nature.   Having washed my face and hands in the true Chinese style, I intimated my wish to go out and inspect the hills and temples in the neighbourhood.

Calling Sing-Hoo to accompany me, we descended the flight of steps and took the path which led down to the lake at the bottom of the basin.   On our way we visited several temples; none of them, however, seemed of any note, nor were they to be compared with those at Koo-shan near Foo-chow-foo.   In truth the good priests seemed to pay more attention to the cultivation and manufacture of tea than to the rites of their peculiar faith. Everywhere in front of their dwellings I observed bamboo framework erected to support the sieves, which, when filled with leaves, are exposed to the sun and air. The priests and their servants were all busily employed in the manipulation of this valuable leaf.

When we arrived at the lake it presented a fine appearance. The noble leaves of the nelumbium were seen rising above its surface, and gold and silver fish were sporting in the water below, while all around the scenery was grand and imposing. Leaving the lake we followed the path which seemed to lead us to some perpendicular rocks. In the distance we could see no egress from the basin, but as we got nearer a chasm was visible by which the huge rock was parted, and through which flowed a little stream with a pathway by its side. It seemed, indeed, as if the stream had gradually worn down the rock and formed this passage for itself, which was not more than six or eight feet in width.

These rocks consist of clay slate, in which occur, embedded in the form of beds or dykes, great masses of quartz rock, while granite of a deep black colour, owing to the mica, which is of a fine deep bluish-black, cuts through them in all directions. This granite forms the summit of most of the principal mountains in this part of the country.

Resting on this clay slate are sandstone conglomerates, formed principally of angular masses of quartz held together by a calcareous basis, and alter-

nating with these conglomerates there is a fine calcareous granular sandstone, in which beds of dolomitic
limestone occur.   The geologist will thus see what a
strange mixture forms part of these huge rocks of
Woo-e-shan, and will be able to draw his own conclusions.   Specimens of these rocks were brought away
by me and submitted both to Dr. Falconer of Calcutta and Dr. Jameson of Saharunpore, who are well
known as excellent geologists.

The soil of these tea-lands consists of a brownish-
yellow adhesive clay.   This clay, when minutely
examined, is found to consist of particles of the rocks
and of vegetable matter.   It has always a very considerable portion of the latter in its composition in
those lands which are very productive and where
the tea-shrub thrives best.

Threading our way onward through the chasm,
with the rocks standing high on each side and dripping with water, we soon got into the open country
again.   After having examined the rocks and soil,
my object was to get a good view of the surrounding
country, and I therefore made my way to the heights
above the temples.   When I reached the summit the
view I obtained was well worth all my toil.   Around
and below me on every side were the rugged rocks
of Woq-e-shan, while numerous fertile spots in glens
and on hill sides were seen dotted over with the tea-
shrub.   Being on one of the highest points I had a
good view of the rich valleys in which the towns of
Tsong-gan-hien and Tsin-tsun stand.   Far away to
the northward the chain of the Bohea mountains were

seen stretching from east to west as far as the eye
could reach, and apparently forming an impenetrable
barrier between Fokien and the rich and populous
province of Kiang-see.

The sun was now setting behind the Bohea hills,
and, as twilight is short in these regions, the last rays
warned me that it would be prudent to get back to
the vicinity of the temples near which I had taken
up my quarters. On my way back I came upon a
tomb in which nine priests had been interred. It was
on the hill side, and seemed a fit resting-place for the
remains of such men. It had evidently been a kind
of natural cavern under the rock, with an opening in
front. The bodies were placed in it, the arched rock
was above them, and the front was built up with the
same material. Thus entombed amongst their
favourite hills, these bodies will remain until "the
rocks shall be rent," at that day when the trumpet of
the archangel shall sound, and the grave shall give
up its dead.

On a kind of flat terrace in front of this tomb I
observed the names of each of its occupants, and the
remains of incense-sticks which had been burning but
a short time before, when the periodical visit to the
tombs was paid. I was afterwards told by the high
priest that there was still room for one more within
the rocky cave. That one, he said, was himself;
and the old man seemed to look forward to the
time when he must be laid in his grave as not far
distant.

As I was now in the vicinity of the temples, and

there was no longer any danger of my losing my
way, I was in no hurry to go in-doors. The shades
of evening gradually closed in, and it was night on
Woo-e-shan. A solemn stillness reigned around,
which was broken only by the occasional sound of a
gong or bell in the temple, where some priest was
engaged in his evening devotions. In the mean time
the moon had risen, and the scene appeared, if possible, more striking than it had been in daylight.
The strange rocks, as they reared their rugged forms
high above the temples, partly in bright light and
partly in deep shade, had a curious and unnatural
appearance. On the opposite side the wood assumed
a dark and dense appearance, and down in the bottom
of the dell the little lake sparkled as if covered with
gems.

I sat down on a ledge of rock, and my eyes wandered over these remarkable objects. Was it a
reality or a dream, or was I in some fairy land?
The longer I looked the more indistinct the objects
became, and fancy seemed inclined to convert the
rocks and trees into strange living forms. In circumstances of this kind I like to let imagination roam
uncontrolled, and if now and then I built a few castles
in the air they were not very expensive and easily
pulled down again.

Sing-Hoo now came out to seek me, and to say
that our evening meal was ready, and that the priests
were waiting. When I went in I found the viands
already served. We seated ourselves at the table,
pledged each other in a cup of wine, and the meal

went on in the same manner as the former one. Like most of my countrymen, I have a great dislike to the Chinese sam-shoo, a spirit somewhat like the Indian arrack, but distilled from rice. Indeed the kind commonly sold in the shops is little else than rank poison. The Woo-e-shan wine, however, was quite a different affair : it resembled some of the lighter French wines; was slightly acid, agreeable, and in no way intoxicating, unless when taken in immoderate quantities. I had no means of ascertaining whether it was made from the grape, or whether it was a kind of sam-shoo which had been prepared in a particular way, and greatly diluted with water. At all events it was a very agreeable accompaniment to a Chinese dinner.

During our meal the conversation between Sing-Hoo and the priests turned upon the strange scenery of these hills, and the numerous temples which were scattered over them, many of which are built in the most inaccessible places. He informed them how delighted I had been with my walk during the afternoon, and how much I was struck with the strange scenery I had witnessed. Anything said in praise of these hills seemed to please the good priests greatly, and rendered them very communicative. They informed us that there were temples erected to Buddha on every hill and peak, and that in all they numbered no less than nine hundred and ninety-nine.

The whole of the land on these hills seems to belong to the priests of the two sects already mentioned, but by far the largest portion belongs to the

Buddhists. There are also some farms established
for the supply of the court of Peking. They are
called the imperial enclosures; but I suspect that
they too are, to a certain extent, under the management and control of the priests. The tea-shrub is
cultivated everywhere, and often in the most inaccessible situations, such as on the summits and ledges
of precipitous rocks. Mr. Ball states* that chains are
said to be used in collecting the leaves of the shrubs
growing in such places; and I have even heard it
asserted (I forget whether by the Chinese or by
others) that monkeys are employed for the same
purpose, and in the following manner:—These animals, it seems, do not like work, and would not
gather the leaves willingly; but when they are seen
up amongst the rocks where the tea-bushes are growing, the Chinese throw stones at them; the monkeys
get very angry, and commence breaking off the
branches of the tea-shrubs, which they throw down at
their assailants!

I should not like to assert that no tea is gathered
on these hills by the agency of chains and monkeys,
but I think it may be safely affirmed that the quantity procured in such ways is exceedingly small. The
greatest quantity is grown on level spots on the hill-
sides, which have become enriched, to a certain extent, by the vegetable matter and other deposits
which have been washed down by the rains from a
higher elevation. Very little tea appeared to be
cultivated on the more barren spots amongst the

* Cultivation and Manufacture of Tea.

hills, and such ground is very plentiful on Woo-e-shan.

Having been all day toiling amongst the hills, I retired to rest at an early hour. Sing-Hoo told me afterwards that he never closed his eyes during the night. It seems he did not like the appearance of the ill-looking priest; and having a strong prejudice against the Fokien men, he imagined an attempt might be made to rob or perhaps murder us during the night. No such fears disturbed my rest. I slept soundly until morning dawned, and when I awoke felt quite refreshed, and equal to the fatigues of another day. Calling for some water to be brought me, I indulged in a good wash, a luxury which I could only enjoy once in twenty-four hours.

During my stay here I met a number of tea-merchants from Tsong-gan-hien, who had come up to buy tea from the priests. These men took up their quarters in the temples, or rather in the priests' houses adjoining, until they had completed their purchases. Coolies were then sent for, and the tea was conveyed to Tsong-gan-hien, there to be prepared and packed for the foreign markets.

On the morning of the third day, having seen all that was most interesting in this part of the hills, I determined to change my quarters. As soon as breakfast was over I gave the old priest a present for his kindness, which, although small, seemed to raise me not a little in his esteem. The chair-bearers were then summoned, and we left the hospitable roof of the Buddhist priests to explore more distant parts

of the hills.   What roof was next to shelter me I had
not the most remote idea.

Our host followed me to the gateway, and made
his adieus in Chinese style.   As we threaded our way
amongst the hills, I observed tea-gatherers busily
employed on all the hill-sides where the plantations
were.   They seemed a happy and contented race;
the joke and merry laugh were going round, and
some of them were singing as gaily as the birds in
the old trees about the temples.

A Chinese Tomb.

CHAPTER XIV.

Stream of "nine windings"—A Taouist priest—His house and temple
—Du Halde's description of these hills—Strange impressions of
gigantic hands on the rocks—Tea-plants purchased—Adventure
during the night—My visitors—Plants packed for a journey—
Town of Tsin-tsun and its trade—Leave the Woo-e hills—Mountain scenery—The lance-leaved pine—Rocks, ravines, and waterfalls—A lonely road—Trees—Birds and other animals—Town of
She-pa-ky—Productions of the country—Uses of the Nelumbium
—Pouching teas—City of Pouching-hien.

WE now proceeded across the hills in the direction
of the small town of Tsin-tsun, another great mart
for black tea. Our road was a very rough one. It
was merely a footpath, and sometimes merely narrow
steps cut out of the rock. When we had gone about
two miles we came to a solitary temple on the banks
of a small river, which here winds amongst the hills.
This stream is called by the Chinese the river or
stream of nine windings, from the circuitous turns
which it takes amongst the hills of Woo-e-shan. It
divides the range into two districts—the north and
south: the north range is said to produce the best
teas. Here the finest souchongs and pekoes are produced, but I believe these rarely find their way to
Europe, or only in very small quantities.

The temple we had now reached was a small and
insignificant-looking building. It seemed a sort of
half-way resting-place for people on the road from

[A Chinese Bird's eye view of the Stream of "Nine Windings" and strange Rocks.]

Tsin-tsun to the hills; and when we arrived several
travellers and coolies were sitting in the porch drinking tea. The temple belonged to the Taouists, and
was inhabited by an old priest and his wife. The
priests of this sect do not shave their heads like the
Buddhists, and I believe are allowed to marry.

The old priest received us with great politeness,
and, according to custom, gave me a piece of tobacco
and set a cup of tea before me. Sing-Hoo now asked
him whether he had a spare room in his house, and
whether he would allow us to remain with him for a
day or two. He seemed to be very glad of the
chance of making a little money, and immediately
led us up stairs to a room which, as we were not very
particular, we agreed to hire during our stay.

This house and temple, like some which I have
already described, were built against a perpendicular
rock, which formed an excellent and substantial back
wall to the building. The top of the rock overhung
the little building, and the water from it continually
dripping on the roof of the house gave the impression that it was raining.

The stream of " nine windings" flowed past the
front of the temple. Numerous boats were plying up
and down, many of which, I was told, contained
parties of pleasure, who had come to see the strange
scenery amongst these hills. The river was very rapid,
and these boats seemed to fly when going with the
current, and were soon lost to view. On all sides
the strangest rocks and hills were observed, having
generally a temple and tea-manufactory near their

summits. Sometimes they seemed so steep that the buildings could only be approached by a ladder; but generally the road was cut out of the rock in steps, and by this means the top was reached.

Du Halde, in describing these hills, says, " The priests, the better to compass their design of making this mountain pass for the abode of the immortal beings, have conveyed barks, chariots, and other things of the same kind, into the clefts of the steep rocks, all along the sides of a rivulet that runs between, insomuch that these fantastical ornaments are looked upon by the stupid vulgar as real prodigies, believing it impossible that they could be raised to such inaccessible places but by a power more than human."

I did not observe any of these chariots; and if they exist at all, they must either have been made for the express purpose, or brought from some distant country, as none are in use in these parts. Boats are common enough on the river; and if they are drawn up into such places, the circumstance would not be so wonderful.

Some curious marks were observed on the sides of some of these perpendicular rocks. At a distance they seemed as if they were the impress of some gigantic hands. I did not get very near these marks, but I believe that many of them have been formed by the water oozing out and trickling down the surface. They did not seem artificial; but a strange appearance is given to these rocks by artificial means. Emperors and other great and rich men, when visiting these hills, have had stones, with large letters carved upon them, let in or built into the face of these rocks. These, at a distance, have a most curious appearance.

The old priest with whom I had taken up my quarters seemed miserably poor; the piece of ground attached to the temple for his support was very small. Now and then one of his own sect, who came to worship at the temples amongst these hills, left him a small present, but such visits were " few and far between." And there was nothing grand or imposing about his temple to attract the rich and great, except indeed the scenery which surrounded it.

Having given the old man some money to purchase a dinner for myself and my men, I made a hasty meal and went out to explore the hills. I visited many of the tea-farms, and was successful in procuring about four hundred young plants. These were taken to Shanghae in good order, and many of them are now growing vigorously in the Government tea plantation in the Himalayas.

The old priest and his wife could not afford to burn either candle or oil, and were therefore in the habit of retiring very early to rest. As the night was wet and my quarters far from comfortable, I soon followed their example. Sing-Hoo, who was in the room with me, said he had no confidence in these Fokien men, as he called them, and that he would let down the trap-door of our garret and make all fast for the night before we went to sleep. However soundly I sleep, the least noise of an unusual kind is

sure to awake me. Somewhere about midnight I
awoke, and for a second or two I heard nothing
except the heavy rain pattering on the roof of our
room. Shortly afterwards, however, a slight noise
below attracted my attention, and my eye naturally
turned to the trap-door. What was my surprise to
see it slowly open and the head of a man make its
appearance in the room where we were! I scarcely
knew how to act, but at last determined to lie still
and watch his motions, and to be ready if necessary
to defend myself as well as I could. Gradually a
man's figure appeared, and entering the room he
began to grope about, muttering some indistinct
words. This awoke Sing-Hoo, who jumped out of
bed in a great fright and called out to me to get up.
" The rain is coming through the roof of the house
into our bed," said the man, whom we immediately
recognised to be the poor old priest. We now
breathed freely and had a good laugh at our being so
alarmed. The old man, after putting some mats
above the place through which the rain was coming
in, descended the stairs to his own room. " Shut
down the door," said Sing-Hoo to him as he went
out. " It is much better up," said the old priest, " it
is much cooler: don't be afraid, there is nothing to
harm you amongst these mountains." Sing-Hoo did
not contradict him, but, when he was gone, got up
and quietly shut down the door. Nothing else disturbed our slumbers during the night.

These old people had not the slightest idea that I
was a foreigner; but I was subjected to some incon-

venience through my servant informing them that I was a mandarin from Tartary. Sometimes, when I was in my room, the country people who were passing, and who had just laid down their burdens to take a cup of tea, expressed great anxiety to see a traveller who had come so far. On several occasions some of them walked up stairs without any ceremony. I believe I always received them with the utmost politeness and sustained my character tolerably well. On one occasion, however, I nearly lost my gravity. An old priest, apparently in his second childhood, came in to see me, and the moment he entered my room he fell upon his knees and kow-towed or prostrated himself several times before me in the most abject manner. I raised him gently from this humiliating posture, and intimated that I did not wish to be so highly honoured. Another priest came and expressed a desire for me to go and visit his temple, which was on an adjoining hill, and which he told me had been honoured with a visit from a former emperor.

I remained two days under the roof of the hospitable Taouist, and saw a great part of the Woo-e hills and their productions. On the evening of the second day, having entered into a fresh agreement with my chairbearers and coolies, I intimated to the old priest that I intended to proceed on my journey early next morning. He kindly pressed me to stay a little longer, but, when he saw I was in earnest, he went out to his tea plantations and brought me some young plants which he begged me to accept. I felt highly

pleased with his gratitude for the small present I had
given him, and gladly accepted the plants, which increased my store very considerably; these with the
other plants were carefully packed with their roots in
damp moss, and the whole package was then covered
with oil-paper. The latter precaution was taken to
screen them from the sun, and also from the prying
eyes of the Chinese, who, although they did not seem
to show any great jealousy on the point, yet might
have annoyed us with impertinent questions. Early
in the morning, our arrangements being completed,
we bade adieu to our kind host and hostess, and set
off across the hills in the direction of Tsin-tsun.

Tsin-tsun is a small town built on the banks of one
of the branches of the river Min. This stream divides
the northern ranges of Woo-e-shan from the southern.
The town is built on both banks of the river, and is
connected by a bridge. Here are great numbers of
inns, eating-houses, and tea-shops for the accommodation of the tea-merchants and coolies. A great
quantity of tea, produced in the surrounding hills, is
brought here for sale, before it finds its way to
Tsong-gan-hien, and thence across the Bohea mountains to Hokow.

When I arrived at Tsin-tsun I felt strongly inclined to go down the river Min to Foo-chow-foo.
This could have been accomplished in about four
days without trouble or inconvenience, as the whole
journey could be performed in one boat. There
were two objections, however, to this route; one was
that I should not have seen much more new ground,

and the other was the difficulty of getting away from
Foo-chow when once there.

After weighing the matter in my mind I determined
neither to go down to Foo-chow-foo, nor to return by
the way I came, but to take another route, which led
eastward to the town of Pouching-hien, then across
the Bohea mountains and down their northern sides
into the province of Chekiang. I ascertained that
the distance from Woo-e-shan to Pouching-hien was
280 le, and that, as the road was mountainous, the
journey would occupy from three to four days.

We halted in Tsin-tsun only long enough to procure refreshment, and then pursued our way. Turning our faces eastward we crossed one of the branches
of the river, which here flows round the foot of the
hills.

I now bade adieu to the far-famed Woo-e-shan,
certainly the most wonderful collection of hills I had
ever beheld. In a few years hence, when China
shall have been really opened to foreigners, and when
the naturalist can roam unmolested amongst these
hills, with no fear of fines and imprisonments to haunt
his imagination, he will experience a rich treat indeed.
To the geologist, in particular, this place will furnish
attractions of no ordinary kind. A Murchison may
yet visit them who will give us some idea how these
strange hills were formed, and at what period of the
world's existence they assumed those strange shapes
which are now presented to the traveller's wondering
gaze.

The direct road from Woo-e-shan to Pouching-

hien led through the city of Tsong-gan; but there
was another road which kept more to the southward,
and joined the Tsong-gan road about a day's journey
from Pouching-hien; this road I determined to take.
Our course was in an easterly direction. A small
stream, another of the tributaries of the Min, had its
source amongst the mountains in this direction, and
for a great part of the way our road led us along its
banks.

This river had many rapids, its bed was full of
large rocks and stones, and it was not navigable even
for small boats. On the morning of the third day
after leaving the Woo-e hills we arrived at the foot
of a very high range of mountains, and at the source
of the river along whose banks we had been travelling.
This was a little beyond a small town named She-
mun, where we had passed the night.

The scenery which presented itself as we ascended
the gigantic mountain surpassed anything I had seen
in China. It had quite a different character from
that of Woo-e-shan. The sides of the mountains
here were clothed with dense woods of the lance-
leaved pine (*Cunninghamia lanceolata*). This was
the first time I had seen this fir-tree of sufficient
size to render it of value for its timber. Many of the
specimens were at least eighty feet in height, and
perfectly straight. There was a richness too in the
appearance of its foliage which I had never seen
before; sometimes it was of a deep green colour, while
at others it was of a bluish tint. There are, doubtless, many varieties of this tree amongst these hills.

It must be of great value as a timber-tree in this part of China.

An excellent paved road led us up through a deep ravine. Frequently the branches of the trees met above our heads and darkened the way. Everything had a wild appearance. Streams were gushing from the mountain sides and fell over rocky precipices, when they were lost to the eye amidst the rich and tropical-looking foliage of the pines. Uniting at the bottom of the mountains, they form a river and flow onward to swell the waters of the Min.

When we had got some distance from the base of the mountain the road became so steep that I was obliged to get out of my chair and walk. Once or twice, when I found myself a considerable way in advance of my men, the road seemed so wild and lonely that I felt almost afraid. It seemed a fit place for tigers and other ferocious animals to spring upon one out of the dense brushwood. We reached the top of the pass in about an hour from the time we commenced the ascent. As the day was close and hot, I was glad to find there a small inn, where I procured some tea, which was most acceptable and refreshing.

Resting awhile on the top of the mountain I enjoyed one of those glorious prospects which well reward the traveller for all his toil, and then pursued my journey. I have already said that immense forests of the lance-leaved pine covered the sides of these mountains. Besides these the *Pinus sinensis*, camphor and tallow trees, were most abundant—the latter did not appear to be cultivated here as it is in many other parts of the country which I had passed through. Eugenias, guavas, and other myrtaceous genera were most numerous—the guava was cultivated extensively for the sake of its fruit. Some evergreen oaks,* with large glossy leaves, were also met with, and were highly ornamental. A deciduous species, not very unlike the English oak, also grew near the tops of these mountains. Azaleas were common, and I found one rhododendron.

The most beautiful bird seen during our journey was the red-billed pie. This bird is scarcely so large as the English species, is of a beautiful light-blue colour, and has several long feathers in the tail tipped with white. It is generally met with in flocks of ten or a dozen, and as they fly across the ravines with their tails spread out they look very beautiful. Several species of jay were also observed, apparently new. Pheasants, partridges, and woodcocks were plentiful and very tame. They did not seem to be molested by the Chinese sportsman. Many other small birds, which I had never seen in other parts of the country, were continually showing themselves, and making me regret that I had no means at hand of adding them to my collections. A small species of deer—the one formerly noticed—was most abundant, and I was told by the Chinese that wild boars and tigers are not unfrequently seen here.

On the third evening after leaving Woo-e-shan we arrived at a bustling little town named She-pa-ky,

* Quercus sclerophylla, Q. inversa, &c.

which was on the main road between Tsong-gan-hien
and Pouching-hien.   Here we spent the night.   Up
to this point our road had in many places been very
bad, but now we were told it was an excellent one all
the way to Pouching-hien, which was only about a
day's journey farther on.   She-pa-ky is situated in
the midst of a fine valley, which is extremely fertile.
Rice is the staple production, but I also observed
large quantities of nelumbium cultivated in the low
irrigated lands.   The rhizoma, or underground stem,
of this plant is largely used by the Chinese as an
article of food, and at the proper season of the year
is exposed for sale in all the markets.   It is cut into
small pieces and boiled, and, like the young shoots of
the bamboo, is served up in one of the small dishes
which crowd a Chinese dinner-table.   An excellent
kind of arrowroot is also made from the same part of
this useful plant.   Tobacco is also grown extensively
in this part of the country, as it is in all parts of the
province of Fokien.   The hills around this plain were
in some parts prettily covered with trees, while in
others they seemed uncultivated and barren.

As we approached Pouching-hien we again entered
a tea-country, and the shrub was observed growing
on many of the lower hills.   Whether it be owing to
the poorness of the soil, or to an inferior mode of
manipulation, I cannot say ; but Pouching teas are
not valued so highly in the market as those of Woo-
e-shan.   There is no doubt that the plant is the same
variety in both districts.

Our road, which had wound amongst hills during

the whole of the day after we left the little town of She-pa-ky, now led us into a wide and beautiful valley, in the centre of which appeared the town of Pouching-hien.   A pretty river, one of the tributaries of the Min, passes by its walls; a bridge is thrown over it at this point.   The suburbs were rather poor in appearance, and indeed the whole place did not strike me as being one of very great importance.   It is more like a country market-town than anything else. I believe it is supposed to contain about a hundred and fifty thousand inhabitants.   The walls and ramparts are apparently of a very ancient date; they are completely overgrown with weeds and straggling bushes, and are surrounded by a canal or moat, as is the case with many other Chinese towns.

A considerable trade in tea is carried on here. It is packed in baskets and sent across the mountains into Chekiang, from whence it finds its way down the rivers to Hang-chow-foo, Soo-chow-foo, and Ning-po ; but I believe little, if any, is exported.   A considerable portion is also sent down the river Min to Foo-chow-foo.

As I had left behind me the great black-tea countries of China, which have been long famed for the production of the best black teas of commerce, this seems a fit opportunity, before proceeding with the narrative of my " adventures," to condense into the next few pages all the information connected with tea which I have gleaned during my journey.

CHAPTER XV.

Some advice to the reader — Botany of the black-tea country — Geological features — Soil — Sites of tea-farms — Temperature — Rainy season — Cultivation and management of tea-plantations — Size of farms — Mode of packing — Chop names — Route from the tea-country to the coast — Method of transport — Distances — Time occupied — Original cost of tea in the tea-country — Expenses of carriage to the coast — Sums paid by the foreign merchant — Profits of the Chinese — Prospect of *good* tea becoming cheaper — Tüng-po's directions for making tea — His opinion on its properties and uses.

As this chapter is intended for the man of science and the merchant, it may not contain much of interest to the general reader, who, if he pleases, may pass it over and go on to the next. Having been thus fairly warned, he must not blame me if I bring into it some hard botanical names which are necessary to the elucidation of my subject.

It is generally admitted that nothing can give a botanist a better idea of the climate of a locality than a list of the plants which are indigenous to it. This knowledge, in the absence of thermometrical observations, is oftentimes of great value. Fully impressed with the importance of this subject, I took care to jot down in my note-book the more important species of plants which I observed, either wild or cultivated, in the great black-tea country about Woo-e-shan.

On referring to these memoranda, I find the following species enumerated: — the camphor-tree (*Laurus camphora*), various species of bamboo, the Chinese pine (*Pinus sinensis*), *Cunninghamia lanceolata*, the tallow-tree, *Vitex trifoliata*, *Buddlea Lindleyana*, *Abelia uniflora*, a spiræa like *Spiræa bella*, *Hamamelis chinensis*, *Eurya chinensis*, Macartney and other wild roses, brambles and raspberries, *Eugenias*, *Guavas* and other myrtaceous plants of a like kind, *Gardenia florida* and *G. radicans*, and various species of violets, Lycopods, and ferns. There were, of course, many other genera besides these, but enough have been mentioned to give a fair idea of the vegetation of these wonderful hills.

I have already given some account of the geological features of the Woo-e hills. As it is not unlikely that the success which has attended the cultivation of tea in this part of China may be traced to have had some connection with the peculiar formation and properties of these rocks, I may be excused if I repeat here what I have before said about them.

The rocks consist of clay-slate, in which occur embedded in the form of beds or dykes great masses of quartz rock, while granite of a deep black colour, owing to the mica, which is of a fine deep bluish black, cuts through them in all directions. This granite forms the summit of most of the principal mountains in this part of the country.

Resting on the clay-slate are sandstone conglomerates, formed principally of angular masses of quartz, held together by a calcareous basis, and alternating with these conglomerates there is a fine calcareous granular sandstone in which beds of dolomitic limestone occur.

The soil of the tea-lands about Woo-e-shan seemed to vary considerably. The most common kind was a brownish-yellow adhesive clay. This clay, when minutely examined, is found to contain a considerable portion of vegetable matter mixed with particles of the rocks above enumerated.

In the gardens on the plains at the foot of the hills the soil is of a darker colour, and contains a greater portion of vegetable matter, but generally it is either brownish yellow or reddish yellow. As a general rule the Chinese always prefer land which is moderately rich, provided other circumstances are favourable. For example, some parts of Woo-e-shan are exceedingly sterile, and produce tea of a very inferior quality. On the other hand, a hill in the same group, called Pa-ta-shan, produces the finest teas about Tsong-gan-hien. The earth on this hillside is moderately rich, that is, it contains a considerable portion of vegetable matter mixed with the clay, sand, and particles of rock.

By far the greatest portion of the tea in this part of the country is cultivated on the sloping sides of the hills. I observed a considerable quantity also in gardens on the level land in a more luxuriant state even than that on the hill-sides; but these gardens were always a considerable height above the level of the river, and were consequently well drained. It will be observed, therefore, that the tea-plants on

Woo-e-shan and the surrounding country were growing under the following circumstances :—

1. The soil was moderately rich, of a reddish colour, well mixed with particles of the rocks of the district.

2. It was kept moist by the peculiar formation of the rocks, and the water which was constantly oozing from their sides.

3. It was well drained, owing to the natural ·declivities of the hills, or, if on the plains, by being a considerable height above the watercourses.

These seem to be the essential requisites as regards soil, situation, and moisture.

Temperature.—With regard to the temperature of the country about Woo-e-shan, I must draw my conclusions from observations which were made at Foochow-foo on the one side and Shanghae on the other. At Foo-chow (lat. 25° 30' north), in the month of June and in the beginning of July, the thermometer ranged from 85° to 95° Fahr., and about the middle of the latter month it rose to 100°, which I believe it rarely exceeds. In the winter of 1844-5, during the months of November, December, and January, the maximum shown by the thermometer was 78°, and the minimum 44°. Snow is sometimes seen on the tops of the mountains, but it does not remain for any great length of time.

Shanghae is in latitude 31° 20' north. The variation of temperature here is much greater than at Foo-chow-foo. In the months of June, July, and

August the thermometer has frequently marked 105°
Fahr. This is not very different from Foo-chow as
far as the summer-heat is concerned, but we find a
great difference in winter. In the end of October
the thermometer frequently sinks as low as the
freezing-point, and the cold destroys what remains
of the cotton-crop, and those half-tropical productions
which are cultivated in the fields. December, January, and February are not unlike the same months in
the south of England, the thermometer often falls as
low as 12° Fahr., and snow covers the surface of the
ground.

With these facts before us, therefore, it will not be
very difficult to arrive at a correct estimate of the
temperature in the black-tea districts of Fokien.
Tsong-gan-hien is in latitude 27° 47′ 38″ north.
Situated as it is almost exactly between these two
places, but a little further to the westward, we shall
not be far from the truth if we suppose that the
variations of temperature are greater there than about
Foo-chow, but considerably less than about Shanghae.
I have no doubt that, taking the summer and winter
months as before, we should find that in June, July,
and August the thermometer at Woo-e-shan would
frequently rise as high as 100° Fahr., while in the
winter months of November, December, and January
it would sink to the freezing-point, or even to 28°.

Rains.—In all observations connected with the
cultivation of tea, there is another matter of great
importance to be taken into consideration, and that is
the period of the summer rains. Every one at all

acquainted with the principles of vegetable physiology must be aware that the practice of constantly pluck-ing the leaves from the tea-bushes must be very injurious to their health. But it so happens that at the period when this operation takes place there is a great deal of moisture in the air, caused by frequent showers, which fall copiously about the time when the monsoon changes from north-east to south-west. The buds burst out again with fresh vigour, and the bushes are soon covered with new leaves. After a careful consideration of this subject, it seems plain to me that, however favourable the climate may be as regards temperature, and however good the soil and situation of the plantations may be, yet without these early summer rains it would not be possible to culti-vate the tea-plant with success. This only shows how many things have to be considered before one can assign the true reason for the success of any natural production in one place, or for its failure in another.

Cultivation and management of plantations.—In the black-tea districts, as in the green, large quan-tities of young plants are yearly raised from seeds. These seeds are gathered in the month of October, and kept mixed up with sand and earth during the winter months. In this manner they are kept fresh until spring, when they are sown thickly in some corner of the farm, from which they are afterwards transplanted.* When about a year old they are from nine inches to a foot in height, and ready for

* Sometimes the seeds are sown in the rows where they are destined to grow, and, of course, are in that case not transplanted.

transplanting. They are planted in rows about four feet apart. Five or six plants are put together in each hole, and these little patches are generally about three or four feet from each other in the rows. Sometimes, however, when the soil is poor, as in many parts of Woo-e-shan, they are planted very close in the rows, and have a hedge-like appearance when they are full grown.

The young plantations are always made in spring, and are well watered by the rains which fall at the change of the monsoon in April and May. The damp, moist weather at this season enables the young plants to establish themselves in their new quarters, where they require little labour afterwards, except in keeping the ground free from weeds.

A plantation of tea, when seen at a distance, looks like a little shrubbery of evergreens. As the traveller threads his way amongst the rocky scenery of Woo-e-shan, he is continually coming upon these plantations, which are dotted upon the sides of all the hills. The leaves are of a rich dark green, and afford a pleasing contrast to the strange and often barren scenery which is everywhere around.

The natives are perfectly aware that the practice of plucking the leaves is very prejudicial to the health of the tea-shrubs, and always take care to have the plants in a strong and vigorous condition before they commence gathering. The young plantations are generally allowed to grow unmolested for two or three years, or until they are well established and are producing strong and vigorous shoots: it would be considered very bad management to begin to pluck the leaves until this is the case. Even when the plantations were in full bearing I observed that the natives never took many leaves from the weaker plants, and sometimes passed them altogether, in order that their growth might not be checked.

But, under the best mode of treatment, and with the most congenial soil, the plants ultimately become stunted and unhealthy, and are never profitable when they are old: hence in the best-managed tea-districts the natives yearly remove old plantations and supply their places with fresh ones. The length of time which a plantation will remain in full bearing depends of course on a variety of circumstances, but with the most careful treatment, consistent with profit, the plants will not do much good after they are ten or twelve years old; they are often dug up and the space replanted before that time.

Size of tea farms and mode of packing.—The tea-farms about Tsong-gan, Tsin-tsun, and Woo-e-shan are generally small in extent. No single farm which came under my observation could have produced a chop of 600 chests. But what are called chops are not made up by the growers or small farmers, but in the following manner:—A tea-merchant from Tsong-gan or Tsin-tsun goes himself or sends his agents to all the small towns, villages, and temples in the district, to purchase teas from the priests and small farmers. When the teas so purchased are taken to his house, they are then mixed together, of course keeping the different qualities as much apart as pos-

sible.   By this means a chop of 620 or 630 chests
is made, and all the tea of this chop is of the same
description or class.*   If it was not managed in this
way there would be several different kinds of tea in
one chop.   The large merchant in whose hands it is
now has to refire it and pack it for the foreign
market.

When the chests are packed the name of the chop
is written upon each.   Year after year the same
chops, or rather chops having the same names, find
their way into the hands of the foreign merchant.
Some have consequently a higher name and command a higher price than others.   It does not follow,
however, that the chop of this year, bought from the
same man, and bearing the same name as a good one
of last year, will be of equal quality.   Mr. Shaw
informed me that it was by no means unusual for the
merchant who prepares and packs the tea to leave
his chests unmarked until they are bought by the
man who takes them to the port of exportation.
This man, knowing the chop names most in request,
can probably find a good one to put upon his boxes ;
at all events he will take good care not to put upon
them a name that is not in good repute.

*Route of teas from the black-tea country to Canton
and Shanghae.*—My principal object in collecting
the information that follows was to ascertain, if
possible, the precise amount of charges upon each

---

* Sometimes a chop or parcel is divided into two packings, consisting
generally of 300 chests each.—BALL's " *Cultivation and Manufacture
of Tea.*"

chest or picul of tea when it arrives at the port whence it is to be exported. If I am able to give this information with any degree of accuracy, we shall then see what amount of profits the Chinese have been in the habit of making by this trade, and whether there is any probability of their being able to lower their prices, and so, with a reduction of our own import duties, to place a healthful and agreeable beverage—

> " The cup
> That cheers, but not inebriates,"—

within the reach of the whole of our population.

I shall, therefore, endeavour to give a description of the route by which the black teas are brought from the country where they are made to the ports of exportation—Canton or Shanghae. We have already seen that nearly all the teas grown in the fine districts about Woo-e-shan are brought to the city of Tsong-gan-hien by the merchants who buy them from the small tea-farmers, and that they are there made into chops, and sold to the dealers connected with the foreign tea-trade, the chief part of whom are Canton men.

A chop of tea having been purchased by one of these merchants, a number of coolies are engaged to carry the chests northward, across the Bohea mountains, to Hokow, or rather to the small town of Yuen-shan, a few miles from Hokow, to which it is sent by boat. If the teas are of the common kind, each coolie carries two chests slung over his shoulders on his favourite bamboo. These chests are often much knocked about during the journey over the steep and rugged mountains, as it is frequently necessary to rest them on the ground, which is often wet and dirty. The finest teas, however, as I have already stated, are never allowed to touch the ground, but are carried on the shoulders of the coolies.

The distance from Tsong-gan-hien to Yuen-shan is 220 le, or to Hokow 280 le. A merchant can perform it in his chair in three or four days, but coolies heavily laden with tea-chests require at least five or six days.

In the country about Yuen-shan and Hokow— that is, on the northern side of the great mountain range—a large quantity of tea is cultivated and manufactured for the foreign market. Thousands of acres were observed under tea-cultivation, but apparently the greater part of this land had been cleared and planted within the last few years. The teas made here, as well as those on the southern side of the Bohea mountains, are brought to Hokow on their way to one of the ports of exportation. What are called Moning or Ning-chow teas, made in a country further to the westward, near to the Poyang lake, are also brought up the river, and pass Hokow on their way to Shanghae.

The town of Hokow—or Hohow, as it is commonly called by Canton men—is situated in latitude 29° 54′ north, and longitude 116° 18′ east. It stands on the banks of the river Kin-keang,* which

---

* This is the name the river bears near its mouth. Further up it is called in the map Long-shia-tong-ho.

rises amongst the hills to the north-east of Yuk-shan, and, flowing westward, empties its waters into the Poyang lake. Hokow is a large and flourishing town, abounding in tea-hongs, which are resorted to by merchants from all parts of China. Many of these men make their purchases here, without going further, while others cross the Bohea mountains to Tsong-gan-hien. When China is really opened to foreigners, and when our merchants are able to go into the country to make their own purchases of black teas, Hokow will probably be chosen by them as a central place of residence, from which they can radiate to Woo-e-shan and Ning-chow, as well as to the green-tea country of Mo-yuen, in Hwuy-chow.

The teas, having arrived at Hokow, are put into large flat-bottomed boats, and proceed on their journey either to Canton or to Shanghae. If intended for the Canton market, they proceed down the river in a westerly direction towards the Poyang lake. Ball says that they are "conducted to the towns of Nan-chang-foo and Kan-chew-foo, and then suffer many transshipments on their way to the pass of Ta-moey-ling, in that part of the same chain of mountains which divides Kiang-see from Quan-tung. At this pass the teas are again carried by porters; the journey occupies one day, when they are re-shipped in large vessels, which convey them to Canton. The time occupied in the entire transport from the Bohea country to Canton is about six weeks or two months."*

If intended for the Shanghae market, the tea-

* Cultivation and Manufacture of Tea.

boats proceed up the river, in an easterly direction, to the town of Yuk-shan. This place is in latitude 28° 45' north, in longitude 118° 28' east, and distant from Hokow 180 le. The stream runs very rapidly, and, upon an average, at least four days are required for this part of the journey. In coming down the river the same distance is easily accomplished in one day.

When the tea-chests arrive at Yuk-shan they are taken from the boats to a warehouse. An engagement is then entered into with coolies, who carry them across the country, in an easterly direction, to Chang-shan, in the same manner as they were brought from Tsong-gan to Hokow. The town of Yuk-shan is at the head of a river which flows west to the Poyang lake, while that of Chang-shan is situated on an important river which falls into the bay of Hang-chow on the east. The distance across the country from one town to the other is about 100 le. Travellers in chairs accomplish it easily in one day, but coolies laden with tea-chests require two or three days.

When the teas arrive at Chang-shan they are put into boats and conveyed down the river. The distance from Chang-shan to Hang-chow is about 800 le, and as it is all down-stream it may be performed in five or six days with perfect ease. At Hang-chow the chests are transshipped from the river boats to those which ply upon the canals, and in the latter are taken on to Shanghae. The distance from Hang-chow-foo to Shanghae is 500 le, and occupies about five days.

We have traced in this manner the route which the black teas travel on their way from Woo-e-shan to Shanghae. The distance travelled and time occupied will stand thus :—

	Le.	Days.
Tsong-gan-hien to Hokow	280	6
Hokow to Yuk-shan	180	4
Yuk-shan to Chang-shan	100	3
Chang-shan to Hang-chow-foo.	800	6
Hang-chow-foo to Shanghae	500	5
Total	1860	24

Three le are generally supposed to be equal to one English mile, and in that case the exact distance would be, of course, 620 miles. I am inclined, however, to think that there are more than three le to a mile, perhaps four, or in some parts of the country even five. If this is the case we may be possibly nearer the mark if we estimate the whole distance at 400 miles. In calculating the time it will be necessary to allow about four days for time consumed in changing boats, for bad weather, &c. This will make the whole journey occupy 28 days, which is about the average time.

With regard to the next item in my account,— namely, the cost and expenses upon these teas,—I must confess that I cannot speak with the same confidence of accuracy as I have done on the previous items. Having myself travelled up and down their rivers, and over their mountains, I was in no necessity of depending at all upon Chinese statements having reference to distance or time. Their statements upon all subjects, and especially upon those relating to the interior of their country, must be received with a great degree of caution. I have, however, been favoured with the assistance of Mr. Shaw, of Shanghae, who adds to his abilities as a merchant a knowledge of the Chinese language, which enabled him to give me valuable aid in the item of *expense*.

In the first place, let us examine the expenses upon what is called good common Congou. By this is meant such tea as was selling in England in December, 1848, at about 8*d.* per pound. This tea was sold in Shanghae at about 12 taels per picul in 1846, 11 taels in 1847, from 9 to 10 taels in 1848, and 11 taels in July, 1849. These prices included the export duty.

I will suppose this tea to be brought from the town of Tsong-gan-hien by the route which I have already described. The expenses for coolie and boat hire upon it will be nearly as follows:—

	Cash.	
Tsong-gan-hien to Hokow (by land) . . .	800	per chest.
Hokow to Yuk-shan (by water)	150	,,
Yuk-shan to Chang-shan (by land)	400	,,
Chang-shan to Hang-chow-foo (by water) . .	200	,,
Expenses for coolies at Hang-chow-foo . . .	10	,,
Hang-chow-foo to Shanghae (by water) . .	180	,,
Total for carriage	1740	,,

1740 cash per chest would amount to 2718 cash per picul, which, converted into silver, would be about 1 dollar 80 cents, or 1.359 taels. To this sum must be added the cost of tea in the tea-country, the expenses of the wholesale dealers for inspection, charcoal, and labour in extra firing, the cost of the chest and packing, and custom-house and export duties.

Such tea as that above referred to is sold by the cultivators and small farmers at about 80 cash a catty, which is equal to 4 taels per picul. The following table will show the total amount of these expenses:—

Cost of tea at 80 cash per catty . . .	4	taels per picul.
Do. of chest and packing	0·847	,,
Wholesale dealer's extra expenses . .	1	,,
Carriage, as above	1·359	,,
Hang-chow-foo custom-house . . .	0·037	,,
Export duty at Shanghae	2·530	,,
	9·773	,,

If these different items are as correct as I believe them to be, it would appear that the profit upon common teas is very small, so small indeed as to make it a matter of doubt whether they will ever be produced at a reduced rate.

It must be borne in mind, however, that all the expenses just enumerated, excepting the original cost of tea, are as heavy upon the common kinds as upon those of a finer quality, for which much higher prices are paid. Take for example the good and middling Ohows, and finest teas, which sold in Shanghae, December 1846, at from 20 to 28 taels, long price;* in 1847 at 18 to 26 taels; in 1848 at 14 to 22 taels; and in July 1849 at 16 to 25 taels per picul. Such tea in November 1847 was worth from 1s. to 1s. 4d. per lb. in England.

These fine teas are said to be sold by the small farmers to the dealers at, on an average, 160 cash a

* Long price [l. p.] means that the export duty is included.

catty, a sum probably higher than that which is actually paid. But suppose 160 cash per catty is the original cost, the matter would stand thus:—

Cost of tea at 160 cash per catty . . . 8   taels per picul.
Total charges, as before, less the cost of tea 5·773   ,,
                                              ─────────
                                              13·773   ,,

In round numbers, the whole cost of bringing these fine teas to the port of Shanghae is 14 taels. The average price received from the English merchant during these four years appears, from the above prices, to have been about 22 taels, thus showing a clear profit of 8 taels per picul.

Before drawing our conclusions, however, it may be proper to mention that in the years 1846 and 1847 the trade in Shanghae was chiefly carried on by barter, which was managed through some Canton brokers then resident in Shanghae. Under these circumstances, it was difficult for any one not in the brokers' secret to say what was the exact sum paid to the Tsong-gan tea-dealer. It was probably, however, something considerably less than what it appears to have been by the above statements. Again, it is to be remarked that in 1848, when the prices were from 14 to 22 taels, the Chinese complained that they were ruinously low. But the average of even these prices would be 18 taels, thus showing an average profit of 4 taels per picul. Considering that this large trade is in comparatively few hands, even this, the lowest class of profits, must amount to a very large sum. It seems even a question whether the

Chinese dealers and brokers could not be amply remunerated by a lower price than any yet quoted.

The above statements would seem to show that it is greatly to the interest of the Chinese merchant to encourage the production of the finer classes of tea, those being the kinds upon which he gets the largest profits.

I have now shown in detail the cost of the different classes of tea in the tea country, the distance which it has to travel before it reaches the seaport towns, and the total expenses upon it when it reaches the hands of the foreign merchant. It forms no part of my plan to say what ought to be a sufficient remuneration for the Chinese tea-dealer or broker;* but if the above calculations are near the truth, we may still hope to drink our favourite beverage, at least the middling and finer qualities of it, at a price much below that which we now pay.

While I encourage such hopes, let me confer a boon upon my countrywomen, who never look so charming as at the breakfast-table, by a quotation or two from a Chinese author's advice to a nation of tea-drinkers how best to make tea. "Whenever the tea is to be infused for use," says Tüng-po, "take water from a running stream, and boil it over a lively fire. It is an old custom to use running water boiled over a lively fire; that from springs in the hills is said to be the best, and river-water the next, while well-water is the worst. A lively fire is a clear and bright charcoal fire.

* I do not think the small farmer and manipulator is overpaid; the great profits are received by the middlemen.

" When making an infusion, do not boil the water too hastily, as first it begins to sparkle like crabs' eyes, then somewhat like fish's eyes, and lastly it boils up like pearls innumerable, springing and waving about.   This is the way to boil the water."

The same author gives the names of six different kinds of tea, all of which are in high repute.   As their names are rather flowery, I quote them for the reader's amusement.   They are these: the "first spring tea," the "white dew," the "coral dew," the "dewy shoots," the "money shoots," and the "rivulet garden tea."

" Tea," says he, " is of a cooling nature, and, if drunk too freely, will produce exhaustion and lassitude ; country people before drinking it add ginger and salt to counteract this cooling property.   It is an exceedingly useful plant ; cultivate it, and the benefit will be widely spread ; drink it, and the animal spirits will be lively and clear.   The chief rulers, dukes, and nobility esteem it; the lower people, the poor and beggarly, will not be destitute of it; all use it daily, and like it."   Another author upon tea says that "drinking it tends to clear away all impurities, drives off drowsiness, removes or prevents headache, and it is universally in high esteem."

CHAPTER XVI.

Geography of the tea-shrub — Best tea districts of China — Names of
tea-plants — Black and green tea made from the same variety — My
Chinamen asked to make tea from *Pongamia glabra* — They succeed ! — Difference between black and green tea depends upon manipulation — Method of making green tea — Of making black — Difference in the manipulation of the two kinds — Mr. Warrington's
remarks on this subject — A familiar illustration — The tea-plant
— Inferior teas made from *Thea bohea* — Best teas made from *Thea
viridis* — The Woo-e-shan variety — The tea-plant affected by climate and reproduction — Tea cultivation in America and Australia
— In English gardens.

THE cultivation of the tea-shrub, although confined,
until very lately, to the eastern parts of Asia, is
carried on over a large tract of country. Thunberg
informs us that it grows plentifully in Japan both in
a wild and cultivated state, and Dr. Wallich says that
it is found in Cochin China. I have met with it in
cultivation in China, from Canton in the south up to
the 31st degree of north latitude, and Mr. Reeves
says it is found in the province of Shan-tung, near the
city of Tang-chow-foo, in latitude 36° 30' north.

The principal tea districts of China, however, and
those which supply the greater portion of the teas
exported to Europe and America, lie between the
25th and 31st degrees of north latitude, and the best
districts are those between 27° and 31°.

The plant in cultivation about Canton, from which

the Canton teas are made, is known to botanists as
the *Thea bohea*, while the more northern variety,
found in the green-tea country, has been called *Thea
viridis*.   The first appears to have been named upon
the supposition that all the black teas of the Bohea
mountains were obtained from this species, and the
second was called *viridis* because it furnished the
green teas of commerce.   These names seem to have
misled the public, and hence many persons, until a
few years back, firmly believed that black tea could
be made only from *Thea bohea*, and green tea only from
Thea viridis.

In my 'Wanderings in China,' published in 1846,
I made some observations upon the plants from which
tea is made in different parts of China.   While I
acknowledged that the Canton plant, known to botanists as *Thea bohea*, appeared distinct from the more
northern one called *Thea viridis*, I endeavoured to
show that both black and green teas could be made
from either, and that the difference in the appearance
of these teas, in so far as colour was concerned, depended upon manipulation, and upon that only.   In
proof of this I remarked that the black-tea plant
found by me near Foo-chow-foo, at no great distance
from the Bohea hills, appeared identical with the
green-tea plant of Chekiang.

These observations were met by the objection, that,
although I had been in many of the tea districts near
the coast, yet I had not seen those greater ones inland
which furnish the teas of commerce.   And this was
perfectly true.   The same objection can hardly be

urged now, however, as I have visited both the green-
tea country of Hwuy-chow, and the black-tea districts
about Woo-e-shan, and during these long journeys
I have seen no reason to alter the opinions I had previously formed upon the subject.

It is quite true that the Chinese rarely make the
two kinds of tea in one district, but this is more for
the sake of convenience and from custom than for any
other reason. The workmen, too, generally make
that kind of tea best with which they have had most
practice. But while this is generally the case in the
great tea districts, there are some exceptions. It is
now well known that the fine Moning districts near
the Poyang Lake, which are daily rising in importance on account of the superior character of their
black teas, formerly produced nothing else but *green*
teas. At Canton green and black teas are made from
the *Thea bohea* at the pleasure of the manufacturer,
and according to demand.

But I must relate an occurrence that took place on
my arrival at Calcutta, which is more curious than
the making of black and green teas from one variety
or species of the tea-plant. I was then on my way to the
Government tea plantations in the north-west provinces
of India, with six Chinese tea-manufacturers, and a
large supply of plants and implements used in making
tea. Dr. Falconer, of the Calcutta garden, with
whom we were staying for a few days, expressed a
wish to see the process of tea manufacture, and asked
me to communicate his wishes to the Chinamen. He
also invited the late Mr. Bethune and some other

friends to witness the operation. I told the Chinese what was proposed, and desired them to unpack a sufficient number of implements for the purpose. This was soon done, a little furnace built, and two pans fixed above the fireplaces, exactly as they are seen in the manufactories in China.

Thus far everything went on well, but where were the tea-leaves to be procured? There were none in the Calcutta garden, nor in any place nearer than the Himalayas. "How can we make tea without tea-leaves?" said the astonished Chinamen. I now explained to them that Dr. Falconer and his friends wanted to see the mode of manipulation only, that the article so made was to look at, not to drink, and that they must go out into the garden and try to find a substitute for tea-leaves. This explanation being deemed satisfactory, they went out to examine the trees of the garden. In a short space of time they returned bringing several parcels of leaves, one of which proved to belong to *Pongamia glabra*, and seemed the most likely to suit the purpose. Orders were now given to some of the natives to collect a large quantity of these leaves and bring them into the room which had been fitted up for the occasion.

In the mean time the Chinamen had the fires lighted and everything in readiness to commence operations. The leaves were now thrown into the pans and heated for a few minutes, then taken out and rolled, then shaken out thinly on bamboo trays to dry off the superfluous moisture, and finally thrown again into the pans and tossed about by the hand until perfectly twisted and dry. They were afterwards sifted and sorted into the various kinds known as hyson skin, hyson, young hyson, imperial, and gunpowder. Some of the sorts were refired several times, and portions of some of them were coloured. When the operations were completed, the samples were so like the teas of commerce, that nineteen persons out of twenty would never have suspected them to be anything else. Here, then, were very fair-looking green teas made from the leaves of a large tree, as unlike the tea-shrub as it could well be. And an article as closely resembling black tea could have been just as easily made out of these leaves.

It is not my intention to enter minutely into the subject of the manipulation of black and green teas, but I will point out, in as few words as possible, the method of treating each kind during the process of manufacture. These methods, it will be observed, differ from each other in some material points, which are quite sufficient to account for the difference in colour. It is scarcely necessary to remark that both kinds of tea are gathered from the bushes in the same way, and are made from the same description of leaves, namely, those which are young and lately formed.

Green tea.—When the leaves are brought in from the plantations they are spread out thinly on flat bamboo trays, in order to dry off any superfluous moisture. They remain for a very short time exposed in this manner, generally from one to two hours; this however depends much upon the state of the weather.

In the mean time the roasting-pans have been heated with a brisk wood fire. A portion of leaves are now thrown into each pan and rapidly moved about and shaken up with both hands. They are immediately affected by the heat, begin to make a crackling noise, and become quite moist and flaccid, while at the same time they give out a considerable portion of vapour. They remain in this state for four or five minutes, and are then drawn quickly out and placed upon the rolling table.

The rolling process now commences. Several men take their stations at the rolling table and divide the leaves amongst them. Each takes as many as he can press with his hands, and makes them up in the form of a ball. This is rolled upon the rattan worked table, and greatly compressed, the object being to get rid of a portion of the sap and moisture, and at the same time to twist the leaves. These balls of leaves are frequently shaken out and passed from hand to hand until they reach the head workman, who examines them carefully to see if they have taken the requisite twist. When he is satisfied of this the leaves are removed from the rolling table and shaken out upon flat trays, until the remaining portions have undergone the same process. In no case are they allowed to lie long in this state, and sometimes they are taken at once to the roasting-pan.

Having been thrown again into the pan, a slow and steady charcoal fire is kept up, and the leaves are kept in rapid motion by the hands of the workmen. Sometimes they are thrown upon the rattan table and rolled a second time. In about an hour or an hour and a half the leaves are well dried and their colour has become *fixed*, that is, there is no longer any danger of their becoming black. They are of a dullish green colour, but become brighter afterwards.*

The most particular part of the operation has now been finished, and the tea may be put aside until a larger quantity has been made. The second part of the process consists in winnowing and passing the tea through sieves of different sizes, in order to get rid of the dust and other impurities, and to divide the tea into the different kinds known as twankay, hyson skin, hyson, young hyson, gunpowder, &c. During this process it is refired, the coarse kinds once, and the finer sorts three or four times. By this time the colour has come out more fully, and the leaves of the finer kinds are of a dull bluish green.

It will be observed, then, with reference to green tea—1st, that the leaves are roasted almost immediately after they are gathered ; and 2nd, that they are dried off quickly after the rolling process.

Black tea.—When the leaves are brought in from the plantations they are spread out upon large bamboo mats or trays, *and are allowed to lie in this state for a considerable time.* If they are brought in at night they lie until next morning.

The leaves are next gathered up by the workmen with both hands, thrown into the air and allowed to separate and fall down again. They are tossed about in this manner, and slightly beat or patted with the

* I am not now alluding to teas which are coloured artificially.

hands, for a considerable space of time.   At length, when they become soft and flaccid, they are thrown in heaps and allowed to lie in this state for about an hour or perhaps a little longer.   When examined at the end of this time, they appear to have undergone a slight change in colour, are soft and moist, and emit a fragrant smell.

The next part of the process is exactly the same as in the manipulation of green tea.   The leaves are thrown into an iron pan, where they are roasted for about five minutes and then rolled upon the rattan table.

After being rolled, the leaves are shaken out, thinly, on sieves, and exposed to the air out of doors. A framework for this purpose, made of bamboo, is generally seen in front of all the cottages amongst the tea-hills.   The leaves are allowed to remain in this condition for about three hours: during this time the workmen are employed in going over the sieves in rotation, turning the leaves and separating them from each other.   A fine dry day, when the sun is not too bright, seems to be preferred for this part of the operation.

The leaves, having now lost a large portion of their moisture, and having become reduced considerably in size, are removed into the factory.   They are put a second time into the roasting-pan for three or four minutes, and taken out and rolled as before.

The charcoal fires are now got ready.   A tubular basket, narrow at the middle and wide at both ends, is placed over the fire.   A sieve is dropped into this

tube and covered with leaves, which are shaken on it
to about an inch in thickness. After five or six
minutes, during which time they are carefully watched,
they are removed from the fire and rolled a third
time. As the balls of leaves come from the hands of
the roller they are placed in a heap until the whole
have been rolled. They are again shaken on the
sieves as before and set over the fire for a little while
longer. Sometimes the last operation, namely, heating and rolling, is repeated a fourth time: the leaves
have now assumed their dark colour.

When the whole has been gone over in this
manner it is then placed thickly in the baskets,
which are again set over the charcoal fire. The
workman now makes a hole with his hand through
the centre of the leaves, in order to allow vent to any
smoke or vapour which may rise from the charcoal,
as well as to let the heat up, and then covers the
whole over with a flat basket: previous to this the
heat has been greatly reduced by the fires being
covered up. The tea now remains over the slow
charcoal fire until it is perfectly dry; it is, however,
carefully watched by the manufacturer, who every
now and then stirs it up with his hands, so that the
whole may be equally heated. The black colour is
now fairly brought out, but afterwards improves in
appearance: the after processes, such as sifting, pick-
ing, and refining, are carried on at the convenience of
the workmen.*

* If the reader is desirous of obtaining more information upon this subject, he should consult Mr. Ball's ' Cultivation and Manufacture of Tea.'

It will be remarked, therefore, with reference to the leaves which are to be converted into black tea,— 1st, that they are allowed to lie for some time spread out in the factory after being gathered and before they are roasted; 2nd, that they are tossed about until they become soft and flaccid, and then left in heaps, and that this also is done before they are roasted; 3rd, that after being roasted for a few minutes and rolled, they are exposed for some hours to the air in a soft and moist state; and 4th, that they are at last dried slowly over charcoal fires. The differences in the manufacture of black and green teas are therefore most marked, and I think fully account for the difference in colour, as well as for the effect produced on some constitutions by green tea, such as nervous irritability, sleeplessness, &c. This is shown in some observations made by Mr. Warrington, of Apothecaries' Hall, in his paper which I have already quoted.

"The question presents itself, then," says Mr. Warrington, alluding to the variation of physical and chemical properties in green and black teas, "from whence do these distinguishing peculiarities arise, and to what are they to be attributed? From observations made in other directions, in the course of the routine work of the establishment to which I am attached, I had formed in my own mind certain conclusions on this subject. I allude to the exsiccation of medicinal herbs; these are for the most part nitrogenous plants, as the *Atropa belladonna*, the *Hyoscyamus niger*, the *Conium maculatum*, and others.

The plants are brought to us by the growers or col-
lectors from the country, tied up in bundles, and
when they arrive fresh and cool they dry of a good
bright green colour; but on the contrary, it is found
that if they are delayed in their transit, or remain in
a confined state for too long a period, they become
heated, from a species of spontaneous fermentation,
and when loosened and spread open emit vapours,
and are sensibly warm to the hand: when such
plants are dried, the whole of the *green colour* is
found to have been destroyed, and a *red-brown* and
sometimes a *blackish-brown result* is obtained.   I had
also noticed that a clear infusion of such leaves eva-
porated carefully to dryness was not *all* undissolved
by *water*, but left a quantity of *brown oxidised extractive matter*, to which the denomination *Apothem*
has been applied by some chemists; a similar result
is obtained by the evaporation of an infusion of black
tea.   The same action takes place by the exposure
of the infusions of many vegetable substances to the
oxidising influence of the atmosphere; they become
darkened on the surface, and this gradually spreads
through the solution, and on evaporation the same
oxidised extractive matter will remain insoluble in
water.   Again, I had found that the green teas, when
wetted and re-dried, with exposure to the air, were
nearly as dark in colour as the ordinary black teas.
From these observations, therefore, I was induced to
believe that the peculiar characters and chemical differences which distinguish black tea from green were
to be attributed to a species of heating or fermenta-

tion, accompanied with oxidation by exposure to the
air, and not to its being submitted to a higher temperature in the process of drying, as had been generally concluded. My opinion was partly confirmed
by ascertaining from parties conversant with the
Chinese manufacture, that the leaves for the black
teas were always allowed to remain exposed to the
air in mass for some time before they were roasted."

Here, then, we have the matter fully and clearly
explained; and, in truth, what Mr. Warrington observed in the laboratory of Apothecaries' Hall may
be seen by every one who has a tree or bush in his
garden. Mark the leaves which are blown from trees
in early autumn; they are brown, or perhaps of a
dullish green, when they fall, and yet, if they are examined some time afterwards, when they have been
exposed to air and moisture in their detached state,
they will be found quite as black as our blackest
teas.

I must now make some observations upon the tea-
plant itself. It has already been remarked that two
tea-plants, considered to be distinct varieties, are met
with in China, both of which have been imported into
Europe. One, the Canton variety, is called *Thea
bohea;* the other, the northern variety, is called *Thea
viridis.* The former produces the inferior green and
black teas which are made about Canton, and from
the latter are made all the fine green teas in the great
Hwuy-chow country and in the adjoining provinces.
Until a few years back it was generally supposed that
the fine black teas of the Bohea hills were also made

from the Canton variety, and hence its name. Such, however, is not the case.

When I visited Foo-chow-foo for the first time in 1845, I observed that the tea-plant in cultivation in that neighbourhood was very different from the Canton variety, and apparently identical with the *Thea viridis* of Chekiang. Foo-chow-foo was not a very great distance from the Bohea hills, and I had good reasons for believing that the Bohea plant was the same as the Foo-chow one; but still I had no positive proof. Now, however, having been on Woo-e-shan itself, and over a great deal of the surrounding country, and having dried specimens of all these plants before me, I am better able to give an opinion upon this long-disputed subject.

I believe that the Woo-e-shan plant is closely allied to the *Thea viridis* and originally identical with that species, but slightly altered by climate. On the closest examination I was only able to detect very slight differences, not sufficient to constitute a distinct variety, far less a species, and in many of the plants these differences were not even visible. The differences alluded to were these—the Woo-e plant showed less inclination to throw out branches than the Hwuy-chow one, and its leaves were sometimes rather darker and more finely serrated.

But it is possible to go into a tea-plantation in any part of China, and to find more marked distinctions amongst its plants than these I have noticed. The reason of this is obvious. The tea-plant is multiplied by seed like our hawthorns, and it is perfectly impossible that the produce can be identical in every respect with the parent.   Instead therefore of having one or two varieties of tea-plant in China, we have in fact many kinds, although the difference between them may be slight.   Add to this, that the seeds of this plant are raised year after year in different climates, and we shall no longer wonder that in the course of time the plants in one district appear slightly different from those of another, although they may have been originally produced from the same stock.

For these reasons I am of opinion that the plants of Hwuy-chow and Woo-e are the same species, and that the slight differences observed are the results of reproduction and difference of climate.

With regard to the Canton plant—that called *Thea bohea* by botanists—different as it appears to be, both in constitution and habit, it too may have originally sprung from one and the same species.

These changes, however, do not alter the commercial value of those plants found cultivated in the great tea-countries of Fokien and Hwuy-chow, where the finest teas are produced; for, while the tea-shrub may have improved in the course of reproduction in these districts, it may have become deteriorated in others.   For this reason seeds and plants ought always to be procured from these districts for transmission to other parts of the world where it is desirable to grow tea.

Of late years some attempts have been made to cultivate the tea-shrub in the United States of America, and also in our own Australian colonies.*   I believe all such attempts will end in failure and disappointment.   The tea-plant will grow wherever the climate and soil are suitable, and, were it merely intended as an ornamental shrub, there could be no objections to its introduction into those countries. But if it is introduced to be cultivated as an object of commercial speculation, we must not only inquire into the suitableness of climate and soil, but also into the price of labour.   Labour is cheap in China.   The labourers in the tea-countries do not receive more than twopence or threepence a day.   Can workmen be procured for this small sum either in the United States or in Australia ?   And if they cannot be hired for this sum, nor for anything near it, how will the manufacturers in such places be able to compete with the Chinese in the market ?

The tea-plants of China are common enough in this country.   In the Royal Botanic Garden at Kew they have been growing in the open air for some years.   They are also to be met with in many other gardens, and almost in every nursery.   They are pretty evergreen bushes, and produce a profusion of single white flowers in the winter and spring, about the time that camellias are in bloom.   It is not, however, for the beauty of their flowers that they are grown—although there is much in them to admire—but on account of their being the plants which produce our favourite beverage.

* I shall have to speak of tea cultivation in India in a future chapter.

Those persons in England who possess tea-plants, and who cultivate them for pleasure, should always bear in mind that, even in the tea-districts of China, this shrub will not succeed when planted in low wet land: and this is doubtless one of the reasons why so few persons succeed in growing it in this country. It ought always to be planted on a warm sloping bank, in order to give it a fair chance of success. If some of the warm spots of this kind in the south of England or Ireland were selected, who knows but our cottagers might be able to grow their own tea? at all events they might have the fragrant herb to look upon.

CHAPTER XVII.

Inn at Pouching-hien — Opium-smokers and gamblers — Value of life
in China — A midnight disturbance — Sing-Hoo fights with a joss-
stick — Difficulty of procuring men next day — Sing-Hoo carries the
luggage, and we march — His bamboo breaks — Scene amongst
beggars — Description of beggars in China — A "king of the
beggars" — Charity always given — I continue my journey —
Mountain passes and Buddhist temples — A border town and Tartar
guard — We are inspected and allowed to pass on.

HAVING left tea and the tea-hills behind me, I shall
now go on with my narrative. When I arrived at
the city of Pouching-hien it was nearly dark. It
had been raining heavily all the afternoon, and, being
wet and uncomfortable, I was glad of the shelter
afforded by a Chinese inn. The one which I entered
did not appear to be so respectable as I could have
wished, and I would have left it and sought another
had the weather been better, but as the night was so
wet I determined to stop where I was.

The chair-bearers and coolie, who had been re-
engaged at Woo-e-shan, had now arrived at the end
of their journey, according to agreement, and intended returning home again next day. They generally took care to be paid the proportion of their fare
at the end of each day's journey, and I now desired
Sing-Hoo to pay them the remainder and get rid of
them as soon as possible. He informed me he had

done so, but that they intended to remain in the same inn with ourselves for the night.

A hot dinner was at length placed upon the table. Rough and unpalatable as this would have appeared in other circumstances, I was now so accustomed to the Chinese style of living, that what was placed before me seemed tempting enough, and I believe I did full justice to it. My chair-bearers, having received their wages, were now seated at a side-table in another room absorbed in the mysteries of gambling, and Sing-Hoo was quietly smoking his pipe with the landlord. A number of other travellers were also loitering about, some of whom had an appearance which did not produce a favourable impression on me. They were evidently opium-smokers, from the sallow colour of their cheeks, probably gamblers, and altogether such characters as one would rather avoid than be on intimate terms with.

It still continued to rain heavily, and as all out of doors seemed dark and dismal, and all within uninviting, I retired early to rest. Tired with the exertions of the day, I was soon fast asleep in spite of my suspicious inn and strange companions. It might have been about midnight when I was awakened by the sounds of angry voices, and amongst them I could distinguish those of my chair-bearers and Sing-Hoo. I jumped up with strong suspicions that something serious was about to happen to us. The noise still increased, and, from the scuffle which reached my ears, I feared they were seizing my servant with the intention of robbing us, and perhaps of taking our lives.

U

Human life is not much valued in some parts of the country, and the province of Fokien does not bear a high character, and for aught I knew I might be in a den of thieves and robbers. Sing-Hoo, but a short time before, had been telling me of an occurrence which took place in the wild mountain country between Hoo-chow-foo—the famous silk town—and Hwuy-chow, his native place. Four travellers, he said, took up their quarters one evening in an inn on the roadside. They called for a good dinner, and afterwards smoked opium and gambled until nearly midnight. Next morning three of them paid their bills of fare and took their departure, but the fourth was nowhere visible. His body was afterwards found in a pit near the house, doubled up in his own box, and from its appearance there was no doubt the man had met with a violent death from the hands of his companions.

With this story in my mind, I could not endure the suspense any longer, and throwing on my clothes I opened the door and walked into the place where the disturbance was. What I saw was quite sufficient to alarm a bolder man, and yet there was something in it laughable too. Eight or ten stout fellows, including the chair-bearers, were attacking my servant, who was standing, like a tiger at bay, up against the wall of the house. He had a large joss-stick in his hand which every now and then he was poking at the faces of those who threatened to close with him. The most adventurous sometimes got a poke which sent them back, cursing and swearing, rather faster than they came. The whole scene brought vividly to my mind Bailie Nicol Jarvie's fight with the red-hot poker, so admirably described by Sir Walter Scott.

Had I been an uninterested spectator, I might have enjoyed a hearty laugh at the scene before me; but I was in the midst of a strange country and hostile people, and, being the weaker party, I felt really alarmed. The only weapon in my possession was a small pocket-pistol, one of those which are loaded by unscrewing the barrel. Thinking that if matters came to the worst this might be of some use, either in frightening our assailants or in saving my life, I went back to my bed-room and got it out. When I examined it I found that the wet had rusted the barrel, and it would not unscrew; it was therefore of no use.

The noise still continued, and if possible got louder. I determined, therefore, to present a bold front, and walked straight in amongst the combatants, clearing a space between my servant and the others, and asked the reason of the disturbance. My chair-bearers and coolie, who had always treated me with every respect, immediately fell back in the rear, grumbling at the same time about some cash which they had not received. On inquiring into the business, I found that Sing-Hoo, Chinaman-like, not content with what he got from me, had been trying to *squeeze* the chair-bearers and coolie out of 300 cash —about a shilling of our money. He denied the accusation most stoutly, but I had no doubt in my own mind that what the men said was true; besides

I was not going to have a disturbance, and perhaps
lose my life, for a shilling, so I ordered him to pay
the money without further delay.

This had the effect of restoring something like
quietness to the house. I now ordered Sing-Hoo
into my room and shut the door. The business, however, had gone too far, for the other men were
highly incensed at his conduct, and threatened to be
revenged upon him. For hours after this I could
hear them talking about the matter, even after they
had lain down in their beds. Sing-Hoo listened
eagerly to every word of their conversation, and was
evidently in a state of great alarm. He begged me
to allow a candle to be lighted and kept burning in
our apartment during the night.

In the room next to mine, and only separated from
it by a wooden partition, about a dozen opium-
smokers had taken up their quarters. The soft,
sickening fumes of the drug found their way through
the chinks of the partition, and were most disagreeable. In a short time the opium began to operate upon
the smokers; they talked and laughed loudly, and
were evidently in their " heaven of bliss." Sing-Hoo's
affair was uppermost in their minds, and it seemed
as if they could think or talk of nothing else. What
madmen might do under the circumstances—for madmen they were while under the influence of the drug
—I could not possibly foresee. This kept me awake
for several hours. At last, however, I dropped off to
sleep, and did not awake until daylight was streaming
into our miserable apartment. All was perfectly quiet.

Sing-Hoo was lying on his bed fast asleep with his clothes on, and the opium-smokers had gone off at last into the land of dreams.

Rousing Sing-Hoo, I desired him to go and look after another chair and coolies to take me onwards across the Bohea mountains into the province of Chekiang. He returned saying that all was arranged, and that the men would come to the inn as soon as they had taken their breakfast. In the mean time we ordered breakfast, and began to make preparations for our departure. I felt anxious to leave Pouching-hien before Sing-Hoo's enemies could put into execution any scheme of revenge, which I had no doubt they would attempt if they had time. It turned out afterwards that my fears were not without foundation.

While we were at breakfast one of the men who had been engaged in the brawl on the evening before went out and endeavoured to prevent us from getting men for our journey. He represented that Sing-Hoo was a bad man, and, however fair he promised, yet he would not pay at the end of the journey. He succeeded but too well, for a message came from the men who had been engaged informing us that they declined going.

" Well, you see what you have done by your foolish conduct," said I to Sing-Hoo; " it is no use attempting to get a chair and coolies in this quarter; these men will prevent you by every means in their power." " Yes," said he, " I see the only way is to leave this house at once, and cut off all connection

with it and with those who were here last night. I
will carry the luggage myself until we have done
this, and then we can easily engage a chair and
coolies as before." This seemed the most feasible
plan to adopt, and indeed the only one likely to
succeed under the circumstances in which we were
placed. I therefore desired him to go and purchase
a bamboo and some rope by which he could carry
the luggage on his shoulders. In the mean time I
busied myself in packing up my plants and other
things in as small bulk as possible.

When Sing-Hoo returned with the ropes and bamboo, he got the luggage on his shoulders, and we left
the inn, in which we had spent a most uncomfortable
night.

It had been raining heavily for many hours, and
it was now pouring in torrents. The streets were
completely flooded, and almost impassable. We
plunged along, however, and were soon clear of the
city, and on the great north road which leads to the
passes across the Bohea mountains. When about a
mile from the city walls, the bamboo with which
Sing-Hoo was carrying our luggage suddenly snapped
in two, and the whole of our effects were deposited in
the mud and water with which the road was flooded.
This part of the road was in the midst of a rice-field;
no houses were near into which we could go for
shelter, or where it was possible to purchase another
bamboo.

I confess I felt a strong inclination to lose my
temper, and to give utterance to some ill-natured re-

proaches; but when I looked at my servant, who stood covered with perspiration and dripping with rain, I had not the heart to reproach him. With the broken pieces of the bamboo in his hand, and the luggage (which included his own packages of grass-cloth) scattered about in the mud and water, he looked perfectly miserable.

About half a mile farther on I observed one of those sheds which are often built across the road in this country for the accommodation of travellers, and determined to make for it, as we could at least obtain shelter there from the rain. Shouldering part of the luggage, and desiring Sing-Hoo to take the remainder, I hurried onwards towards this place of shelter. These sheds are generally tenanted at night by beggars, who have nowhere else to lay their heads. When we entered we found a number of them fast asleep, and one preparing breakfast. Our arrival did not seem to attract more notice from them than a passing glance. Some of the sleepers lazily opened their eyes, but soon closed them again, and the cook went on with his culinary preparations.

It being impossible to proceed in the plight we were now in, I despatched Sing-Hoo back to the town for a chair and coolies, whilst I remained amongst the beggars to look after the luggage. Being afraid that he might fall into the hands of his enemies, who might detain him, or do him a serious injury, I desired him on no account to go near that part of the city where they were. I believe he was fully alive to the importance of taking these precautions.

He left me on his errand, and I sat down amongst the beggars. Never before had I had the honour of such company, and I devoutly hope I may never have again. Some of them were covered with natural sores, and others with artificial ones; while the low forehead, restless eye, and sturdy form of others told of a mind diseased. All were unshaven, and covered with dirt and filth. Beggars are numerous in China, and generally belong to three very distinct classes. The first are really objects of pity, and consist of the blind, the lame, and others who are covered with filthy cutaneous diseases; the second are those who endeavour to make themselves pitiable objects by artificial means; the third and largest class consists of persons who are weak-minded or insane. The community of beggars is found scattered over the empire in large numbers: it has its own regulations or laws, and there is really a "king of the beggars." The beggars in China are a privileged class, and, as they beg from door to door, seem to demand charity as their right more than as a favour. They are a great nuisance to the shopkeepers in large towns, who cannot get rid of them without giving them alms. Although a shopkeeper or householder is thus compelled to give a little to each, yet the sums given are often exceedingly small. The coin of the country is well adapted to this state of things. A hundred Chinese copper "cash" are worth only about fourpence of our money, and a beggar rarely receives more than one cash. Often he gets even less than this, and in the following curious manner:—In every string of a hundred cash there are a number of small inferior ones: these are either given to beggars, or the beggar lays down one of them for the shopkeeper, who gives in return one of the usual size, so that in this case the beggar receives about the value of half a cash, or the fiftieth part of a penny! I believe, in many cases, it is not unusual for the inhabitants of a city to compound with the heads of this strange community. When this is done a slip of paper is pasted on the doorposts of the person who has made this arrangement, and no beggar troubles him during the space of time for which he has paid.

Such were the kind of persons with whom I shared the shelter of a public building on this eventful morning. They were not inquisitive, but left me to my own meditations, which were not very pleasant ones. I had three hundred le of a mountain road before me ere I could reach the head of the river, which has one of its sources on the northern side of the Bohea mountains, and in its course joins the Green River, which falls into the bay of Hang-chow. This was a most serious undertaking; and if I could not procure a chair I should be obliged to discard the greater part of my luggage, amongst which were the tea-plants I had procured on the Woo-e hills. I began to wish now that I had gone down the river Min to Foo-chow-foo, instead of coming across these mountains; but there was no use in repining, the die was cast, and I must press onwards.

In about an hour Sing-Hoo returned, bringing a chair and men, whom he had procured without any difficulty in another part of the town from that in which we had spent the night. Silently but heartily I bade adieu to Pouching-hien and the beggars, and getting into my chair continued my journey.

The road from Pouching-hien to the foot of the mountains (I was now travelling in a northerly direction) led through an undulating country. Rice was the principal crop in the fields, but considerable quantities of tobacco were cultivated on all the spots a little higher than the irrigated rice-lands. The tallow-tree was again met with in great abundance.

Forty le north from Pouching-hien we passed through a large town, the name of which I neglected to write down at the time, and which I now forget. We stopped here about two hours for refreshment, and pushing onwards arrived the same evening at a small place amongst the Bohea mountains, named Tsong-so. Determined not to run the risk of meeting disreputable company, I ordered Sing-Hoo to go to the principal inn of the town. The landlord received me at the door, and conducted me to the upper part of the hall, on each side of which the bedrooms were placed. Having chosen one, and deposited my luggage in it, I returned to the hall and partook of the usual beverage—tea. In due time an excellent dinner was set before me, and so ended in a peaceful and agreeable manner a most exciting and disagreeable day.

The next morning we had an early breakfast, and then continued our journey. The road was a good one, but, being entirely mountainous, it was very

fatiguing.   We crossed over three passes during the
day.   These mountains, like the Woo-e hills, seem
to be the strongholds of Buddhism.   This morning,
on reaching the top of the first pass, I found we were
within the precincts of a temple.   It was on the left-
hand side of the road, while on the right there was a
large tea-house for the refreshment of travellers; a
kind of awning connected the two buildings, and
formed a covered way which served as a protection
from sun and rain.

A young priest, who observed us, ran and made
a table ready and set tea before me.   When I had
finished tea he returned, carrying a large book in his
hand, in which subscriptions for the support of the
temple were entered with the names of the donors.
This he presented to me, and intimated that "the
smallest sum would be thankfully received."   Sing-
Hoo now explained to him that I was not a Buddhist,
and would not subscribe to the support of that religion.   Giving him a small sum for the tea, and
thanking him for his civility, I took my departure.
He closed the book and carried it off, apparently
perfectly satisfied.

About mid-day we reached the top of another pass
having a temple somewhat like the last, and a large
tea-house or refreshment room attached to it.

We were now on the borders of two provinces,
namely, Fokien and Chekiang, and had to pass
through a border-town where a number of troops
were stationed.   This place is called Ching-che, and
stands on the banks of a small mountain-stream

which flows to the westward. As we entered the town I observed soldiers idling about in all directions; some were washing their clothes in the river, others were smoking in the tea-shops, while many were sitting chatting at the doors. All seemed to have eager eyes for the passing traveller, whom it was their duty to examine.

When we had got about half way through the town we stopped at a tea-shop for refreshment. Sing-Hoo begged me to remain in my chair until we had passed the Tartar lines, and I judged it prudent to do so. During the time we stopped, a mandarin of an inferior grade came and examined us, and seeing nothing out of the common way he merely inquired of Sing-Hoo where we had come from, and where we were going to. When he had obtained the requisite information, he walked away, seemingly perfectly satisfied.

We now crossed the river, which, I believe, here divides Fokien from Chekiang. Another high hill was before us, and we began to ascend it soon after we had crossed the river; and here an accident happened, which, had it taken place in the midst of the town through which we had just passed, might have been attended with disagreeable results. One of the bamboo levers of my chair, which I had often thought rather unsound, suddenly snapped in two, and the chair came down upon the road. This was very annoying, yet I felt thankful that it had not occurred while we were within the Tartar lines.

The chair-bearers said they could procure another bamboo at some cottages close by, so, leaving Sing-

Hoo to look after the luggage and broken chair, I went on towards the pass, examining the botany of this remarkable district by the way. I met again with the pretty *Spiræa* which I had first seen on the western ranges of the Bohea mountains. Here also it had chosen its home at a high elevation, and was never met with in the valleys, or on the lower sides of the hills.

When I reached the top of the pass I observed my chairmen and coolies far below. They had evidently got everything right again, and were coming onward as fast as they could. I waited for them on the top of the mountain. They said they had been obliged to pay the sum of 200 cash for a pair of new bamboos, a sum which I told them should be repaid to them at the end of their journey. They seemed very much pleased, and afterwards showed their gratitude in many little ways.

The day was now far advanced, and we had still a considerable distance to go before reaching the town in which we intended to spend the night. Almost every evening we had had a terrific thunder-storm amongst these mountains, and several hours of heavy rain. The clouds were already threatening, so we pressed on as fast as we could.

The town came at last into view, beautifully situated in the bosom of the hills. It is called Er-she-pa-tu. Just as we entered it the storm came on, the thunder sounded nearer and nearer, large drops of rain began to fall, and there was no time to lose in seeking an inn. We soon found a comfortable one, and spent the night agreeably enough.

CHAPTER XVIII.

A celebrated Buddhist temple — Scenery around it — Its trees and
    shrubs — Buddhist worship — Leave the temple — Reflections on
    Buddhism — Important station for Christian missionaries — Priva-
    tions they would have to endure — Roman Catholics and their
    labours — Christian charity — Protestant missionaries — Their views
    as to the interior of China — A day-dream of China opened —
    Bamboo paper — A mandarin on a journey — Town of Ching-hoo
    — Engage a boat for Nechow — Return to Shanghae.

THE next day's journey was still mountainous. The
roads, although narrow, were excellent, and showed
the indefatigable industry of the Chinese. I have
already stated that many of these mountain passes
have gates, which are constructed not unlike those at
the entrance to a city. On the borders of Chekiang,
where we now were, I observed three of these gates
on the top of one of the mountains, each placed at
a short distance from the other. A long row of
houses, evidently built as barracks, were observed
between the gates, but all ruinous and unoccupied.
I suppose that troops are thrown into these places
in troubled times only, and that in times of peace
they prefer remaining in the towns or villages below,
to being perched up at a high elevation amongst the
barren mountains.

When we reached the top of this mountain, the
Chinamen told us we should pass a celebrated temple

on the northern side, which we had now to descend.
This temple, they said, was called Shan-te-Maou,
and was situated amongst the most beautiful mountain
scenery, besides being a famous place for refreshment
and rest.   It was evidently a place in high repute
amongst the Chinese, so we pushed on for it, deter-
mining to dine and spend the remaining portion of
the day there.   We had not gone very far when our
road led through some beautiful bamboo woods.
These and other large trees told, in language not
to be mistaken by the Chinese traveller, that we
were within the precincts of the Buddhist temple.

Shan-te-Maou is built upon a steep hill-side.   As
we approached it, the temples were seen on the right-
hand side of the road, and the refectory on the left,
while the space between was thatched over to afford
protection from the sun and rain.   The temples
were in three grand divisions, each rising one behind
the other up the hill-side.   They were crowded with
images, many of which were very large.   The refectory was also upon a large scale, and was evidently
a source of considerable profit to the priests of Buddha,
who inhabit this mountain.   In its centre there was
a large space, roofed over, but open at the sides, and
crowded with tables, forms, and chairs for the guests.
On each side there were kitchens, bake-houses, and
all the appurtenances of a large inn.

As the place was so beautiful, and its productions
so interesting to me, I determined to halt for a day or
two at this temple, before bidding adieu for ever to
the Bohea mountains.   The good priests had no

objections to this arrangement; on the contrary, they offered me a room in which I could lock up my luggage during the day, and in which I could sleep at night.

The beauty of the scenery around had not been exaggerated by the Chinese. It was grand and imposing. High mountains rose behind the temple, while in front some glimpses were obtained through the trees of a wide and fertile valley. Besides the fine thickets of bamboo, there were in the vicinity of the buildings some noble specimens of different species of fir-trees. Amongst them, and most conspicuous, was the beautiful *Cryptomeria*, or Japan cedar, to which I have more than once alluded in these pages. It is evidently in high favour with the priests of Buddha, and well deserves to be so. I observed also two specimens of evergreen oak (*Quercus sclerophylla*, and *Q. inversa*), with large and glossy leaves, not unlike the Portugal laurel at a distance. Amongst shrubs there were *Spiræa callosa*, *S. Reevesiana*, *Hydrangeas*, *Azaleas*, wild roses, brambles, &c. Insects, too, were most numerous, many of which were new and hitherto undescribed.

I have remarked that these mountains appear to be the strongholds of Buddhism. I will now endeavour to describe the Buddhist form of worship, which I witnessed in this temple.

Anxious to see the whole of the service, I took my station at one of the passages leading to the large temple a few minutes before the priests assembled. I had not been there long before an old priest walked

past me to a huge block of wood, carved in the form
of a fish, which was slung from the roof of one of the
passages.   This he struck several times with a wooden
pole, and a loud hollow sound was given out which
was heard over all the building.   The large bronze
bell in the belfry was now tolled three times; and
the priests were observed coming from all quarters,
each having a yellow robe thrown over his left shoulder.
At the same time an old man was going round
beating on a piece of square board, to awake the
priests who might be asleep, and to call the lazy
ones to prayer.

The temple to which the priests were hurrying
was a large building, fully 100 feet square, and about
60 feet in height.   Its roof was supported by numerous
massive wooden pillars.   Three large idols—the
Past, the Present, and the Future—each at least 30
feet in height,—stood in the middle of the temple.
An altar was in front of them, and more than a
hundred hassocks were on the floor in front of the
altar for the priests to kneel on during the service.
Ranged on each side of this spacious hall were numerous idols of a smaller size; said to be the repre-
sentatives of deified kings and other great men who
had been remarkable for piety during their lifetime.

Entering with the priests, I observed a man light-
ing the candles placed upon the altar and burning
incense.   The smoke of the incense as it rose in the
air filled the place with a heavy yet pleasing perfume.
A solemn stillness seemed to pervade the temple.
The priests came in one by one, in the most devout

X

manner,—scarcely lifting their eyes from the ground,
and arranged themselves on the right and left sides
of the altar, kneeling on the hassocks, and bending
down lowly several times to the idols. Again the
large bell tolled,—slowly and solemnly at first, then
gradually quicker; and then everything was perfectly still.

The priests were now all assembled—about eighty
in number—and the services of the temple began.
I took a seat near the door. The priest nearest to
the altar now rang a small bell,—another struck a
drum; and the whole eighty bent down several times
upon their knees. One of them then struck a round
piece of wood, rather larger than a man's skull, and
hollow inside, alternately with a large bronze bell.
At this stage of the ceremonies a young priest stepped
out from amongst the others, and took his station directly
in front of the altar, bowing lowly and repeatedly as
he did so. Then the hymn of praise began. One of
the priests, apparently the leader, kept time by beating upon the hollow piece of wood, and the whole of
the others sang or chanted the service in a most
mournful key. At the commencement of the service,
the priests who were ranged in front of the altar, half
on the right side and half on the left, stood with their
faces to the large images. Now, however, they suddenly wheeled round and faced each other. The
chanting, which began slowly, increased in quickness
as it went on, and when at the quickest part suddenly
stopped. All was then silent for a second or two.
At last, a single voice was heard to chant a few notes

by itself, and then the whole assembly joined, and went on as before.

The young priest who had come out from amongst the others now took his station directly in front of the altar, but near the door of the temple, and bowed lowly several times upon a cushion placed there for that purpose. He then walked up to the altar with slow and solemn steps, took up a vessel which stood on it, and filled it with water. After making some crosses and gyrations with his hand, he sprinkled a little of the water upon the table. When this was done, he poured a little from the vessel into a cup, and retired slowly from the altar towards the door of the temple. Passing outside, he dipped his fingers in the water and sprinkled it on the top of a stone pillar which stood near the door.

While this was going on the other priests were still chanting the service. The time of the music frequently changed :—now it was fast and lively,—now slow and solemn,—but always in a plaintive key. This part of the service being ended, all knelt lowly before the altar, and when they rose from their knees a procession was formed. The priests on the right of the altar filed off to the right, and those on the left to the left, each walking behind the other up the two sides of the spacious hall, and chanting as they went a low and solemn air, time being kept by the tinkling of a small bell. When the two processions met at the farther end of the building, each wheeled round and returned in the same order as it came. The procession lasted for about five minutes, and then the priests took up their stations in front of the altar, and the chanting went on as before. A minute or two after this the whole body fell upon their knees, and sang for a while in this posture. When they rose, those on the left sang a part of the service by themselves, then knelt down. The right side now took up the chant, and, having performed their part, also knelt down. The left side rose again, and so they went on for ten minutes, prostrating themselves alternately before the altar. The remainder of the service was nearly the same as that at the commencement.

This striking ceremony had now lasted for about an hour. During the whole time a thick screen had been hanging down in front of the large door, to keep out the sun's rays. Just before the conclusion of the service the curtain was drawn aside, and a most striking and curious effect was produced. Streams of ruddy light shot across the temple, the candles on the altar appeared to burn dimly, and the huge idols seemed more massive and strange than they had done before. One by one the priests slowly retired as solemnly as they came, and *apparently* deeply impressed with the services in which they had been engaged. Nearly all the priests adjourned to the refectory, where dinner was served immediately. The Buddhists eat no animal food; but they manage to consume a very large quantity of rice and vegetables. I have been perfectly astonished at the quantity of rice eaten by one of these priests at a meal. And yet, generally, they look poor and emaciated beings, which is probably owing as much to the sedentary lives which they lead as to the nature of their food.

On the morning of the third day, after refreshing myself with a cup of the pure bohea, probably the last which I shall drink on these mountains, from which it gets its name, I bade adieu to the priests and left the temple. Leaving my men to finish a substantial meal of rice, I strolled down the hill by myself. The road had been made in a zigzag manner, owing to the steepness of the hill. Now I was in a dense tropical-looking forest, and now by some turning of the road I obtained a view down into the valley, which was covered with rice-fields of the most luxuriant green.

Looking up behind me, I got a glimpse of the temple peeping out from amidst the rich woods which surrounded it. The sun was shining gaily upon it, and making the tiled roof sparkle as if covered with precious stones. It looked more like an enchanted palace than the dwelling-place of man. And yet it was melancholy to think that, however fair and enchanting to look upon, and however beautiful the scenery around it, a cloud more dark than the thunder-cloud rested upon it, for it was but "an altar erected to the unknown God."

When China is really opened these mountains may become important stations for the labours of the Christian missionary. It will doubtless be a sacrifice of no ordinary kind for men to immure themselves and their families in such places, far away from any means of communicating with their friends or rela-

tions at home.   But the Roman Catholic church has
led the way, and amidst many dangers and difficulties
has given us some noble examples of self-denial and
heroism.   I know very well that some persons imagine that these men have other objects in view than
the advancement of the Redeemer's kingdom upon
earth.   I trust I am a consistent Protestant, but I
am not one of these who are uncharitable enough to
try to find out other reasons than the true one to
account for the conduct of men who have left all that
is dear on earth—friends, home, and country—in
many instances for ever, to preach the Gospel to the
heathen.   A good cause can always afford to give
praise where praise is due.   I confess it pains me to
hear the labours of these men undervalued, for I
know well what they have to undergo.

The Protestant church has many champions as
bold and undaunted as it had in the days of the Refor-
mation.   To these missionaries the way into the heart
of the Chinese empire may not be very clear.   They
may not consider it their duty to press beyond the
wide field which exists already at the five ports where
foreigners reside.   There is no doubt, however, that
a few years will see a vast change in China; it may
be that another war and all its horrors is inevitable,
and whenever that takes place this vast country will
be opened up to foreigners of every nation.   Then
the Christian missionary will be able to extend his
labours to those far-distant stations amongst the Bohea
hills which I have just been describing.   With the
blessing of God these temples may yet be the spots

from which the Sun of righteousness shall shine. The "glad news of the Gospel" may yet be proclaimed in them, and spread from hill to valley, and from valley to hill, until the whole of this vast country shall hear the glad and joyful tidings.

While seated at the bottom of the hill under the shade of a large camphor-tree waiting for my men, it was pleasant to dream of all these vast changes, and to picture to the mind future scenes amongst these mountains. Absorbed in thought, I could fancy I heard the sound of the sabbath-bell tolling the hour of prayer—I could almost see the crowds coming up from the valley dressed in their holiday attire, and could hear them chanting the beautiful Morning Hymn :—

> " Awake, my soul, and with the sun
> Thy daily stage of duty run."

While these thoughts were passing through my mind, my people arrived, and, getting into my chair, I proceeded across the valley. About a mile below the temple I observed a manufactory for making paper out of the bamboo. Large water-tanks were constructed in the fields for the purpose of steeping the bamboo stems. They appeared to be steeped for a length of time in some solution of lime. They were then taken out and beaten upon stones until they became quite soft, or till all the flinty matter which abounds in their stems was removed.

After passing through this rice-valley we ascended another hill, from the top of which an excellent view was obtained. We were now fairly on the northern side of the Bohea range. The hills appeared to fall back in all directions, and thus a wide expanse of valley was exposed to view. We were now near the source of the river to which we were bound, and in the evening we arrived at a town named Sha-co, which is built on both sides of its banks.

We put up for the night at the principal inn of this town. A young lady, apparently the landlord's daughter, amused us during dinner, and for several hours in the evening, by playing upon a stringed instrument, not unlike a guitar, accompanying it with her voice. It was really pretty music, and I believe I enjoyed it as much as the Chinese themselves did. During the evening the landlord informed us that he expected a mandarin of high rank to stay in his house next night. This personage, he said, was on his way from the court of Peking to Foo-chow-foo, and runners had been sent on before to make preparations for his reception.

The next morning I met the old gentleman and his family at a Buddhist temple on the plain, where they had stopped to refresh themselves. He had several women and children with him, besides several inferior mandarins, and a large number of servants and soldiers. When we met the cavalcade at the temple it completely blocked up the road. We were therefore obliged to wait patiently until they had finished their meal before we could get on. They took the road across the Bohea mountains, over which we had come, and we that to the town of Ching-hoo, which we reached early in the afternoon. It is a small bustling town, and a place of considerable importance, being at the head of one of the branches of the river which flows into the bay of Hang-chow. All the traffic carried on between the towns near the sea, such as Hang-chow-foo, Shanghae, &c., and those on the eastern Bohea mountains, as Pouching-hien, must pass through Ching-hoo. All the basket teas manufactured in the Pouching districts are brought here on their way to the fertile and populous countries in the north-east.

As soon as we arrived we went to an inn to dine and make inquiries regarding a boat. In this instance I took care to pay the chairbearers and coolie myself, not wishing to have another scene like that at Pou-ching-hien. The men had behaved very well during the journey, so I paid them, in addition to their wages, a small sum for the accident that had happened to the chair ; I also gave them the usual gratuity for wine, or sam-shoo, which they always expect on these occasions. They appeared perfectly satisfied, and, after making many low bows, went their way back to Pouching-hien.

Sing-Hoo now went out to engage a boat to take us down the river. While he was absent a barber came into the room where I was, and politely asked me if I wanted my head shaved after coming off such a long journey across the mountains. I need scarcely say I begged to decline any attention of this kind. My servant soon came back, bringing a boat-man with him, whom he had engaged to take us down to Nechow, a small town near the mouth of the river.

As I glided smoothly and quickly down the river I looked upon the difficulties and dangers of my journey as at an end. Although between two and three hundred miles to the westward of any of the ports at which foreigners reside, yet the river seemed like an old friend who had met me at Ching-hoo to carry me safely home.

Nothing further happened to damp the pleasure of my journey. On my way down I paid another visit to the pretty town of Nan-che ; I also stopped a day at Yen-chow-foo to procure some plants of the weeping cypress for Mr. Beale's garden at Shanghae, and arrived at last at Nechow.

The route which I had now before me has been already fully described. I arrived at Shanghae in due time, having been absent on this long journey nearly three months. Although I had been eating with chopsticks all this time, I had not forgotten the use of knives and forks, and I need scarcely say I heartily enjoyed my first English dinner. The tea-plants procured in Woo-e-shan reached Shanghae in good order, and most of them are now flourishing on the slopes of the Himalayas.

CHAPTER XIX.

Tea-plants, &c., taken to Hong-kong — Shipped for India — I sail
again for the north — Shanghae gardens in spring — " South Garden "—Double-striped peach and other plants — Moutan gardens
— Fine new varieties of the tree-pæony — Chinese method of propagating them — Mode of sending them to Canton — Value there —
Introduction to Europe — Size in England—Azalea gardens—
Skimmia Reevesiana — New Azaleas — The " Kwei-wha "— The
Glycine — Its native hills — Chinese mode of training it — The
yellow Camellia.

IN the month of August the weather was excessively
hot. As exposure to the sun at this time of the
year is attended with great danger, and as I had
some hard work before me in the autumn, I did not
wish to run the risk of being laid up with fever. I
therefore remained quietly under Mr. Beale's hospitable roof until the end of September.

In October and November I procured a large
supply of tea-seeds and young plants from Hwuy-
chow, and from various parts of the province of Chekiang. These were all brought to Shanghae in order
to be prepared and packed for the long voyage to
India. When they were all gathered together into
Mr. Beale's garden they formed a collection of great
interest. Here were tea-plants, not only from Silver
Island, Chusan, and the districts about Ning-po,
but also from the far-famed countries of Sung-lo-
shan and the Woo-e hills. A number of Ward's
glazed cases were now got ready for the reception of

the plants, and the whole of them were taken down to Hong-kong under my own care. They were then divided and sent on to Calcutta by four different vessels, in case of accident.

As soon as I had got all the plants put on board I left Hong-kong again for the north. My object now was to engage some first-rate tea manufacturers for the Indian plantations, to procure a supply of the implements used in the best districts for the manufacture of tea, and to get together another large collection of tea-plants.

I reached Shanghae in the month of April, 1850. The winter had passed away, and spring was just commencing. Trees and shrubs were bursting into leaf and flower, birds were singing gaily in every bush, and all nature was teeming with life and joy.

Taking advantage of the fine weather and a few days of leisure I determined to make a tour of the gardens near Shanghae, some of which are of considerable interest.

The first I visited is about two miles from the south-west corner of the city, and is now well known to the foreign residents as the "South Garden." It was one of those in which I had found many new plants on my first visit to China.

This little garden covers about an acre of land, and is surrounded, like many of these places, by a ditch, which is connected with canals through which the tide ebbs and flows. On entering the gate, the first object which one notices is the gardener's house. It is a rude building of one story, and contains the

old couple, two sons with their wives, and a large
number of young children.   The Chinese in the
country always live in little colonies of this description.   When a son marries, the wife is brought home,
and a portion of the building is set apart for their
use.   Here they live together in the most harmonious
manner, and the grandchildren, when they grow up
and marry, occupy a part of the same buildings,
rarely leaving the place of their birth.

"Ah, you have come back!"   "Are you well?"
"How did the plants get home?"   "Were they
much admired in England?" were the questions
which were rapidly put to me by the old nurseryman
and his sons; at the same time they brought a chair,
and asked me to sit down under the awning of the
cottage.   I told them that most of the plants had
arrived safely in England, that they had been greatly
admired, and that the beautiful *Weigela* had even
attracted the notice of her Majesty the Queen.   All
these statements, more particularly the last, seemed
to give them great pleasure; and they have doubtless
fancied the *Weigela* of more value ever since.

This garden contains many of the beautiful plants
introduced by the Horticultural Society of London
from 1843 to 1846.   Amongst some pots at the
entrance there were fine plants of the now well-
known *Weigela*, the pretty *Indigofera decora, Forsythia viridissima*, and a fine white variety of *Wistaria sinensis*.   Round the sides of the ditch were
many magnificent specimens of *Edgeworthia chrysantha*, and *Gardenia florida Fortuniana*, growing

in the open ground. Some of the Gardenias were 4 feet high and 15 feet in circumference. When covered with its large camellia-looking blossoms it is extremely handsome, and at all times forms a pretty evergreen bush. In a bed in the middle of the garden the white variety of *Platycodon grandiflorus* was in full bloom, and near it another bed of *Dielytra spectabilis.* Both these looked very handsome, particularly the latter; its large purse-like blooms of a clear red colour, tipped with white, and hanging down gracefully from a curved spike, and its moutan-like leaves, render it a most interesting plant, and one which will become a great favourite in English gardens. Several kinds of roses were growing in pots, and amongst them the new yellow, or salmon-coloured, introduced by the Horticultural Society. This rose deserves more notice at home than it has yet had; doubtless it will be more thought of when it is better known and properly treated. It should be planted out at the foot of a wall with a southern or western aspect, and allowed to scramble over it. It grows rapidly; the flowers are of a striking colour, and are produced in great profusion. Fine plants of *Viburnum plicatum,* and *V. macrocephalum,* were also noticed, both in pots and also in the open ground.

I also observed some young plants of the interesting palm-tree (*Chamærops* (?) *excelsa*) which I have already noticed in the earlier pages of this work. It is perfectly hardy about Shanghae, and thrives there unprotected throughout the severest winters. There were other palms, but this was the only one that seemed hardy.

Here were also some beautiful peach-trees with double flowers. Two of these have been already described by Dr. Lindley in the 'Journal of the Horticultural Society,' and named the "double white" and "double crimson" peaches. But, fine as these undoubtedly are, there is a third far more beautiful and striking than either of them. This produces large double white flowers, which are striped with red or crimson lines like a carnation. A tree of this variety in full bloom is one of the most beautiful objects that can be imagined. Sometimes the branches "sport," and produce self-coloured flowers—the colours being, in this case, either white or crimson. This fine tree is now safely in England, and in a few years it may be expected to produce a marked effect in our gardens early in spring.

These double peach-trees seem to be particularly well adapted for forcing, as they form their flower-buds fully in autumn, and are ready to burst into bloom with the first warm days in spring. A little artificial heat, therefore, will bring them into full flower about the new year, or any time from that period up to March.

As spring flowers they are highly prized by the Chinese. Itinerant gardeners carry them about the streets for sale in the northern Chinese towns. The flower-buds are then just beginning to expand; the buyer puts them into pots, gives them a little water, and places them in his window or sitting-room. In a

day or two the buds burst, and the little tree is one
mass of bloom.   In this state all the three varieties
are very beautiful, but I think the carnation-striped
one is the handsomest of them all.

In the centre of the South Garden there is the
family tomb—a large mound of earth covered with
many pretty flowers.   Here the old man's forefathers
for many generations lie buried, and here he will
sleep among the flowers he loved in his lifetime.
This garden contains a good assortment of shrubs and
trees which have been longer known than those I
have enumerated.   There are some beds of Reeves'
Spiræa (*S. Reevesiana*), a beautiful shrub ; the Chinese juniper, *Hibiscus syriacus*, *Wistaria sinensis*,
Lagerstrœmias, plums, and the favourite la-mae (*Chimonanthus*), with which Chinese ladies decorate their
hair.

I had now made the circuit of the garden, and
came to the little wooden bridge by which I entered,
and to the gardener's house.   Having rested there, I
walked on to the Moutan Gardens.   They are
situated about five or six miles west of Shanghae,
and in the midst of an extensive cotton country.   On
the road I met a number of coolies, each carrying
two baskets filled with moutans (tree-pæonies) in full
flower, which were being taken to the markets for
sale.   When I reached the gardens I found many of
the plants in full bloom, and certainly extremely
handsome.   The purple and lilac-coloured kinds were
particularly striking.   One, a very dwarf kind, and
apparently a distinct species, had finely cut leaves,

and flowers of a dark velvety purple, like the Tus-
cany rose of our gardens.   This the Chinese call the
" black" moutan, and I believe it is the same which
Dr. Lindley has described in the Journal of the
Horticultural Society, and named *Pæonia atrosan-
guinea*.   Another kind, called the " tse," or purple,
has double flowers of a large size ; this is probably
the variety reported to have 1000 petals, and which
is said to exist only in the garden of the emperor.
The third is called the " lan," or blue ; this is a lilac
variety, with flowers of the colour of *Wistaria sinensis*.
There are others of various shades of purple, perfectly distinct from these, and equally fine.

The double whites are also numerous and handsome.   The largest of these Dr. Lindley has named
P. globosa, but there are four or five others nearly as
large and double.   Some of them have a slight lilac
tinge, which gives a richness to the colour.   The
most expensive is one called " wang," or yellow, by
the Chinese : it is a straw-coloured variety, rather
pretty, but not so handsome as some of the others.

The reds (hong) are also numerous.   Curiously
enough, those kinds which are common in Canton
and England are rare here.   There are about half-a-
dozen new varieties of reds in these gardens : one of
them, called " Van-yang-hong," is the finest flower I
ever saw.   The flowers are of a clear red colour,
unlike any of the others, perfectly double, and each
measures 10 inches across.   Altogether I numbered
about thirty distinct varieties in these gardens.

Nearly all these fine varieties of the moutan are

quite unknown in Canton. This may seem strange
in a country where the people are proverbially fond
of flowers, but the Chinese are so machine-like in all
their movements, that after a little acquaintance with
them we cease to wonder at the apparent anomaly.
The fact is, the Canton gardens are supplied with
moutans by another district, which lies much further
to the west than Shanghae. From time immemorial
the same gardens have supplied these flowers; they
came always by the same road and at the same time
of the year. Shanghae, until the close of the last
war, never seems to have had any connection with
Canton in so far as flowers were concerned, consequently these fine varieties of the tree-pæony never
found their way to the south and from thence to
Europe.

The moutan gardens are numerous, but each is
upon a very small scale. They look more like cottage gardens than anything else, and are managed in
the same way as gardens of this description generally
are, namely, by the members of the family. The
female part of the community seem to take as much
interest in the business as the males, and are very
avaricious and fond of money. I invariably found
that I had to pay a higher price for a plant when
they were consulted on the matter. The soil of
these gardens is a rich loam, well manured, and thus
rendered lighter in texture than that of the surrounding country in which the cotton grows.

The propagation and management of the moutan
seem to be much better understood at Shanghae than

in England.   Our nurserymen always complain that they cannot propagate it with facility, and consequently this fine flower is invariably high in price. The Chinese method is as follows:—

In the beginning of October large quantities of the roots of a herbaceous pæony are seen heaped up in sheds and other outhouses, and are intended to be used as stocks for the moutan.   The bundle of tubers which forms the root is pulled to pieces, and each of the finger-like rootlets forms a stock upon which the moutan is destined to be grafted.   Having thrown a large number of these rootlets upon the potting bench, the scions are then brought from the plants which it is desirable to increase.   Each scion used is not more than 1½ inch or 2 inches in length, and is the point of a shoot formed during the bygone summer.   Its base is cut in the form of a wedge, and inserted in the crown of the finger-like tuber.   This is tied up or clayed round in the usual way, and the operation is completed.   When a large number of plants have been prepared in this manner they are taken to the nursery, where they are planted in rows about a foot and a half apart, with the same distance between the rows.   In planting, the bud or point of the scion is the only part which is left above ground; the point between the stock and scion, where the union is destined to take place, is always buried beneath the surface.   Kæmpfer states that the Chinese propagate the moutan by budding ; but this must be a mistake, as budding is never practised in the country, and is not understood.   He was probably deceived by the small portion of scion which is employed, and which generally has only a single bud at its apex.

Many thousands of plants are grafted in this manner every autumn, and the few vacant spaces which one sees in the rows attest the success which attends the system; indeed it is rare that a graft fails to grow. In about a fortnight the union between the root and the scion is complete, and in the following spring the plants are well-established and strong. They frequently bloom the first spring, and rarely later than the second, when they are dug up and taken to the markets for sale. When each has only one stem and one flower-bud, it is of more value in the eyes of the Shanghae nurseryman than when it becomes larger. In this state it is more saleable; it produces a very large flower, and is easily dug up and carried to the market. I could always buy moderately large plants at a cheaper rate than small ones, owing to these circumstances.

In the gardens of the mandarins the tree-pæony frequently attains a great size. There was one plant near Shanghae which produced between 300 and 400 blooms every year. The proprietor was as careful of it as the tulip fancier is of his bed of tulips. When in bloom it was carefully shaded from the bright rays of the sun by a canvas awning, and a seat was placed in front on which the visitor could sit down and enjoy the sight of its gorgeous flowers. On this seat the old gentleman himself used to sit for hours every day, smoking pipe after pipe of tobacco, and drinking cup after cup of tea, while all the time he was gazing on the beauties of his favourite " Moutan-wha." It was certainly a noble plant, and well worthy of the old man's admiration.

The tree-pæony is found wild on the mountains of the central provinces of China, and is cultivated as a garden-plant in all parts of the empire. It is called the *Mou-tan-wha*, or Moutan flower, by the natives, and hence botanists in Europe, retaining the Chinese name for the species, call it Pæonia moutan. It was first seen by Europeans in the gardens about Canton, but it is not indigenous to that part of China. The Canton gardeners carry on a large trade with the moutan growers, who bring the plants yearly in boats from the provinces of Hoo-nan and the western parts of Kiang-nan, a distance of at least one thousand miles. This takes place in the winter months when the plants are leafless and in a state of rest. The roots are packed in baskets, and have scarcely any soil adhering to them; in this simple manner they are distributed over all the empire without suffering any injury. On their arrival in the south they are immediately potted by the purchasers, and, owing to the difference in the temperature, soon come into bloom. In the winter months snow is rarely seen on the hills about Canton or Hong-kong, and oftentimes the weather is very warm. The change, therefore, acts upon the plants like a forcing-house, and soon brings the leaves and flowers to maturity. As soon as the flower-buds are fairly formed, the plants are eagerly bought up by the natives to ornament their balconies, halls, and gardens. The price of each plant depends not upon its size or strength, but upon the number of flower-buds which it has upon it. The first thing the Canton nurseryman does, when asked the price of a moutan, is to count the number of flowers which it is likely to produce; if it has only one bud, it may be worth a quarter of a dollar; if two, half a dollar, and so on. This is reasonable enough, when the circumstances of the case are considered. The moutan, when brought down into the hot climate of the south, will not thrive for any length of time. Being strong and vigorous when received, it blooms well the first year, but, being deprived of its natural period of rest—that is, a cold winter—it gets out of health, and, although it may continue to exist, is ever afterwards quite worthless as an ornamental flower. The southern Chinese, therefore, never attempt to preserve it after it has once bloomed, and hence the value of the plant to them depends entirely upon the manner in which it blooms during the first year after being brought away from its native climate. This circumstance keeps up the constant yearly trade between the moutan country and Canton.

According to Loudon, the first plant of the tree-pæony reached Europe in 1787. In the ' Arboretum et Fruticetum Britannicum' we find the following notice of it from the pen of that indefatigable author: —" From Chinese drawings, and from the extravagant praises bestowed upon this plant in the 'Mémoires sur la Chine,' published by the missionaries, an ardent desire was excited, in Sir Joseph Banks and others, to import plants into England; and, pre-

viously to 1786, Sir Joseph Banks engaged Mr.
Duncan, a medical gentleman attached to the East
India Company's service, to procure a plant for the
Royal Garden at Kew, where it was first received,
through Mr. Duncan's exertions, in 1787.

" One of the largest tree-pæonies within ten miles
of London stood, till lately, in the grounds at Spring
Grove, where it was planted by Sir Joseph Banks.
It was 6 feet or 8 feet high, and formed a bush 8 feet
or 10 feet in diameter, in 1825.   South of London
there are equally large plants at Rook's Nest, near
Godstone, Surrey, which were planted in 1818.
North of London the largest plant in the country is
at the seat of Sir Abraham Hume, at Wormleybury,
in Hertfordshire.   It is 7 feet high, and forms a bush
14 feet in diameter, after having been planted thirty
years.   It stands the winter, in general, very well,
but, if the flower-buds swell too early in February, it
becomes advisable to cover the plant slightly with a
mat.   In the year 1835 this plant perfected 320
flowers; but it has been known to bear three times
that number.   In most parts of Scotland the tree-
pæony will grow without protection, and near the sea-
coast nearly as well as in England.   The largest
plants are at Hopeton House and in Dalkeith Park.
In Ireland the plant attains a large size with little or
no protection, as will appear by the notice of one
12 feet high at Lord Ferrand's."

A few days after visiting the moutan district I
went to see the azalea gardens, which are equally interesting.   About five miles from the city there are

two nurseries, each of which contains an extensive and valuable collection. They are usually known as the Pou-shan Gardens, and are often visited by the foreign residents in Shanghae.

My road led me through a country which is perfectly level and in a high state of cultivation. The deciduous trees were covered with fresh green leaves, as yet uninjured by the attacks of insects; wheat and barley were in the ear, and the air was scented with the field-bean, which was now in full bloom. Clumps of trees were dotted over the country, generally divided pretty distinctly into two kinds—deciduous and evergreen. The deciduous clumps marked the spots where the villages and farm-houses were situated; the evergreens, consisting chiefly of cypress and juniper trees, were growing about the tombs of the dead.

Little more than an hour's walk brought me to the garden I had come to visit. There were no external marks, such as a name or signboard, to direct the stranger to the garden; indeed, a person unacquainted with the customs of the Chinese would never have dreamed of finding such a beautiful place as this in a poor country village. Going up a narrow passage between two houses, I reached the residence of the nurseryman. He received me with great politeness, asked me to sit down in his house, and called to one of his sons to bring me a cup of tea. Having drunk the refreshing beverage, I walked out with him to inspect his garden.

In the front of the house three or four flat stages

were covered with Japanese plants, of which the old man had a good collection. A small species of pinus was much prized, and, when dwarfed in the manner of the Chinese, fetched a very high price; it is generally grafted on a variety of the stone pine. The *Azalea obtusa*, and some varieties of it with semi-double flowers, were in full flower, and are highly prized by the Chinese. The colour of this species is much more brilliant and dazzling in China than I have ever seen it in England. A beautiful variety, quite new, had small semi-double pink flowers, which it produced in great profusion. This will be a great favourite in England when its merits are known. Its novel colour, small leaves, and neat habit will render it most desirable for bouquets and for decorative purposes. I have named it *Azalea amœna*, and it is now in England.

On the same stage with this Azalea I observed a fine new shrub, which I mistook for a holly. It turned out to be a species of *Skimmia*, and I observe that Dr. Lindley has described it as *Skimmia japonica*. It is however quite a different plant from that known by the name in the gardens of this country, and I propose to call it *Skimmia Reevesiana*.* It produces a profusion of whitish flowers, deliciously scented, and afterwards becomes covered with bunches of red berries like our common holly. Its glossy ever-green leaves and neat habit add greatly to its beauty,

---

* In compliment to John Reeves, Esq., who has introduced many Chinese plants into this country, and who has been of great service to me while in China.

and will make it a general favourite when it becomes
better known.   The Chinese call this the Wang-shan-
kwei, and it is said to have been discovered on Wang-
shan, a celebrated mountain in the district of Hwuy-chow.

After looking over the plants upon the stage, I
passed on to the main portion of the nursery, which is
situated behind the house.   Here a beautiful sight was
presented to the eye.   Two large masses of Azaleas,
arranged on each side of a small walk, were covered
with flowers of the most dazzling brightness and
beauty.   Nor were they common kinds.   Generally
they belonged to the same section as *A. indica* (the
varieties of *A. variegata* do not flower so early), but
the species so common in Canton and the south were
comparatively rare here.   A most beautiful kind,
having the habit of *A. indica* and half deciduous, had
its flowers striped with pale blue or lilac lines, and
sometimes blotches of the same colour upon a white
ground.   Not unfrequently it "sports" like the double-
blossomed peach already described, and then, in addition to its carnation-striped flowers, has some self-
coloured purple ones on the same plant.   This species
has been named *Azalea vittata*.

Another species allied to this, which I have named
A. Bealei, had red stripes, and a third was mottled and
striped in its flowers, the colours being still the same.
These are all quite new, and they flower early in the
season, fully three weeks or a month before that section
to which *A. variegata* belongs.   A red variety, which
flowers later, is particularly worthy of notice.   Its
habit is different from any known species; its leaves are

dark green, shining, and evergreen; and its flowers
are of a deep clear red, and very large.   Each flower
measures from three to four inches in diameter.   It is
said to be a Japanese species.   Specimens of all these
fine plants are now to be found in English gardens.

Passing over a little wooden bridge, I entered the
third compartment of the nursery, which contained a
collection of the common shrubs of the country.
Along the banks of a ditch, through which the tide
ebbs and flows, there is a row of the *Olea fragrans.*
This is the famous Kwei-wha of the Chinese, and one
of their most favourite flowers.   It forms a good-sized
bush, about as large as a lilac, and flowers in the
autumn.   There are three or four varieties, the main
difference between them consisting in the colour of
their blossoms.   Those kinds which produce brownish-
yellow flowers are the finest and are most highly
esteemed by the natives.   The bushes are seen growing near all the villages in the north-eastern provinces
of the empire, and are plentiful in gardens and nurseries.   When they are in flower in the autumnal months,
the air in their vicinity is literally loaded with the
most delicious perfume.   One tree is enough to scent
a whole garden.

In England we know nothing of the beauty of this
charming plant.   But there is no other amongst all
the beautiful productions of the East which more
deserves our care, or that would more richly reward
it.   And I am quite sure that English gardeners have
only to take the subject in hand to ensure the most
complete success.   Look at *Camellias, Azaleas, Gar-*

denias, and a host of other things, all natives of China, and most of them much better grown, and brought to a greater state of perfection in England than amongst the Chinese themselves. And why should one of the most delightful plants of China be so neglected? All that is required is a span-roofed conservatory, where the bushes can be planted out in the bed, and liberally supplied with fresh air. During the summer months, when they are growing, they must be kept warm and moist, in order that the young wood may be well matured. In the autumn let them be kept rather dry, and give the house little or no artificial heat during winter. The plants will thus be subjected to a system of treatment similar to that which they receive in their native country. In the central and northern provinces of China, where the plant succeeds much better than it does in the warmer climate of the south, the winters are often extremely cold. The thermometer (Fahr.) is sometimes within a few degrees of zero. The summers are very hot: in the months of June, July, and August, the thermometer ranges, during the day, between 80 and 100 degrees, and the weather is generally very wet in May and June.

The flowers of the Kwei-wha are a source of great profit to the Chinese cottager, as well as to the nurserymen, who produce them in large quantities for the market. There is a great demand for them in all the large towns. Ladies are fond of wearing wreaths of them in their hair; they are also dried and placed in ornamental jars, in the same way as we do rose-leaves in Europe, and they are used largely for mixing with the finer kind of tea, in order to give it an agreeable perfume.

In all these gardens the Azalea is propagated readily and extensively. Layering is the common method employed, but grafting and striking from cuttings are also resorted to with success. During the hot summer months, both young and old plants are shaded from the mid-day sun. Most of these new kinds which I have been describing flower early, that is, in March and April: the section to which the *A. variegata* belongs flowers in May. After the flowering season has passed, the weather is generally moist, owing to a change in the monsoon. It is at this period that the plants grow most luxuriantly, and form their young wood, and this growth is completed and the wood ripened during the fine summer and autumn which follow. These northern Azaleas are exposed to severe colds during the winter. As I have already observed, the thermometer often sinks to within a few degrees of zero, and the weather is not unlike that which we have in England.

The Azalea is indigenous to China, and is found wild on every hill side, like the heath of our own country. About Hong-kong and Canton it is usually found in a wild state high up on the sides of the mountains, from 1000 to 2000 feet above the level of the sea. In latitude 25° north, in the province of Fokien, it is met with in less elevated situations, that is, from 500 to 1000 feet high ; and when we reach Chusan, in latitude 30° north, we find it growing plentifully on the lower sides of all the hills, and never, or at least rarely, at a high elevation. We thus see how plants, which are naturally fitted for the temperature of one part of the globe, can accommodate themselves to another by choosing a higher or lower situation on the hills.

Although this genus is thus found spreading itself over a vast tract of country, yet the northern parts just indicated are evidently those in which it is most at home. All who have been in the island of Chusan will remember how beautiful the hill sides and woods were in the months of April and May, when the Azaleas were in bloom. Every hill was a garden gay with flowers, planted and reared by the hand of Nature herself. Before I saw these hills I thought nothing could be more magnificent than those gorgeous displays of Azaleas at our flower-shows, and certainly, if we look merely at individual specimens, many of those reared by the skill of English gardeners surpass those which we find in a state of nature. But Nature plants and rears with no sparing hand; her colours are clear and brilliant, and she is not confined to greenhouses and flower-tents in which to display her productions, but scatters them with wild profusion over the sides of the hills. It is here that she is inimitable, and it is thus that she produces effects which, once seen, can never be forgotten.

Before leaving these Shanghae Azalea gardens, I must notice one plant which was in flower at the time I paid this visit to them. It was a specimen of *Wistaria chinensis,* in a dwarfed state, growing in a pot. The tree was evidently aged, from the size of its stem. It was about six feet high, the branches came out from the stem in a regular and symmetrical manner, and it had all the appearance of a tree in miniature. Every one of these branches was now loaded with long racemes of pendulous lilac blossoms. These hung down from the horizontal branches, and gave the whole the appearance of a floral fountain.

The Glycine, or *Wistaria Chinensis*, has been long known in Europe, and there are large trees of it on many of our house and garden walls. It was introduced into this country from a garden near Canton, belonging to a Chinese merchant named Consequa; but it is not indigenous to the south of China, and is rarely seen in perfection there. Indeed the simple fact of its being perfectly hardy in England shows at once that it has a more northern origin.

Before the last war with China foreigners were confined to narrow limits about Canton and Macao, where they had no means of knowing anything of the more hardy plants of the north, which they sometimes met with in gardens, and introduced into Europe. Now, however, we can prosecute our botanical researches in a country which is nearly a thousand miles further to the north-east, and at many other places which lie along that line of coast. The island of Koo-lung-sû, for example, near Amoy, was taken by our troops during the war, and occupied by them for some years, according to treaty, until a portion of the ransom-money was paid. It seemed to have been a place of residence for many of the mandarins and principal merchants in peaceful times, and boasted of its gardens and pretty fish-ponds. When I first saw these gardens they were mostly in a ruinous condition, and everywhere exhibited the fatal effects of war. Many beautiful plants, however, still continued to grow and scramble about over the ruined walls. Captain Hall, of the Madras army, who was stationed there for some time, was very fond of botany, and took great pleasure in pointing out to me all the plants which he met with in his rambles. "I have good news for you," said he one morning when I met him; "come with me and I will show you the most beautiful plant on the island. I have just discovered it. It is a creeper, produces fine long racemes of lilac flowers before it puts forth its leaves, and is deliciously fragrant." What could it be? was it new? would it produce perfect seeds? or could young plants be procured to send home? were questions which rapidly suggested themselves. It is only the enthusiastical botanical collector who can form an idea of the amount of excitement and pleasure there is when one fancies he is on the eve of finding a new and beautiful flower. Captain Hall led the way, and we soon reached the spot where the plant grew. There had been no exaggeration in his description; there it was, covering an old wall, and scrambling up the branches of the adjoining trees; it bore long racemes of pea-shaped flowers, and scented the surrounding air with its odours. Need I say it was the beautiful *Wistaria?* But it was not found in a wild state even at Amoy, and had evidently been brought from more northern latitudes.

When I reached Chusan, in latitude 30° north, I found a remarkable change in the appearance of the vegetation. Tropical forms had entirely disappeared, or were rarely met with. Although the summers were as warm, or even warmer, than they were in the south, yet the winters were nearly as cold as those we have in England. At this place, and all over the provinces of Chekiang and Kiang-nan, the Glycine seemed to be at home. It grew wild on every hill-side, scrambling about in the hedges by the footpaths, and hanging over and dipping its leaves and flowers into the canals and mountain-streams.

But by far the most beautiful effect is produced when it attaches itself to the stems and branches of other trees. This is not unfrequent in nature, and is often copied by the Chinese and introduced into their gardens. One can scarcely imagine anything more gorgeous or beautiful than a large plant of this kind in full bloom. Its main and larger branches are entwined round every branch and branchlet of the tree, and from them hundreds of small ones hang down until they nearly touch the ground. The whole of the branches are covered with flower-buds, which a day or two of warm weather brings rapidly forward into bloom. To form an idea of the effect produced by these thousands of long lilac racemes, one must imagine a floral cascade, or a weeping willow covered with the flowers of the Glycine. There are some large specimens of this kind on the island of Chusan. One, in particular, was most striking. Not content with monopolising one tree, it had scrambled over a whole clump, and formed a pretty arbour underneath. When I saw it last it was in full flower, and had a most charming appearance.

The Chinese are fond of growing the Glycine on trellis-work, and forming long covered walks in the garden, or arbours and porticos in front of their doors. I have already noticed a large specimen of this description in the garden of the British consulate at Shanghae. There is another remarkable one in the garden of a mandarin at Ning-po. Growing in company with it is the fine new variety introduced lately by the Horticultural Society of London, and described in the Journal of the Society. In foliage and general habit the two kinds are nearly alike, but the new one bears long racemes of pure white flowers. The kind old gentleman to whom the garden belonged (he is dead now) allowed me to make layers of this plant on the top of his house, and during the summer months, when I was travelling in other districts, attended to them and watered them with his own hands. When I saw him about a year ago he told me he was then nearly eighty years old. One of the gentlemen who accompanied me (Dr. Kirk, of Shanghae), being introduced to him as a medical man, was asked if he could live one year more. The old man said he knew he must die soon, but he was most anxious to live for another year, but feared he should not. His presentiment was but too correct, for the next time I visited Ning-po, about six months after, I found the door of the mansion bricked up, and the garden neglected and overrun with weeds.

I visited several other nursery gardens about ten or twelve miles to the eastward of Shanghae. One of them contained a very remarkable plant which I must not omit noticing. Those who have read my 'Wanderings in China' may remember a story I told of my endeavours to find a *Yellow Camellia*,—how I offered five dollars for one—how a Chinaman soon found two instead of one—and how he got the money and I got taken in!

In one of these nurseries, however, I found a yellow Camellia, and it was in bloom when I bought it. It is certainly a most curious plant, although not very handsome. The flowers belong to the anemone or Warratah class; the outer petals are of a French white, and the inner ones are of a primrose yellow. It appears to be a very distinct species in foliage, and may probably turn out more hardy than any of its race.

CHAPTER XX.

Safe arrival of tea-plants in India — Means taken in China to engage tea manufacturers — I visit Chusan — My lodgings — A mandarin who smoked opium — His appearance at daylight — A summer morning in Chusan — An emperor's edict — The Yang-mae — Beauty of its fruit — City of Ting-hae — Poo-too, or Worshipping Island — Ancient inscriptions in an unknown language — A Chinese caught fishing in the sacred lake — He is chased by the priests — The bamboo again — The sacred Nelumbium — My holidays expire — Collections of tea-seeds and plants made — Return to Shanghae — Tea manufacturers engaged — We bid adieu to the north of China.

DURING the summer of 1850 I had the satisfaction of hearing that my collections of tea-plants had arrived safely at Calcutta. Owing to the excellent arrangements made there by Dr. Falconer, and at Allahabad by Dr. Jameson, they reached their destination in the Himalayas in good order. One of the objects of my mission to China had been, to a certain extent, accomplished. The Himalayan tea plantations could now boast of having a number of plants from the best tea-districts of China, namely, from the green-tea country of Hwuy-chow, and from the black-tea country of the Woo-e hills.

I had now, however, what I believed to be a much more difficult and uncertain task before me. This was to procure tea manufacturers from some of the best districts. Had I wanted men from any of the towns on the coast, they might have been procured with the greatest ease. A shipload of emigrants had been induced to embark for California only a short time before, and emigration was carried on most extensively both at Amoy and Canton. But I wanted men from districts far inland, who were well acquainted with the process of preparing the teas.

In order that I might accomplish this in a satisfactory manner, Mr. Beale kindly lent me his aid. His Compradore, who was a man highly respected by the Chinese and well known, undertook to conduct the negotiations. In the mean time I left Shanghae for the tea-districts about Ning-po, in order to make arrangements for another supply of seeds and young plants from that country.

In the end of June the weather, as usual, became excessively hot, and it was dangerous to be out in the sun, more particularly in an inland district. I determined, therefore, to leave the old monastery where I was staying, and take up my quarters on some of the islands in the Chusan archipelago.

I was anxious to see the island of Chusan, which we had held for some years after the war, but which is now once more in the possession of the Chinese. I found it a bustling place, and apparently greatly improved. The fine harbour was full of junks, some bound for the south, others for the north, and all seemed to make Chusan a kind of starting point. A large town had been built along the shore, and it was difficult to find out the old houses in which the

English lived when the island was in possession of the Queen's troops.

The large hospital built by the English was still standing, and, being now converted into a kind of customhouse and used for public purposes, I went there to look for quarters during my stay. Here I found an old mandarin, who received me politely, and offered me a room upstairs next to his own.

This old man was an inveterate opium-smoker. In the evening, when my servant was spreading out my bed, he happened to lay it by the wall next to the old man's room. "You had better not put your master's bed there," said one of the people connected with the office; "the Loi-ya smokes opium, and makes a disagreeable noise in his sleep." I found this was too true.

About nine o'clock in the evening the old man lay down in his bed, lighted his little lamp, and began to inhale the fumes of the intoxicating drug. He was smoking, at intervals, until I went to bed, and for some time afterwards. Between one and two o'clock in the morning I was awakened out of a sound sleep by a strange and unusual noise. It was some seconds before I could call to mind where I was or who was my neighbour. At last I remembered the warning which my servant had received. The drug had done its work; the old opium-smoker was evidently asleep and in the land of dreams. His nasal organs were producing most discordant sounds, and it was these and a harsh moaning noise which awoke me.

At daybreak I rose and passed through his room, on my way out of the building. He was now sleeping soundly and quietly. The opium-pipe was placed on a table at the side of his bed, and the little lamp was standing by the side of it. The heavy fumes of opium still filled the apartment, and made me glad to get out into the open air.

What a change was now presented to my view! I had been looking on a pitiable depraved specimen of man—"the lord of creation;" I now looked on creation itself. The air was cool, soft, and refreshing, as it blows at this time of the year from the south, and consequently comes over the sea. The dew was sparkling on the grass, and the birds were just beginning their morning song of praise.

When I returned from a morning stroll I found the old mandarin up at breakfast. About this time an edict had been promulgated by the new Emperor, not only condemning opium-smoking, but threatening with severe punishment all who indulged in the habit. Any officer in the service of Government who was an opium-smoker was to lose his appointment and also his rank, and the disgrace and degradation were to be extended to his family and children for some generations. But the most curious part of the proceeding remains to be told, and shows how very considerate his Celestial Majesty is to his subjects in matters of this kind. The celebrated edict was not to be enforced for some months. The opium-smoker had begun the year smoking, and he was to be allowed to continue to smoke until its close! Of course an edict of this kind was sure to create a considerable sensation, not only amongst the Chinese, but also amongst the importers of the drug. The best informed, however, and those who had some experience of the character of the Chinese, treated it as so much waste paper—as a collection of high-sounding words without meaning. Nor were they wrong, for when the new year arrived the edict had been long forgotten, and opium-smokers went on smoking as they had done before.

The Chusan people had received the edict about the time of my visit, and this old gentleman evidently knew all about it. "Well," said I to him, "how is this? you were smoking opium last night; have you not seen the edict?" "Oh yes," he replied, "but it does not come into force until next year." Every night afterwards during my stay here he used to walk into my room about nine o'clock with a smile on his countenance and say, "I am going to smoke now; you know I shall not be allowed to smoke next year." And I firmly believe the old man smoked more than he had been accustomed to do, and likewise enjoyed it more.

As I have given a full description of the island of Chusan in my former work, I shall not again describe it; but I must not fail to notice a fruit which is cultivated on the sides of the hills here, and in various parts of the province of Chekiang. It is called the *Yang-mae,* and appears to be a species of *Myrica,* allied to the Himalayan *M. sapida,* noticed by Frazer, Royle, and other writers. The Chinese variety is, however, much superior to the Indian. Indeed, I believe the Chinese have both, but use the Indian one as a stock for grafting upon.

There is a very large plantation of this tree in Chusan, and the fruit was beginning to be brought to the market during my stay there. It was sold at a very cheap rate, and was considered a great luxury by the natives.

I had frequently seen the trees of the *Yang-mae*, but never when in fruit, so I determined to visit one of the plantations. Starting very early one morning, I crossed over the first range of hills, and found myself in the centre of the island with my view bounded by hills in all directions. On the sides of these inland hills there were large quantities of the *Yang-mae*. The trees were bushy, round-headed, and from fifteen to twenty feet in height. They were at this time loaded with dark-red fruit, not unlike, at first sight, the fruit of our Arbutus, although very differently formed and much larger. I observed two kinds, one with red fruit, and the other with fruit of a yellowish colour. The trees formed most striking objects on the hill side.

The natives were busily engaged in gathering the fruit and packing it in baskets for the markets. Large quantities are consumed in the city of Ting-hae, the capital of Chusan, and a great deal is taken across to the main land. The streets of Ning-po used to be crowded with it during the season. The gatherers appeared delighted to see a stranger, and offered me liberal supplies of this fine fruit. It looked very beautiful and inviting, both upon the trees and also as it lay crowded in the little baskets.

On my return from the Yang-mae plantations I spent some time in the old city of Ting-hae. All marks of English possession had entirely disappeared. Tailors, shoemakers, and other tradesmen, with their quaint English names and signboards, so amusing in former days, were now nowhere to be seen. Everything was purely Chinese, and no one, unacquainted with the history of the place, would have suspected that it had been in the hands of the English a year or two before.

After staying for a few days at Chusan I went onward to another of the islands named Poo-too. This is commonly called by foreigners the "Worshipping Island," and is inhabited by the priests of Buddha and their followers. I had two objects in visiting it at this time; the first was on account of my health, which was getting affected by the excessive heat of the weather, and the second was to obtain a copy of some inscriptions which I had observed on a former occasion.

When I landed I walked over the hill in the direction of one of the principal temples, which had been built in a little valley or glen between the hills. On the roadside, by the way, I came to the stones on which the inscriptions had been carved. There were two of them; they looked like little grave-stones, and, as usual in such cases, each had a small place near its base for burning incense.

The characters upon them were not Chinese, and

no Chinaman could read them. I applied to some
of the *most learned* priests in Poo-too, but without
success. They could neither read them, nor could
they give me the slightest information as to how
they came to be placed there.

The characters looked like those of some northern
Indian language. One of the stones was evidently
less aged than the other. In this, the unknown characters were placed along the top, and a row of Chinese ones below. The latter, when read, appeared to
be nothing more than an unmeaning phrase used by
the Buddhist priests at the commencement of their
worship, " *Nae mo o me to fa.*" What the upper
line means, some oriental scholar may possibly be
able to say.

南 無 阿 彌 陀 佛

The second stone was evidently very ancient.
There were no Chinese characters upon this.

How, or when, these stones were placed there, it is
difficult to form even a conjecture. Buddhism, we
know, was imported from India to China, and it is
just possible that under these old stones may lie the
remains of some of its earliest preachers. Persecuted,
perhaps, by the heathens of the time, they sought a

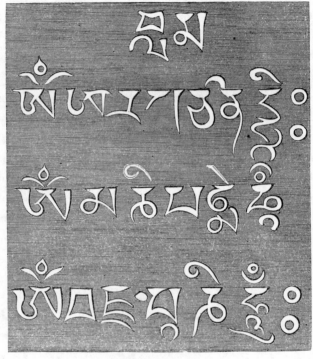

[Old Stone at Poo-too.]

home on the small and solitary island where their remains are now reposing.

Having made copies of the characters, I went onwards down the hill, in the direction of a large group of temples. At the bottom of the hill, and in front of the temples, there is a pretty lake filled with the Nelumbium, which was now in full bloom. As I came near, I observed a Chinaman fishing in the lake. This rather surprised me, as the Buddhists in this part of China do not take the life of any animal, and never eat animal food,—at least such is their pro-

fession.   The man evidently knew he was doing
wrong, and was hiding behind the pillars of a bridge
which is here thrown over the lake.   His occupation,
however, was soon put a stop to in a most laughable
manner.   At a little distance on the other side of
the bridge stood a group of men whose long flowing
garments and shaved tailless heads denoted that they
belonged to the Buddhist priesthood.   They were
evidently watching the movements of the angler with
considerable anxiety and interest.   At last one of
their number, with a bamboo in his hand, left the
others and moved towards the bridge by a circuitous
route, so as not to be observed by the man who was
fishing.   The priest managed this so cleverly that he
was on the bridge and by the side of the angler before
the latter knew that he had been observed; indeed
the first intimation he received of his being discovered was from the bamboo, which the priest did
not fail to lay pretty smartly over his shoulders.

This scene was now most laughable to all except
the trespasser.   He seemed at first inclined to turn
upon his assailant, but the priest, who was a stout
young fellow, laid the bamboo on without mercy.
The other priests were also fast coming upon the
scene of action.   When the delinquent observed
them, he evidently considered that " discretion was
the better part of valour," and took to his heels,
running up the hill with the whole party of priests in
full chase after him.   He would most likely have
been caught, had not my appearance on the scene
attracted the notice of his pursuers.

As soon as the priests saw me they gave up the pursuit, and, coming up to me, received me with much politeness, and asked me to visit the temples. In the mean time the unfortunate angler was making the best of his way over the hills in the direction of the sea. Having returned the salutations of the priests, I asked them to explain the cause of the extraordinary scene which I had just witnessed. They informed me that the man I had seen was a thief and a pirate, who had come from some of the neighbouring islands to fish in the sacred lake and kill their fishes!

I now walked down to the lake accompanied by the priests. No flower could be more beautiful or more majestic than the Nelumbium was at this season. As I stood on the little romantic bridge I looked to the right and left; my eye rested on thousands of these flowers, some of which were white, others red, and all were rising out of the water and standing above the beautiful clear green foliage. The leaves themselves, as they lay upon the smooth surface of the lake, or stood erect upon long footstalks, were scarcely less beautiful than the flowers, and both harmonized well together. Gold, silver, and other kinds of fishes were seen swimming swiftly to and fro, and apparently enjoying themselves under the shade of the broad leaves, in happy ignorance of the encounter between their protectors and their piratical enemy.

The surrounding scenery was strikingly picturesque. On all sides of the lake were well-wooded hills, whose summits were about fifteen hundred feet

above the level of the sea.   The ancient pile of temples, which covered many acres of land, was situated
on the northern side of the lake, while others of a less
pretending character were seen peeping out from
amongst the trees on every hill-side.

The lake, covered with flowers, the wooded mountains, the ancient temples, and the glorious flood of
light which was scattered over the scene from a clear
sky, made one almost fancy oneself in some scene of
enchantment.

In the garden of a mandarin at Ning-po I once
observed a very beautiful variety of the Nelumbium,
different from the red and white kinds already noticed,
and which I may distinguish by the name of *N. vitta-
tum*, its flowers being finely striped.   It was evidently
extremely rare in that part of China, so rare indeed
that I could not succeed in procuring a plant to send
to England.

Although these plants are generally grown in the
stove when their cultivation is attempted in this
country, they are fitted by nature to endure a very
low degree of temperature in winter.   They are
abundant in all parts of the province of Kiang-nan,
at Shanghae, Soo-chow, and Nanking, where the
winters are very severe.   The ponds and lakes are
often frozen up, and the thermometer frequently
sinks to within a few degrees of zero.   During the
spring and summer months the plants form and perfect their leaves, flowers, and fruit; in autumn, all
the parts which are visible above water gradually
decay, and nothing is left in a living state except the

large roots, which remain buried deep in the mud, and they continue in a dormant state until the warmth of spring again calls vegetable life into action. This is the treatment which Nature gives this beautiful plant, and we shall never succeed with its cultivation in this country unless we follow her example. Our summers are probably not hot enough for it to succeed if planted out in our lakes and ponds, but, if we find it necessary to give it artificial heat in summer, we must not forget that it requires a period of rest during winter. In China the lotus-ponds are generally nearly dry in winter, when the plants are in a state of rest; this is another point for our consideration when we cultivate them artificially.

The Nelumbium, or *Lien-wha*, is cultivated very extensively in China for the sake of its roots, which are esteemed an excellent vegetable, and are much used by all classes of the community. The roots attain their largest size at the period when the leaves die off; and are dug up and brought to market during the winter months in the north of China. The stalls of the greengrocers are always loaded with them at that season of the year. Although in high repute amongst the natives, being served up with many of their dishes and forming part of others, I must say that I never liked them, nor are they generally liked by foreigners. An excellent description of arrowroot is made from them, which is considered equal in quality to that which we import from the West Indies. The seeds are also held in high estimation; they are commonly roasted before being served up to table.

In the beginning of September, my two months' holiday having expired, I left the islands of the Chusan archipelago for the main land. The south-west monsoon was nearly over, northerly winds were not unfrequent, and the weather was already much cooler. Responsible men on whom I could depend, or rather on whom I had sufficient checks, were now despatched to the great tea districts of Hwuy-chow and Fokien for collections of tea-seeds, and I took up my quarters in the districts near Ning-po. On many occasions during these campaigns I was greatly indebted to the British consuls here for much kindness and hospitality—in the first instance to Mr. Sullivan, now at Amoy, and latterly to Mr. Brooke Robertson. There is an excellent garden at the Ning-po Consulate, and I often took advantage of it for the protection of my plants.

Having procured a large quantity of tea-seeds and young plants, I left the Ning-po districts in the end of December for Shanghae. On my arrival there I found that some good tea manufacturers and lead box makers had been engaged, and everything had succeeded far beyond my most sanguine expectations. A large assortment of implements for the manufacture of tea had also arrived. Nothing therefore remained for me to do except to pack my plants and proceed on my voyage to India.

It was an amusing scene to see these inland China-men taking leave of their friends and their native country. A large boat was engaged, and lay along-side the jetty, to take them and their effects from

2 A

Shanghae down to the mouth of the river, where the
" Island Queen" was at anchor, to start for Hong-
kong next morning. The landing-place was crowded
with the emigrants and their friends. When the
hour of departure arrived, the eight Chinese walked
on board, and the boat was immediately pushed out
into the stream. Now the emigrants on board, and
their friends on shore, with clasped hands, bowed to
each other many, many times, and the good wishes
for each other's health and happiness were not few,
nor apparently insincere. Next morning the " Island
Queen," Captain M'Farlane, got under way, and we
bade adieu to the north of China.

CHAPTER XXI.

Experiments with tea-seeds — Best method of sending them to distant countries — How oaks and chestnuts might be transported — Arrive at Calcutta — Condition of the collections — East India Company's botanic garden — Amherstia and other plants in bloom — Proceed onwards — The Sunderbunds — Arrive at Allahabad — Land journey — Reach Saharunpore — State of the tea-plants — Saharunpore garden — Mussooree garden — Its trees and other productions — Its value to the country and to Europe.

In the autumn of 1848 I sent large quantities of tea-seeds to India. Some were packed in loose canvas bags, others were mixed with dry earth and put into boxes, and others again were put up in very small packages, in order to be quickly forwarded by post; but none of these methods were attended with much success. Tea-seeds retain their vitality for a very short period if they are out of the ground. It is the same with oaks and chestnuts, and hence the great difficulty of introducing these valuable trees into distant countries by seeds.

In 1849, however, I succeeded in finding a sure and certain method of transporting tea-seeds to foreign countries in full life; and as this method will apply to all short-lived seeds as well as to those of the tea-plant, it is important that it should be generally known. It is simply to sow the seeds in Ward's cases soon after they are gathered.

2 a 2

My first experiment was tried in the following manner. Having procured some fine mulberry-plants from the district where the best Chinese silk is produced, I planted them in a Ward's case in the usual way, and watered them well. In two or three days, when the soil was sufficiently dry, a large quantity of tea-seeds were scattered over its surface, and covered with earth about half an inch deep. The whole was now sprinkled with water, and fastened down with a few crossbars to keep the earth in its place. The case was then screwed down in the usual way, and made as tight as possible.

When the case reached Calcutta the mulberry-plants were found to be in good condition, and the tea-seeds had germinated during the voyage, and were now covering the surface of the soil. Dr. Falconer, writing to me upon the receipt of this case, says, "The young tea-plants were sprouting around the mulberries as thick as they could come up."

During this year (1849) large quantities of seeds were sown in other cases between the rows of young tea-plants. These also germinated on their way to India, and reached their destination in the Himalayas in good condition.

When the news of the success of these experiments reached me from India, I determined to adopt the same plan when I packed the cases which I was now taking round under my own care. Tea-seeds were therefore sown in all the cases between the rows of young plants.

Fourteen cases having been packed and prepared

in this manner, I had still a large quantity of seeds
—about a bushel—remaining on hand.   These I determined to dispose of in the following manner.   Two
glazed cases had been prepared to take a collection
of camellias from China to the Botanic Garden at
Calcutta.   The tea-seeds were emptied out in front
of these cases and a small portion of earth thrown in
amongst them.   A layer of this mixture, which now
consisted of about one part earth and two parts seeds,
was laid in the bottom of each case, and the camellia-
plants were lifted gently out of their pots and placed
upon it.   The spaces between the plants were then
filled up to the proper height with this mixture of
tea-seeds and earth, and a little soil was sprinkled
upon the surface to cover the uppermost seeds.   The
whole was then well watered, bars were nailed across
to keep the earth in its place, and the lids of the
cases were fastened down in the usual manner.

My collections of plants and seeds, which now
filled sixteen glazed cases, were in this state when I
left Shanghae with the Chinese manufacturers and
implements, as described in the last chapter.   This
was on the 16th of February, 1851.   The north-east
monsoon was now blowing steadily along the coast of
China.   This being a fair wind, all sail was set, and
in four days we anchored in the bay of Hong-kong,
having run little less than one thousand miles.   We
at once went onwards in the steam-ship " Lady Mary
Wood," and arrived at Calcutta on the 15th of
March.   Here we took up our abode with Dr. Falconer, the superintendent of the H.C. Botanic Garden,

and it was at this time that the counterfeit tea was made from the leaves of *Pongamia glabra*, the account of which I have given in a former chapter. All the glass cases were taken to the garden to be examined and put in order for the next part of the journey.

When the cases were opened in Calcutta the young tea-plants were found to be in good condition. The seeds which had been sown between the rows were also just beginning to germinate. These, of course, were left undisturbed, as there was room enough for them to grow; but it was necessary to take other measures with those in the camellia cases. On opening the latter, the whole mass of seeds, from the bottom to the top, was swelling, and germination had just commenced. The camellias, which had now arrived at their destination, were lifted gently out and potted, and appeared as if they had never left their native country. Fourteen new cases were got ready, filled with earth, and these germinating seeds were sown thickly over the surface, and covered with soil in the usual way. In a few days the young plants came sprouting through the soil; every seed seemed to have grown; and by this simple plan about twelve thousand plants were added to the Himalayan plantations.

Many attempts are yearly made by persons in Europe to send out seeds of our oaks and chestnuts to distant parts of the world, and these attempts generally end in disappointment. Let them sow the seeds in Ward's cases as I have described, and they are

MACKINTOSH HOUSE

05491

Charles Rennie Mackintosh (1868-1928), the influential Scottish architect and designer, lived at 6 Florentine Terrace, later renamed 78 Southpark Avenue, from 1906 to 1914. Substantial alterations were made to the Victorian house and the principal interiors decorated in his distinctive style. A development of those created for his previous home at 120 Mains Street, Glasgow, the interiors were remarkable in their day for the austerity of the furnishings and decoration. Mackintosh's remodelling demonstrates his architectural approach to the creation of an interior in the manipulation of space and light, and the orchestration of contrasting visual and spatial effects. The furniture, Mackintosh's collection of his own work, documents ten years of his output as a designer from 1896.

In 1914, with his career in decline. Mackintosh and his wife Margaret Macdonald Mackintosh (1864-1933) left Glasgow, and the house together with most of its contents was purchased five years later by William Davidson, Mackintosh's client at Windyhill, Kilmacolm. Following Mr Davidson's death in 1945, his sons presented the contents to the University which purchased the property. The house was used as a residence for senior members of staff till 1963 when, because of the threat posed by subsidence and the University's plans for redevelopment in the area, the house was demolished. Prior to demolition, however, an extensive survey was carried out and all salvageable fitments removed to enable a future reconstruction of the principal interiors: dining room, studio-drawing room and main bedroom, together with the hall and stairway.

The Gallery architects, Whitfield Partners, London, have sought to recreate the original appearance and character of these interiors. The rooms are daylit, are linked by a reconstructed hall and staircase, and enjoy the same orientation as the original. Air-conditioning and security systems have been unobtrusively installed.

As far as possible the original decorative schemes have been recreated. Information has been sought from all available sources which include a few samples of paint, fabric and wallpaper, together with drawings and notes by Mackintosh, descriptions and memories from people who had known the house in Mackintosh's day or shortly after, and the evidence of other projects, particularly the photographs of the architect's previous home in Mains Street.

THE HALL

In the hall the major alteration was the remodelling of the entrance. The outer pair of storm doors was replaced by a single door, the inner half-glazed door removed, the porch step sloped, and the flanking sides panelled with pine. Stained wood strapping was applied to the north and south walls. The height of this strapping and the front door follows that of the dining room arrangement. A horizontal leaded window replaced the original narrow upright on the south wall. The cornice was replaced with a cove.

Four doors led from the hall to the dining room, cloakroom, servant's room and kitchen. The two latter doors have not been reconstructed.

Although no contemporary photographs of the Mains Street hall survive, stylistically the stained oak settle and lead umbrella stand date from 1900 and must have been used there. The stained oak hat, coat and umbrella stand, based on a design for the Argyle Street Tea Rooms in 1897, also came from Mains Street. The beaten lead mirror, entitled "Vanity", was made by Margaret and Frances Macdonald and Herbert MacNair in 1896 and exhibited that year at the Arts and Crafts Exhibition, London. The piece is on loan from Glasgow School of Art (Davidson Bequest).

The colour scheme is based on the memories of those who knew the house during the Mackintosh and Davidson periods. It is possible that the walls between the strapping were originally decorated with a stencilled pattern.

STAIRWAY

Apart from the installation of a new window at first floor level, no alterations were made by Mackintosh to the stairway. The treads were originally stone to the first landing with wood above. A door on the half-landing between ground and first floor, not reconstructed, led to a rear bedroom situated over the kitchen. The decorative scheme with its white treads and balustrade, dark handrail, narrow haircord carpet, papered walls and white ceiling is closest to though less elaborate than that created at Hous'hill, Nitshill, Glasgow (1904).

Desk and Cabinets: The white-painted pieces are oak. The studio bookcase is a version of that designed for Mackintosh's brother-in-law Charles Macdonald, Dunglass Castle, Bowling (1900). One of the collection's outstanding treasures is the mahogany writing cabinet in the studio, purchased for a world-record price in 1979 after an international appeal. Based on a 1904 design for The Hill House, the rigid geometry of square and rectangle is relieved by the restricted use of gently-curving members and decorative inlays of leaded-glass, ivory, mother-of-pearl and pearwood. A chair and a pair of candlesticks accompanied the desk. It is probable the cabinet had a stained and polished finish which matched these pieces. A replica of the chair is on display.

The elaborate cabinets flanking the drawing room fireplace follow a design of 1902 for Mrs Rowat. The white desk (1900) is an ingenious design with deep side cupboards and various internal subdivisions. The silvered beaten copper panels, though unsigned, are probably by Margaret Macdonald Mackintosh.

Bric à Brac: The furnishings included various items by Margaret Macdonald Mackintosh: a silvered beaten copper panel (1899); two circular leaded-glass plaques (1900); and a circular lead plaque (1900).

The studio bookshelves are in process of being filled with a library which reflects the Mackintoshes' known interests and reading. Works with appropriate decorative bindings of the period are also being included.

2nd FLOOR LANDING

Various alterations were made at this level. The existing small bathroom in front of the window was removed, and the skylight filled in. The west stairwell wall was panelled and one of the plaster panels designed for the Willow Tea Rooms (1903) incorporated above.

Two doors led from the landing, one to a short passageway and bathroom converted from an existing bedroom, and the other to the main bedroom. In the reconstruction the former leads to the Mackintosh Exhibition Gallery. The black stairway led to a south-facing attic room and balcony which the Mackintoshes used as a guest bedroom.

BEDROOM

By removing the partition wall dividing the two front bedrooms, an L-shaped apartment was created which would accommodate the white-painted oak suite. The two existing doors were removed, and a new door and arched passageway introduced. The splayed window shutters were replaced with squared-off reveals. The Mains Street bedroom fireplace was installed; a gesso panel was probably intended to fit above.

As at Mains Street, Mackintosh created a white room setting enriched by the stencilled fabrics and the glass and painted insets in the furniture designed in 1900.

The wardrobe, a particularly sculptural piece, constructed in three sections with a removable shelving unit, is closely related to that for The Hill House (1903). The double curve of its handles is taken up in the uprights of the cheval mirror, the most elaborate Mackintosh designed. The detailing of the handles and insets in the mirror is repeated in the bedside tables, a compact design later developed at Windyhill (1902) and Hous'hill (1904). The bed was the first four-poster Mackintosh designed, a format he returned to at Hous'hill in 1904. The original design for the washstand shows that the piece was intended to have an upper section as a splashback. The marks of crude sawing-off, probably by Mackintosh to suit the new window location, can still be seen beneath the white caps.

None of the fabrics for the bed or washstand survive. Replicas based on the evidence of the Mains Street photographs have been made up.

As no bedside lights have survived, fittings from the main bedroom, Windyhill (1901), have been hung at either side of the bed.

The most extensive collection anywhere of the work of Charles Rennie Mackintosh is housed in the Hunterian Art Gallery. Changing selections from the collection and related loans are shown in the Exhibition Gallery at the top of the Mackintosh Wing.

Those areas of the collection not on show may be seen on weekdays by appointment. Applications should be made in writing to the Secretary.

The Mackintosh Wing may have to be closed at certain times. Parties must book in advance. No disabled access.

Hunterian Art Gallery,   Mon.-Fri. 9.30-12.30 **&** 1.30-5.00
University of Glasgow,   Sat. 9.30-1.00
82 Hillhead Street,   041-330 5431
Glasgow, G12 8QQ.

There is a 50 pence admission charge on weekday afternoons and Saturday mornings.

almost sure of success. If they are to be sent to a great distance, they should be sown thinly, not in masses.

The H. C. Botanic Garden at Calcutta is situated on the right bank of the river Hooghly, a little below the " City of Palaces." From the time of Dr. Wallich's retirement until the appointment of Dr. Falconer extensive alterations appear to have been made. It must be confessed, however, that some of these alterations have been most injurious to the garden. For example, many valuable specimens and groups of trees have been cut down, which cannot be replaced in one generation. We look in vain for those noble specimens of palm-trees which must have been planted in the days of Roxburgh and Wallich, while in their places we find some small " botanical arrangements " which cannot be carried out, and which are never likely to answer the purposes for which they were intended.

The alterations now in progress appear to be of a very different kind, and are the first results of a well-digested plan. It is proposed to form a large Arboretum in one portion of the grounds, to contain specimens of all the exogenous trees and shrubs which grow in the climate of Bengal; in another part of the garden the endogens, such as palms, Dracænas, &c., are to be placed ; and no doubt other classifications of herbaceous and medical plants will also be formed. If this plan is carried out as it has been commenced, this noble establishment will present a very different appearance in a few years.

During my stay here I saw two remarkable plants
in full bloom. The one was *Amherstia nobilis*, and
the other *Jonesia Asoca*. The former was considered
rather difficult to manage, but it is now succeeding
admirably under the treatment of Mr. Scott, the head
gardener. Its long racemes of scarlet flowers were
certainly most graceful and pretty. The *Jonesia*,
however, in my opinion is the more beautiful of the
two. I had frequently seen it in our stoves at home,
but I had no idea of its beauty until I saw it in the
Calcutta garden. It was now literally loaded with
its fine orange blossoms, which contrasted so well
with the dark-green leaves. Were the shrub better
known at home, I am sure we should see finer
specimens produced at our metropolitan flower-
shows.

The collections under my care being ready, I received orders from the Indian Government to proceed onwards on the 25th of March in one of the
small river steamers as far as Allahabad. The
Hooghly was shallow at this time of the year, it
being the dry season in India. We were, therefore,
obliged to go down the river to its mouth, and across
amongst the Sunderbunds. This vast country stretches
from the river Hooghly on the western side of the
bay of Bengal, to Chittagong on the east, and is
upwards of two hundred miles across. It is cut up
into hundreds of islands, some having the appearance
of being surrounded by arms of the sea, while others
are formed by rivers which intersect the land in all
directions. These are the many mouths of the

Ganges by which that mighty river empties itself into the bay of Bengal.

I was much struck with the dense vegetation of the Sunderbunds. The trees are low and shrubby in appearance; they grow close to the water's edge, and many dip their branches into the stream. The ground is so low in many places as to be nearly covered at high water or during spring-tides.

A great portion of the Sunderbunds is uninhabited by man. Here the Bengal tiger roams unmolested in his native wilds. I was told that the poor wood-cutters who come here in boats to cut wood are frequently carried off by this animal, notwithstanding all the charms which are used to keep him away. A priest is often brought in the boat, whose duty it is to land on the spot where the wood is to be cut, and to go through certain forms which are supposed to act as a spell upon the tigers. This, however, is frequently of little use, as the following anecdote will show. A short time since a small river steamer, in passing through the Sunderbunds, was in want of fuel. Her chief officer boarded one of these wood-boats in order to get some wood to enable her to proceed to the nearest coaling station. The poor woodman begged and prayed to be allowed to keep the wood which he had been some weeks in procuring, and in obtaining which he had lost six of his crew, who had been all carried off by tigers. " How is that," said the officer; " had you no priest with you to charm the tigers?" "Alas! that was of no use," replied the woodman, " for the priest was the first man the tigers took away."

As we steamed along through these narrow passages, numerous herds of deer were observed quietly feeding on the edges of the jungle. They appeared very tame, and often allowed us to get quite close to them before they took any notice of the steamer.

On the fifth day after leaving Calcutta we entered the main stream of the Ganges. All the towns on its banks have already been frequently described in accounts of India. I may, therefore, simply state that we passed in succession the large towns of Patna, Dinapoor, Ghazepoor, Benares, and Mirzapoor, and reached Allahabad on the 14th of April. Here the river Jumna joins the Ganges, neither of which is navigable for steamers above the fortress of Allahabad; we had, therefore, to continue our journey to Saharunpore by land. All the tea-plants were brought on shore and put in an open shed until arrangements could be made for sending them onward. Mr. Lowther, the Commissioner, who had received instructions from the Government concerning us, appeared most anxious that everything should be done to ensure the speedy and safe arrival of the men, plants, &c., at their destination. My thanks are also due to Mr. Waddington, the Government agent, for the kind manner in which he attended to my suggestions.

The Chinese and their effects, with the tea-plants and implements for manufacture, filled nine waggons. As it was not possible to get bullocks for more than three waggons a day, it was determined to send three on the 16th, three on the 17th, and the remainder on the 18th of the month. I left Allahabad on the evening of the 19th in a Government carriage, and by quick travelling I was enabled to inspect the different parties several times on the road between Allahabad and Saharunpore.

In due time all arrived at their destination in perfect safety, and were handed over to Dr. Jameson, the Superintendent of the Botanical Gardens in the North-West Provinces and of the Government tea-plantations. When the cases were opened, the tea-plants were found to be in a very healthy state. No fewer than 12,838 plants were counted in the cases, and many more were germinating. Notwithstanding their long voyage from the north of China, and the frequent transshipment and changes by the way, they seemed as green and vigorous as if they had been all the while growing on the Chinese hills.

Saharunpore is about thirty miles from the foot of the Himalayas. Its botanical garden is well known. It contains a large collection of ornamental and useful plants suited to the climate of this part of India, and they are propagated and distributed in the most liberal manner to all applicants. Medical plants are also cultivated upon an extensive scale, particularly the Hyoscyamus or Henbane. Upon the whole, this seems a valuable establishment, and exceedingly well managed by Dr. Jameson and the excellent head gardener, Mr. Milner.

But the climate of Saharunpore is too hot in summer for such plants as are commonly found in the open air in England, or which are indigenous to the

higher elevations of the Himalayas. Hence the
Indian Government, at the suggestion of Dr. Royle,
established in 1826 another nursery near the well-
known stations of Mussooree and Landour, and from
six to seven thousand feet above the level of the sea.

As the garden at Mussooree is of more interest to
the English reader than those at Calcutta and Saharunpore, I shall endeavour to give a description
of it. It is situated on the northern side of the first
range of the Himalayas, and extends a considerable
way down a romantic-looking glen. A public road
or bridle-path leads along the brow of the hill above
the garden, and it was from this road that I had the
first view of this pretty and interesting place. A
single glance was sufficient to convince me that this
was the celebrated garden from which so many interesting Himalayan trees and shrubs had found their
way to Europe. Many of the hill pines were most
conspicuous. The beautiful Deodar was seen towering above the other trees, and, although all the
specimens were comparatively young, they were yet
striking and graceful. Near it was the *Abies
Smithiana*. It had a dark and sombre appearance,
yet it was peculiarly graceful, owing to its symmetrical form and somewhat pendulous habit. Then
there was the *Cupressus torulosa*, which stood promi-
nently out from amongst the other trees, and a
distinct variety of the same species said to be from
Cashmere.

On entering the garden I commenced a minute
inspection of its interesting and varied productions.

It has no pretensions to be considered an ornamental garden, in so far as its walks and arrangements are concerned.   Narrow footpaths winding about in all directions amongst the trees, and little terraced patches for the cultivation of the different plants, are all that is to be seen in the way of arrangement.   To introduce the useful and ornamental plants of other countries to the northern provinces of India, and to gather together the productions of the Himalayas and send them out in all directions with a liberal hand, seem to be the principal objects for which this garden is maintained.   And very noble objects these undoubtedly are, and well worthy of the enlightened and liberal Government that supports it.

Our common garden-flowers seemed almost as abundant here as they are in our English nurseries. Pelargoniums, fuchsias, pinks, dahlias, violets, mimuluses, &c., were met with in great profusion, and at the time of my visit nearly all were in bloom.   Many of our English fruit trees and bushes had also been imported, such as apples, pears, plums, raspberries, &c. A quantity of apple and pear trees had just been received from America in a novel manner.   They had been sent out to Calcutta in ice by one of the vessels freighted with that article ; about one-fourth of the original number had reached the Himalayas in good condition.

Amongst Indian fruit-trees I observed a number of Cashmere kinds, which had been introduced here by Drs. Royle and Falconer.   Dr. Jameson had also introduced apples, pears, plums, almonds, &c., from

Cabul. All these things will one day find their way to Europe, and some of them may prove of great value.

As may be expected this little spot is particularly rich in the vegetable productions of the Himalayas. Besides those I have already noticed, I might add *A. Webbiana* and *Pinus excelsa.* Less known than these was a fine horse-chestnut called *Pavia indica,* a noble poplar (*Populus ciliata*), a species of *Buxus* —the box-tree of the hills, *Andromeda ovalifolia,* and *Ilex dipyrena.* Two fine species of evergreen oaks were also observed, named *Quercus dilatata* and *Q. semecarpifolia.* Amongst herbaceous plants I noticed some pretty primroses, *Lilium giganteum* and *Wallichianum,* and *Fritillaria polyphylla.* Here also was the once famous Prangos plant in full bloom.

But this establishment is of great value in another point of view. Connected with it are a number of native gardeners, who are out in the hills for months every autumn, collecting seeds of ornamental and useful trees and shrubs for distribution all over the world where such plants will grow. If we consider the thousands of the Deodar and other Himalayan pine-trees which are now to be found in every English nursery, we must perceive the vast amount of benefit which an establishment of this kind, small as it is, confers upon England.

In these days, when our Indian empire has become so greatly extended that it embraces every variety of climate and soil, one regrets that a place of this kind should be so small. Perhaps the Mussooree garden could not be much extended, but other places might be found even more suitable to carry out the purposes for which it was designed.   It may be very true that we have nearly all the productions of the Himalayas which are of value growing plentifully in our gardens at home, but the inhabitants of India cannot say as much with reference to the valuable productions with which our gardens abound.   In my opinion, one of the great objects of having a Government garden in these hills should be to introduce from Europe trees of a useful kind for the benefit of the natives of this country.

CHAPTER XXII.

Ordered to inspect the tea-plantations in India — Deyra Doon plantation — Mussooree and Landour — Flora of the mountains — Height
and general character — Our mode of travelling — Hill-plants
resemble those of China — Guddowli plantation — Chinese manufacturers located there — I bid them farewell — The country improves in fertility — Tea-plantations near Almorah — Zemindaree
plantations — Leave Almorah for Bheem Tal — View of the Snowy
range — Bheem Tal tea-plantations — General observations on tea
culture in India — Suggestions for its improvement — Other plants
which ought to be introduced — Nainee Tal — Arrive at Calcutta —
The Victoria regia.

Soon after my arrival at Saharunpore I received
through the Lieutenant - Governor of the North-
Western Provinces orders from the Governor-General
of India to visit all the tea plantations in the districts
of Gurhwal and Kumaon, and to draw up a report
upon their condition and future prospects. In this
tour of inspection I was accompanied by Dr. Jameson, who has the charge of all the Government tea
plantations. The first plantations we visited were
those in the Deyra Doon.

The Deyra Doon, or Valley of Deyra, is situated
in latitude 30° 18' north, and in longitude 78° east.
It is about 60 miles in length from east to west, and
16 miles broad at its widest part. It is bounded on
the south by the Sewalick range of hills, and on the
north by the Himalayas proper, which are here nearly

8000 feet above the level of the sea.   On the west
it is open to the river Jumna, and on the east to the
Ganges, the distance between these rivers being about
60 miles.

In the centre of this flat valley the Kaolagir tea
plantation has been formed.   Eight acres were under
cultivation in 1847.   There are now 300 acres
planted, and about 90 more taken in and ready for
many thousands of young plants lately raised from
seeds in the plantation.

The soil is composed of clay, sand, and vegetable
matter, rather stiff and apt to get "baked" in dry
weather, but free enough when it is moist or during
the rains.   It rests upon a gravelly subsoil, consisting
of limestone, sandstone, clay-slate, and quartz rock,
or of such rocks as enter into the composition of the
surrounding mountain ranges.   The surface is comparatively *flat*, although it falls in certain directions
towards the ravines and rivers.

The plants are arranged neatly in rows 5 feet
apart, and each plant is about 4½ feet from the next
one.   A long rank-growing species of grass, indigenous to the Doon, is most difficult to keep from over-
topping the tea-plants, and is the cause of much extra
labour.   Besides the labour common to all tea-countries in China, such as weeding, and occasionally
loosening the soil, there is here an extensive system
of irrigation carried on.   To facilitate this, the plants
are planted in trenches, from four to six inches below
the level of the ground, and the soil thus dug out is
thrown between the rows to form the paths.   Hence

2 B

the whole of the plantation consists of numerous trenches. At right angles with these trenches a small stream is led from the canal, and by opening or shutting their ends irrigation can be carried on at the pleasure of the overseer.

The plants generally did not appear to me to be in that fresh and vigorous condition which I had been accustomed to see in good Chinese plantations. This, in my opinion, is caused, 1st, by the plantation being formed on *flat land*; 2nd, by the system of *irrigation*; 3rd, by too early plucking; and 4th, by hot drying winds, which are not unfrequent in this valley from April to the beginning of June.

Leaving the Doon, we took the hill-road for Paorie, near which was the next tea-plantation on our route. This road led us through the well-known hill stations of Mussooree and Landour. As we ascended the mountains, it was curious to mark the changes which took place in the character of the vegetable productions. On the plains and lower sides of these hills such plants as *Justicia Adhatoda, Bauhinia racemosa* and *variegata, Vitex trifolia, Grislea tomentosa,* &c., grew in the greatest profusion. Higher up, say 3000 or 4000 feet above the level of the sea, *Berberis asiatica* makes its appearance, while nearer the top we find Oaks, Rhododendrons, *Berberis nepalensis, Andromeda ovalifolia,* Viburnums, Spiræas, and many other plants which are either hardy or half-hardy in England.

The mountains about Mussooree and Landour are nearly 8000 feet above the level of the sea. Their sides are steep, and they are generally exceedingly barren; here and there I observed little terraced patches of cultivation, bnt these were few and far between. The view from the tops of these mountains on a clear day is very fine. The Valley of Deyra lies spread out to the southward, and appears as if bounded on all sides by hills, while to the northward nothing is seen but rugged barren mountains and deep glens. The snowy range is also visible when the atmosphere is clear.

Leaving these hill stations on the 30th of May, we went onwards in an easterly direction along the sides of the mountains. The country was very mountainous, and there were no traces of cultivation for many miles on this part of our journey. A long train of Paharies or hill-men carried our tents, luggage, and provisions. Dr. Jameson and myself rode on ponies, while Mrs. Jameson, who accompanied us, was carried in a jaun-pan, or kind of light sedan-chair. In many places our road led along the sides of precipices which it made one giddy to look down, and had we made a single false step we should have fallen far beyond the reach of earthly aid.

On the journey along the upper sides and tops of these mountains, I had a good opportunity of observing the character of their vegetable productions. As Royle and other travellers have told us, the flora of the Himalayas at high elevations bears a striking resemblance to that of European countries; and I can add that it resembles still more the hill vegetation of the same latitudes in China. In fact many of the species found in the Himalayas are identical

2 B 2

with those which I met with on the Bohea mountains,
and on the hills of Chekiang and Kiang-see. I might
here give the names of the different plants met with
on this journey from Mussooree to Paorie, but it will,
perhaps, be better for me to refer the reader for such
information to Royle's 'Illustrations of the Botany
of the Himalayan Mountains.'

On the morning of the 6th of June we arrived at
the Guddowli plantation near Paorie. This plantation is situated in the province of Eastern Gurhwal,
in latitude 30° 8' north, and in longitude 78° 45'
east. It consists of a large tract of terraced land,
extending from the bottom of a valley or ravine to
more than 1000 feet up the sides of the mountain.
Its lowest portion is about 4300 feet, and its highest
5300 feet, above the level of the sea : the surrounding
mountains appear to be from 7000 to 8000 feet
high. The plantation has not been measured, but
there are, apparently, fully one hundred acres under
cultivation.

There are about 500,000 plants, about 3400 of
which were planted in 1844 and are now in full
bearing ; the greater portion of the others are much
younger, having been planted out only one, two, or
three years. There are besides a large number of
seedlings in beds ready for transplanting.

The soil consists of a mixture of loam, sand, and
vegetable matter, is of a yellow colour, and is most
suitable for the cultivation of the tea-plant. It resembles greatly the soil of the best tea districts in
China. A considerable quantity of stones are mixed

with it, chiefly small pieces of clay-slate, of which the mountains here are composed. Large tracts of equally good land, at present covered with jungle, might be made available in this district without interfering in any way with the rights of the settlers.

I have stated that this plantation is formed on the hill side. It consists of a succession of terraces, from the bottom to the top, on which the tea-bushes are planted. In its general features it is very like a Chinese tea-plantation, although one rarely sees tea-lands terraced in China. This, however, may be necessary in the Himalayas, where the rains fall so heavily. Here too a system of irrigation is carried on, although to a small extent only, owing to the scarcity of water during the dry season.

This plantation is a most promising one, and I have no doubt will be very valuable in a few years. The plants are growing admirably, and evidently like their situation. Some of them are suffering slightly from the effects of hard plucking, like those at Kao-lagir; but this can easily be avoided in their future management. Altogether, it is in a most satisfactory condition, and shows how safe it is in matters of this kind to follow the example of the Chinese cultivator, who never makes his tea-plantations on *low rice land* and *never irrigates*.

The country about Paorie is entirely mountainous. Whichever way we look, east, west, south, or north, nothing is seen but mountains and hills, stony ravines, and deep glens. The view is bounded on the north and north-west by the snowy range.

The land is much more fertile than about Mussooree, and more thickly inhabited. Cultivated spots are everywhere visible, particularly on the lower portions of the hills and to about half way up their sides. All above that is generally barren, and, I should think, is rarely visited by man.

The Chinese manufacturers whom I had brought round from China were located on this farm. They had nice cottages and gardens given them, and everything was done which could add to their comfort in a strange land. On the morning I left Paorie the poor fellows got up early, and were dressed in their holiday clothes to bid me good bye. They brought me a packet of letters addressed to their relations in China, which they begged me to forward; they also offered me a small present, which they asked me to accept as a slight token of their gratitude for the kindness I had shown them during our long journey. This, of course, I declined, while I told them how much I was pleased with the motives by which they were actuated. I confess I felt sorry to leave them. We had travelled together for a long time, and they had always looked up to me with the most perfect confidence as their director and friend. While I had always treated them kindly myself, I had taken measures to have them kindly treated by others, and never, from the time of their engagement until I left them in their new mountain home, had they given me the slightest cause for anger.

We now proceeded to visit the plantations in the vicinity of Almorah. The country became more and more fertile as we advanced, and numerous excellent lands, well suited for the cultivation of the tea-plant, were passed on our route.   On the 29th of June we arrived at the Hawulbaugh plantation.

This tea-farm is situated on the banks of the river Kosilla, about six miles north-west from Almorah, the capital of Kumaon.   It is about 4500 feet above the level of the sea.   The land is of an undulating character, consisting of gentle slopes and terraces, and reminded me of some of the best tea-districts in China.   Indeed, the hills themselves, in this part of the Himalayas, are very much like those of China, being barren near their summit and fertile on their lower sides.

Thirty-four acres of land are under tea-cultivation here, including the adjoining farm of Chullar.   Some of the plants appear to have been planted in 1844; but, as at Paorie, the greater number are only from one to three years old.

The soil is what is usually called a sandy loam; it is moderately rich, being well mixed with vegetable matter.   It is well suited for tea-cultivation.   The greater part of the farm is terraced as at Guddowli, but some few patches are left in natural slopes in accordance with the Chinese method.   Irrigation is practised to a limited extent.

All the young plants here are in robust health and are growing well, particularly those that are on land where water cannot flood or injure them.   Some few of the older bushes appear rather stunted; but this is evidently the result of water remaining stagnant

about their roots, and partly also of over-plucking;
both defects, however, admit of being easily cured.

Nearer Almorah, and about 5000 feet above the
level of the sea, there are two small plantations
named Lutchmisser and Kuppeena. The former
contains three acres, and the latter four acres of land
under cultivation. The soil is light and sandy, and
much mixed with particles of clay-slate which have
crumbled down from the adjoining rocks. These
plantations are rarely irrigated, and the land is steep
enough to prevent any stagnant water from remaining
about the roots of the plants.

Most of the bushes here have been planted for
many years. They are in full bearing, and generally
in excellent health. On the whole I consider these
plantations in good order.

I have now described all the Government plantations in Gurhwal and Kumaon, except those at
Bheem Tal. Before visiting these, however, I was
instructed to inspect some others belonging to the
Zemindars, and under the patronage of the Commissioner and Assistant-Commissioner of Kumaon and
Gurhwal.

The first of these is at a place named Lohba,
which is situated in eastern Gurhwal, about fifty
miles to the westward of Almorah, and is at an elevation of 5000 feet above the level of the sea. It is
one of the most beautiful spots in this part of the
Himalayas. The surrounding mountains are high,
and in some parts precipitous, while in others they
consist of gentle slopes and undulations. On these

undulating slopes there is a great deal of excellent land suitable for tea-cultivation. A few tea-bushes have been growing vigorously for some years in the Commissioner's garden, and they are now fully 10 feet in height. These plants having succeeded so well, naturally induced the authorities of the province to try this cultivation upon a more extensive scale. It appears that in 1844 about 4000 young plants were obtained from the Government plantations, and planted on a tract of excellent land, which the natives wished to abandon. Instead of allowing the people to throw up their land, they were promised it rent-free upon the condition that they attended to the cultivation of the tea, which had been planted on a small portion of the ground attached to the village.

This arrangement seems to have failed, either from want of knowledge, or from design, or perhaps partly from both of these causes. More recently, a larger number of plants have been planted, but I regret to say with nearly the same results.

But results of this discouraging kind are what any one acquainted with the nature of the tea-plant could have easily foretold, had the treatment intended to be given it been explained to him. Upon inquiry, I found the villagers had been managing the tea-lands just as they had been doing their rice-fields, —that is, a regular system of irrigation was practised. *As water was plentiful,* a great number of the plants, indeed nearly all, seem to have perished from this cause. The last planting alluded to had been done late in the spring, and just at the commencement of the dry weather, and to these plants little or no water seems to have been given. So that in fact it was going from one extreme to another equally bad, and the result was of course nearly the same.

I have no hesitation in saying that the district in question is well adapted for the cultivation of tea. With judicious management a most productive farm might be established here in four or five years. Land is plentiful, and of little value either to the natives or the Government.

The second Zemindaree plantation is at Kutoor. This is the name of a large district thirty or forty miles northward from Almorah, in the centre of which the old town or village of Byznath stands. It is a fine undulating country consisting of wide valleys, gentle slopes, and little hills, while the whole is intersected by numerous streams, and surrounded by high mountains. The soil of this extensive district is most fertile, and is capable of producing large crops of rice on the low irrigable lands, and dry grains and tea on the sides of the hills. From some cause, however, either the thinness of population, or *the want of a remunerative crop*,* large tracts of this fertile district have been allowed to go out of cultivation. Everywhere I observed ruinous and jungle-covered terraces, which told of the more extended cultivation of former years.

* The crops of this district, such as rice, mundooa, and other grains, are so plentiful and cheap as scarcely to pay the carriage to the nearest market town, much less to the plains. In Almorah a maund of rice or mundooa sells for something less than a rupee, of barley for eight annas, and of wheat for a rupee.

Amongst some hills near the upper portion of this district, two small tea-plantations have been formed under the patronage and superintendence of Captain Ramsay, Senior Assistant-Commissioner of Kumaon. Each of them covers three or four acres of land, and had been planted about a year before the time of my visit. In this short space of time the plants had grown into nice strong bushes, and were in the highest state of health. I never saw, even in the most favoured districts in China, any plantations looking better than these. This result, Captain Ramsay informed me, had been attained in the following simple manner. All the land attached to the two villages with which the tea-farms are connected is exempted from the revenue-tax, a sum amounting to fifty-two rupees per annum. In lieu of paying this, the assamees (cultivators) of both villages furnish manure, and assist at the transplanting season, as well as in ploughing and preparing fresh land. In addition to this, one chowdree and four prisoners are constantly employed upon the plantations. The chief reason of the success of these plantations, next to that of the land being well suited for tea-cultivation, may, no doubt, be traced to a good system of management : that is, the young plants have been carefully transplanted at the proper season of the year, when the air was charged with moisture, and they have not been destroyed by excessive irrigation afterwards. The other Zemindaree plantation at Lohba might have been now in full bearing had the same system been followed.

From the description thus given, it will be observed that I consider the Kutoor plantations in a most flourishing condition; and I have no doubt they will continue to flourish, and soon convince the Zemindars of the value of tea-cultivation, provided three things intimately connected with the success of the crop are strongly impressed upon their minds; viz., the unsuitableness of low wet lands for tea cultivation; the folly of irrigating tea as they would do rice; and the impropriety of commencing the plucking before the plants are strong and of considerable size. I am happy to add that amongst these hills there are no foolish prejudices in the minds of the natives against the cultivation of tea. About the time of my visit a Zemindar came and begged to have 2000 plants to enable him to commence tea-growing on his own account.

It is of great importance that the authorities of a district and persons of influence should show an interest in a subject of this kind. At present the natives do not know its value, but they are as docile as children, and will enter willingly upon tea-cultivation providing the "sahib" shows that he is interested in it. In a few years the profits received will be a sufficient inducement.

About the middle of July we left the Almorah districts in order to visit those of Bheem Tal. Our road led across a high mountain which lies between Almorah and the plains of India. I think it is called the Gaughur mountain, and is nearly 9000 feet above the level of the sea. While winding up the sides of this mountain I had my first good view of the snowy range. We had stopped for the night at a Dâk bungalow. Next morning when we resumed our march a light drizzling rain was falling, and heavy clouds were hanging in masses about the sides of the hills. These clouds were not only above us, but they were also seen far down in the glens below. As I turned to look on this strange and wonderful scenery, the snowy mountains lay before me in all their grandeur, and the sun was shining on them. To say that they rose far above the clouds conveys no idea of their height, for I was above the clouds on the spot where I stood. Their snowy peaks seemed to reach to heaven itself, and to pierce the deep-blue sky.

Never in all my wanderings had such a view been presented to my eyes. It was indeed grand and sublime in the fullest sense of the words. How little the most gigantic works of man seemed when compared with these! The pyramids of Egypt themselves, which I had looked upon in wonder some years before, now sank into utter insignificance! I could have looked for hours upon such glorious objects, but the clouds soon closed in around me, and I saw the snowy range no more.

After crossing the Gaughur we gradually descended its southern sides until we reached the Bheem Tal tea-plantations.

The lake of Bheem Tal is situated in latitude 29° 20′ north and in longitude 79° 30′ east. It is 4000 feet above the level of the sea, and some of the surrounding mountains are said to be 8000 feet. These form the southern chain of the Himalayas, and bound the vast plain of India, of which a glimpse can be had through the mountain passes. Amongst these hills there are several *tals* or lakes, some flat meadow-looking land, and gentle undulating slopes, while higher up are steep and rugged mountains. It is amongst these hills that the Bheem Tal tea-plantations have been formed. They may be classed under three heads, viz.:—

1. *Anoo and Kooasur Plantations.*—These adjoin each other, are both formed *on low flat land,* and together cover about forty-six acres. The plants do not seem healthy or vigorous; many of them have died out, and few are in that state which tea-plants ought to be in. Such situations never ought to be chosen for tea-cultivation. The same objection applies to these plantations as to those at Deyra, but in a greater degree. No doubt, with sufficient drainage, and great care in cultivation, the tea-plant might be made to exist in such a situation; but I am convinced it would never grow with that luxuriance which is necessary in order to render it a profitable crop. *Besides, such lands are valuable for other purposes.* They are excellent rice-lands, and as such of considerable value to the natives.

2. *Bhurtpoor Plantation.*—This plantation covers about four and a half acres of terraced land on the hill-side, a little to the eastward of those last noticed. The soil is composed of a light loam, much mixed with small pieces of clay-slate and trap or greenstone,

of which the adjacent rocks are composed. It contains also a small portion of vegetable matter or *humus*. Both the situation and soil of this plantation are well adapted to the requirements of the tea-shrub, and consequently we find it succeeding here as well as at Guddowli, Hawulbaugh, Almorah, and other places where it is planted on the slopes of the hills.

3. *Russia Plantation.*—This plantation extends over seventy-five acres, and is formed on sloping land. The elevation is somewhat less than Bhurt-poor, and, although terraced in the same way, the angle is much lower. In some parts of the farm the plants are doing well, but generally they seemed to be suffering from too much water and hard pluck-ing. I have no doubt, however, of the success of this farm when the system of cultivation is improved. I observed some most vigorous and healthy bushes in the overseer's garden, a spot adjoining the plantation which could not be irrigated, and was informed they " never received any water except that which fell from the skies."

In the Bheem Tal district there are large tracts of excellent tea-land. In crossing over the hills towards Nainee Tal, with Mr. Batten, Commissioner of Ku-maon, I pointed out many tracts admirably adapted for tea-cultivation, and of no great value to the natives; generally, those lands on which the mundooa is cultivated are the most suitable.

Dr. Jameson now left me and returned to his duties at Hawulbaugh, while I went on to Nainee Tal, on my way to the plains. I have great pleasure

in bearing my humble testimony to the energy and
skill with which Dr. Jameson has managed the tea-
plantations which were placed by Government under
his care.   Considering that until lately we had little
or no information as to how the tea-plant was managed in China, the only wonder is that so few mis-
takes have been made in its cultivation in India.

Having thus described all the tea-plantations in
the provinces of Gurhwal and Kumaon, I shall now
make some general observations upon the cultivation
of the tea-plant in India, and offer some suggestions
for its improvement.

1. *On Land and Cultivation.*—From the observations already made upon the various tea-farms which
I have visited in the Himalayas, it will be seen that
I do not approve of *low flat lands* being selected for
the cultivation of the tea-shrub.   In China, which at
present must be regarded as the model tea-country,
the plantations are never made in such situations, or
they are so rare as not to have come under my notice.
In that country they are usually formed on the lower
slopes of the hills, that is, in such situations as those
at Guddowli, Hawulbaugh, Almorah, Kutoor, &c., in
the Himalayas.   It is true that in the fine green-tea
country of Hwuy-chow, in China, near the town of
Tun-che, many hundred acres of flattish land are
under tea-cultivation.   But this land is close to the
hills, which jut out into it in all directions, and it is
intersected by a river whose banks are usually from
15 to 20 feet above the level of the stream itself, not
unlike those of the Ganges below Benares.   In fact,

it has all the advantages of hilly land such as the tea-plant delights in.   In extending the Himalaya plantations this important fact ought to be kept in view.

There is no scarcity of such land in these mountains, more particularly in eastern Gurhwal and Kumaon.   It abounds in the districts of Paorie, Kunour, Lohba, Almorah, Kutoor, and Bheem Tal, and I was informed by Mr. Batten that there are large tracts about Gungoli and various other places equally suitable.   Much of this land is out of cultivation, as I have already stated, while the cultivated portions yield on an average only two or three annas per acre of revenue.

Such lands are of less value to the Zemindars than low rice-land where they can command a good supply of water for irrigation.   But I must not be understood to recommend poor worn-out hill-lands for tea-cultivation—land on which nothing else will grow. Nothing is further from my meaning.   Tea, in order to be profitable, requires a good sound soil—a light loam, well mixed with sand and vegetable matter, moderately moist, and yet not stagnant or sour. Such a soil, for example, as on these hill-sides produces good crops of mundooa, wheat, or millet, is well adapted for tea.   It is such land which I have alluded to as abounding in the Himalayas, and which is at present of so little value either to the Government or to the natives themselves.

The system of irrigation applied to tea in India is never practised in China.   I did not observe it practised in any of the great tea-countries which I visited.

On asking the Chinese manufacturers whom I brought
to India, and who had been born and brought up in
the tea-districts, whether they had seen such a practice, they all replied, " *No, that is the way we grow
rice ; we never irrigate tea.*" Indeed, I have no hesitation in saying that, in nine cases out of ten, the
effects of irrigation are most injurious. When tea
will not grow without irrigation, it is a sure sign that
the land employed is not suitable for such a crop. It
is no doubt an excellent thing to have a command of
water in case of a long drought, when its agency
might be useful in saving a crop which would otherwise fail, but irrigation ought to be used only on such
emergencies.

I have already observed that good tea-land is
naturally moist, although not stagnant ; and we must
bear in mind that the tea-shrub is *not a water plant*,
but is found in a wild state on the sides of hills.
In confirmation of these views, it is only necessary
to observe further, that all the *best Himalayan plantations are those to which irrigation has been most
sparingly applied.*

In cultivating the tea-shrub much injury is often
done to a plantation by *plucking leaves from very
young plants.* In China young plants are never
touched until the third or fourth year after they have
been planted. If growing under favourable circumstances, they will yield a good crop after that time.
All that ought to be done, in the way of plucking or
pruning, before that time, should be done with a view
to *form the plants*, and make them *bushy* if they do

not grow so naturally. If plucking is commenced too early and continued, the energies of the plants are weakened, they are long in attaining any size, and consequently there is a great loss of produce in a given number of years. A bush that has been properly treated may when eight years of age yield from two to three pounds of tea per annum, while another of the same age, but not a quarter of the size from over-plucking, may not produce more than as many ounces.

The same remarks apply also to plants which become unhealthy from any cause; leaves ought never to be taken from such plants; the gatherers should have strict orders to pass them over until they get again into a *good state* of health.

2. *On Climate.*—I have already stated that eastern Gurhwal and Kumaon appear to me to be the most suitable spots for the cultivation of the tea-plant in this part of the Himalayas. My remarks upon climate will therefore refer to that part of the country.

From a table of temperature kept at Hawulbaugh from November 28th, 1850, to July 13th, 1851, obligingly furnished me by Dr. Jameson, I observe that the climate here is extremely mild. During the winter months the thermometer (Fahr.) was never lower at sunrise than 44°, and only on two occasions so low, namely on the 15th and 16th of February, 1851. Once it stood as high as 66°, on the morning of February the 4th, but this is full ten degrees higher than usual. The minimum in February must, however, be several degrees lower than is shown by

2 c 2

this table, for ice and snow are not unfrequent;
indeed opposite the 16th of February, in the column
of remarks, I find written down "*a very frosty
morning.*" This discrepancy, no doubt, arises either
from a bad thermometer being used, or from its
being placed in a sheltered verandah. We may,
therefore, safely mark the minimum as 32° instead
of 44°.

The month of June appears to be the hottest in
the year. I observe the thermometer on the 5th,
6th, and 7th of that month stood at 92° at 3 P. M.,
and this was the highest degree marked during the
year. The lowest, at this hour, during the month
was 76°, but the general range in the 3 P. M. column
of the table is from 80° to 90°.

The wet and dry seasons are not so decided in the
hills as they are in the plains. In January, 1851,
it rained on five days and ten nights, and the total
quantity of rain which fell, as indicated by the rain-
gauge, during this month, was 5·25 inches; in
February, 3·84 inches fell; in March, 2·11; in
April, 2·24; in May none; and in June 6·13. In
June there are generally some days of heavy rain,
called by the natives Chota Bursaut, or small rains;
after this there is an interval of some days of dry
weather before the regular "rainy season" commences. This season comes on in July and con-
tinues until September. October and November
are beautiful months, with a clear atmosphere and
cloudless sky. After this fogs are frequent in all the
valleys until spring.

In comparing the climate of these provinces with that of China, although we find some important differences, yet upon the whole there is a great similarity. My comparisons apply, of course, to the best tea-districts only, for, although the tea-shrub is found cultivated from Canton in the south, to Tan-chow-foo in Shan-tung, yet the provinces of Fokien, Kiang-see, and the southern parts of Kiang-nan yield nearly all the finest teas of commerce.

The town of Tsong-gan, one of the great black-tea towns near the far-famed Woo-e-shan, is situated in latitude 27° 47' north. Here the thermometer in the hottest months, namely in July and August, rarely rises above 100°, and ranges from 92° to 100° as maximum; while in the coldest months, December and January, it sinks to the freezing point and sometimes a few degrees lower. We have thus a close resemblance in temperature between Woo-e-shan and Almorah. The great green-tea district being situated two degrees further north, the extremes of temperature are somewhat greater. It will be observed, however, that while in the Himalayas the hottest month is June, in China the highest temperature occurs in July and August; this is owing to the rainy season taking place earlier in China than it does in India.

In China rain falls in heavy and copious showers towards the end of April, and these rains continue at intervals in May and June. The first gathering of tea-leaves, those from which the Pekoe is made, is scarcely over before the air becomes charged with moisture, rain falls, and the bushes, being thus placed in such favourable circumstances for vegetating, are soon covered again with young leaves, from which the main crop of the season is obtained.

No one acquainted with vegetable physiology can doubt the advantages of such weather in the cultivation of tea for mercantile purposes. And these advantages, to a certain extent at least, seem to be extended to the Himalayas, although the regular rainy season is later than in China. I have already shown, from Dr. Jameson's table, that spring showers are frequent in Kumaon, although rare in the plains of India ; still, however, I think it would be prudent to adapt the gathering of leaves to the climate, that is, to take a moderate portion from the bushes before the rains, and the main crop after they have commenced.

3. *On the Vegetation of China and the Himalayas.*—One of the surest guides from which to draw conclusions on a subject of this nature is found in the indigenous vegetable productions of the countries. Dr. Royle, who was the first to recommend the cultivation of tea in the Himalayas, drew his conclusions, in the absence of that positive information from China which we now possess, not only from the great similarity in temperature between China and these hills, but also from the resemblance in vegetable productions. This resemblance is certainly very striking. In both countries, except in the low valleys of the Himalayas (and these we are not considering), tropical forms are rarely met with. If we take trees and

shrubs, for example, we find such genera as *Pinus*, *Cupressus, Berberis, Quercus, Viburnum, Indigofera, Andromeda, Lonicera, Deutzia, Rubus, Myrica, Spiræa, Ilex*, and many others common to both countries.

Amongst herbaceous plants we have *Gentiana, Aquilegia, Anemone, Rumex, Primula, Lilium, Leontodon, Ranunculus*, &c., equally distributed in the Himalayas and in China, and even in aquatic plants the same resemblance may be traced, as in *Nelumbium, Caladium*, &c. And more than this, we do not find plants belonging to the same genera only, but in many instances the identical species are found in both countries. The Indigofera, common in the Himalayas, abounds also on the tea-hills of China, and so does *Berberis nepalensis, Lonicera diversifolia, Myrica sapida*, and many others.

Were it necessary, I might now show that there is a most striking resemblance between the geology of the two countries as well as in their vegetable productions. In both the black and green tea countries to which I have alluded, clay-slate is most abundant. But enough has been advanced to prove how well many parts of the Himalayas are adapted for the cultivation of tea ; besides, the flourishing condition of many of the plantations is, after all, the best proof, and puts the matter beyond all doubt.

4. *Suggestions.*—Having shown that tea can be grown in the Himalayas, and that it would produce a valuable and remunerative crop, the next great object appears to be the production of superior tea,

by means of fine varieties and improved cultivation.
It was well known that a variety of the tea-plant
existed in the southern parts of China from which
inferior teas only were made.   That, being more
easily procured than the fine northern varieties,
from which the great mass of the best teas are made,
was the variety originally sent to India.   From it
all those in the Government plantations have sprung.

It was to remedy this, and to obtain the best
varieties from those districts which furnish the trees òf
commerce, that the Honourable Court of Directors
sent me to China in 1848.   Another object was to
obtain some good manufacturers and implements
from the same districts.   As the result of this mission, nearly twenty thousand plants from the best
black and green tea countries of Central China have
been introduced to the Himalayas.   Six first-rate
manufacturers, two lead-men, and a large supply of
implements from the celebrated Hwuy-chow districts
were also brought and safely located on the Government plantations in the hills.

A great step has thus been gained towards the
objects in view.   Much, however, remains still to be
done.   The new China plants ought to be carefully
propagated and distributed over all the plantations;
some of them ought also to be given to the Zemindars,
and more of these fine varieties might be yearly imported from China.

The Chinese manufacturers, who were obtained
some years since from Calcutta or Assam, are, in my
opinion, far from being first-rate workmen; indeed, I

doubt much if any of them learned their trade in China. They ought to be gradually got rid of and their places supplied by better men, for it is a great pity to teach the natives an inferior method of manipulation. The men brought round by me are first-rate green-tea makers ; they can also make black tea, but they have not been in the habit of making so much black as green. They have none of the Canton illiberality or prejudices about them, and are most willing to teach their art to the natives, many of whom will, I have no doubt, soon become excellent tea manufacturers. And the instruction of the natives is one of the chief objects which ought to be kept in view, for the importation of Chinese manipulators at high wages can only be regarded as a temporary measure ; ultimately the Himalayan tea must be made by the natives themselves ; each native farmer must learn how to make tea as well as how to grow it ; he will then make it upon his own premises, as the Chinese do, and the expenses of carriage will be much less than if the green leaves had to be taken to the market.

But as the Zemindars will be able to grow tea long before they are able to make it, it would be prudent in the first instance to offer them a certain sum for green leaves brought to the Government manufactory.

I have pointed out the land most suitable for the cultivation of tea, and shown that such land exists in the Himalayas to an almost unlimited extent. But if the object the Government have in view be the establishment of a company to develop the resources of these hills, as in Assam, I would strongly urge the propriety of concentrating, as much as possible, the various plantations. Sites ought to be chosen which are not too far apart, easy of access, and if possible near rivers; for, no doubt, a considerable portion of the produce would have to be conveyed to the plains or to a seaport.

In my tour amongst the hills I have seen no place so well adapted for a central situation as Almorah or Hawulbaugh. Here the Government has already a large establishment, and tea-lands are abundant in all directions. The climate is healthy, and better suited to an European constitution than most other parts of India. Here plants from nearly all the temperate parts of the world are growing as if they were at home. As examples, I may mention Myrtles, Pomegranates, and Tuberoses from the south of Europe; Dahlias, Potatoes, Aloes, and Yuccas from America; *Melianthus major* and bulbs from the Cape; the Cypress and Deodar of the Himalayas; and the Lagerstræmias, Loquats, Roses, and Tea of China.

In these days, when tea has become almost a necessary of life in England and her wide-spreading colonies, its production upon a large and cheap scale is an object of no ordinary importance. But to the natives of India themselves the production of this article would be of the greatest value. The poor *paharie*, or hill peasant, at present has scarcely the common necessaries of life, and certainly none of its luxuries. The common sorts of grain which his lands produce will scarcely pay the carriage to the nearest market-town, far less yield such a profit as will enable him to purchase even a few of the necessary and simple luxuries of life. A common blanket has to serve him for his covering by day and for his bed at night, while his dwelling-house is a mere mud-hut, capable of affording but little shelter from the inclemency of the weather. If part of these lands produced tea, he would then have a healthy beverage to drink, besides a commodity which would be of great value in the market. Being of small bulk compared with its value, the expense of carriage would be trifling, and he would have the means of making himself and his family more comfortable and more happy.

Were such results doubtful, we have only to look across the frontiers of India into China. Here we find tea one of the necessaries of life in the strictest sense of the word. A Chinese never drinks cold water, which he abhors, and considers unhealthy. Tea is his favourite beverage from morning until night; not what we call tea, mixed with milk and sugar, but the essence of the herb itself drawn out in pure water. Those acquainted with the habits of this people can scarcely conceive the idea of the Chinese existing, were they deprived of the tea-plant; and I am sure that the extensive use of this beverage adds much to the health and comfort of the great body of the people.

The people of India are not unlike the Chinese in many of their habits. The poor of both countries eat sparingly of animal food, and rice with other grains and vegetables form the staple articles on which they live; this being the case, it is not at all unlikely the Indian will soon acquire a habit which is so universal in China. But in order to enable him to drink tea, it must be produced at a cheap rate; he cannot afford to pay at the rate of four or six shillings a pound. It must be furnished to him at four *pence* or six *pence* instead, and this can easily be done, but only on his own hills. If this is accomplished, and I see no reason why it should not be, a boon will have been conferred upon the people of India of no common kind, and one which an enlightened and liberal Government may well be proud of conferring upon its subjects.

But while the cultivation of the tea-plant is of the first importance, there are in China other productions of the vegetable kingdom which ought not to be overlooked, and which, if introduced, would add greatly to the comforts of the people of India. There is a fruit-tree, called by botanists *Myrica sapida*, which is found growing wild on the Himalayas. A very fine variety of this fruit is cultivated in China, and is as superior to the Indian one as the apple is to the crab. It is much esteemed by the Chinese, and would be a great luxury to the inhabitants of northern India. Our English cherries, chestnuts, and the finer sorts of pears, ought also by all means to be introduced to the Himalayas. They would grow in the climate of Almorah as well as they do at home.

The varieties of the bamboo found in the north of

China would be of great value in the Himalayas, more particularly a fine large clean-stemmed kind common about the temples in the tea-districts. Something of this kind appears to be much wanted in the provinces of Gurhwal and Kumaon.*

When I reached Nainee Tal I was kindly received by Captain Jones, who offered me quarters in his house until my dâk was laid for Meerut, to which I was now bound on my way to Calcutta and England. Nainee Tal is one of the prettiest stations I have seen in the Himalayas. Its romantic-looking lake is almost surrounded by richly wooded mountains. A fine broad road has been made round the edge of the lake, and the houses of the inhabitants are scattered on the sloping sides of the hills. Schooners and pleasure-boats are seen daily sailing on the lake, and when viewed from a high elevation have a curious and striking appearance. From one of the positions where I stood I could see the lake, and through an opening in the hills the far-spreading plains of India. Heavy masses of clouds were hanging over the plains far below the level of the lake, and the little vessels were actually sailing about at an elevation higher than the clouds!

On the 28th of July I left Nainee Tal and took the road for the plains. Mr. Batten accompanied me down the hill as far as a little garden which we had agreed to visit, where we found breakfast await-

---

* The observations, in this chapter, upon tea-cultivation in India, are taken, by permission of the Honourable Court of Directors of the East India Company, from a Report which I had the honour to make to the Indian Government.

ing us. The scenery here is so wild and striking as to baffle all attempts at description. Behind us were mountains of all heights, rent and broken up into every variety of form, while before us lay the plains of India stretching away as far as the eye could reach without a mountain or a hill to obstruct the view.

Mr. Batten now left me and returned to his home amongst the mountains, while I pursued my homeward journey. I visited the well-known cities of Delhi and Agra on my route, and arrived at Calcutta on the 29th of August, when I took up my quarters with Dr. Falconer, in the botanic garden, until the mail-steamer was ready to receive her passengers for England.

On the 5th of September I had the pleasure of seeing the *Victoria regia* flower for the first time in India. It was growing luxuriantly in one of the ponds in the botanic garden, and no doubt will soon be a great ornament to Indian gardens. It will soon reign as the queen of flowers in every land, and, like our beloved sovereign whose name it bears, the sun will never set on its dominions.